Communications in Computer and Information Science 1538

More information about this series at https://link.springer.com/bookseries/7899

Edwige Pissaloux · George Angelos Papadopoulos ·
Achilleas Achilleos · Ramiro Velázquez (Eds.)

ICT for Health, Accessibility and Wellbeing

First International Conference, IHAW 2021
Larnaca, Cyprus, November 8–9, 2021
Revised Selected Papers

Springer

Editors
Edwige Pissaloux
Université de Rouen-Normandie
Rouen, France

George Angelos Papadopoulos
University of Cyprus
Nicosia, Cyprus

Achilleas Achilleos
Frederick University
Nicosia, Cyprus

Ramiro Velázquez
Universidad Panamericana
Aguascalientes, Mexico

ISSN 1865-0929 ISSN 1865-0937 (electronic)
Communications in Computer and Information Science
ISBN 978-3-030-94208-3 ISBN 978-3-030-94209-0 (eBook)
https://doi.org/10.1007/978-3-030-94209-0

This Springer imprint is published by the registered company Springer Nature Switzerland AG
The registered company address is: Gewerbestrasse 11, 6330 Cham, Switzerland

Preface

The UN Convention on the Rights of Persons with Disabilities (PwDs), Article 9, defines Information and Communication Technology (ICT) accessibility as an important part of accessibility rights [1]. The World Health Organisation (WHO) estimates that over one billion people live with some form of disability, and in developing nations infirmity and disabilities are real drivers of exclusion and poverty [2]. Moreover, as stated by the WHO, the number of people experiencing disability is dramatically increasing due to demographic trends and increases in chronic health conditions, among other causes [2]. In addition, people with disabilities are disproportionately affected during the COVID-19 pandemic.

ICTs have a crucial role to play. In fact, making technologies and services accessible is not merely a basic human right, but ICTs have the potential to bring a real difference to the quality of life of people living with difficult or debilitating conditions or disabilities. ICTs are advancing exponentially, while the cost is plummeting. Nevertheless, health care demand is rising, accessible technologies and services are required, and the costs continue to rise. This calls for additional research and adoption of technologies that can help to meet these challenges, since ICT for health, accessibility, and wellbeing still continues to lag behind other applications.

There is a need for the design, implementation, user-centered evaluation, and standardization of new and future inclusive and sustainable technologies that benefit all: healthy people, people with disabilities or other impairments, people with chronic diseases, etc. This calls for multi- and interdisciplinary research involving the interplay between ICTs and biomedical, neurocognitive, and experimental research, which puts users with disabilities at the epicenter and aims to engage in a co-creation and co-design approach. Specifically, the focus should be placed on user-oriented design and innovation, as well as user-centered evaluation. New intuitive ways of human-computer interaction (e.g., augmented and virtual reality, natural language processing) and user feedback and acceptance are among the primary factors that need to be examined in order to propose more intuitive and user-tailored ICT solutions.

Therefore, the proceedings of the first International Conference on ICT for Health, Accessibility and Wellbeing (IC-IHAW 2021) present state-of-the-art multi- and interdisciplinary research in this field. We would like to applaud the steering committee, Michal Bujacz, George A. Papadopoulos, Edwige Pissaloux, and Ramiro Velázquez for helping us to assemble and organize a number of high-quality and diverse papers on topics such as active aging, assistive devices and systems, brain functions support, and ICT and wellbeing. This very exciting volume promises to deliver to the readers a broad view of how ICTs can be applied for addressing challenges in terms of health, accessibility, and wellbeing, with accepted papers that showcase research and development of different ICTs and their application in various end-user domains, e.g., older adults, people with dementia, stroke patients.

Part of the series "ICT for Societal Challenges", the IC-IHAW 2021 conference brought together academics, industry experts, and education leaders from all over the world to discuss an incredibly wide array of topics, ranging from machine learning, robotics, and augmented reality to natural language processing, to address problems related to health and disability.

The conference received a total of 36 papers, and the submitting authors originated from 26 countries from all parts of the globe with the Europe, Middle East, and Africa (EMEA) region ranking first with 69% of submissions, the Asia-Pacific Region ranking second with 15%, and the rest being from North and Latin America. From the submitted papers, 12 full papers and seven short papers were accepted for presentation and publication in this Springer conference proceedings, yielding an acceptance rate of 33.3% for full papers. Every paper went through a rigorous review process, in which each paper received at least two expert reviews, with most of the papers receiving more than three reviews.

The technical program of IC-IHAW 2021 consisted of six sessions: Active Ageing, Brain Functions Support (two sessions), ICT & Wellbeing (two sessions), and Assistive Devices & Systems during which 19 papers were presented (12 full papers and 7 short papers) at the virtual event.

We would like to thank everyone involved in the conference for helping to make it a success.

November 2021 Med-Salim Bouhlel
Achilleas Achilleos

References

1. https://www.un.org/development/desa/disabilities/convention-on-the-rights-of-persons-with-disabilities/article-9-accessibility.html
2. https://www.who.int/news-room/fact-sheets/detail/disability-and-health

Organization

Conference Chairs

Honorary General Chair

Edwige Pissaloux	University of Rouen Normandy, France

General Chair

George A. Papadopoulos	University of Cyprus, Cyprus

Scientific Program Chair

Salim Bouhlel	University of Sfax, Tunisia

Scientific Program Vice-Chair

Achilleas Achilleos	Frederick University, Cyprus

Publications Chair

Ramiro Velazquez	Universidad Panamericana, Mexico

Program Committee

Achilleas Achilleos	Frederick University, Cyprus
Tobias Ableitner	University of Applied Science Stuttgart, Germany
Anis Ammous	Ecole Nationale d'Ingénieurs de Sfax and Umm Al-Qura University, Tunisia
Athanasios Anastasiou	National Technical University of Athens, Greece
Dominique Archambault	Université Paris 8, France
Valentina Emilia Balas	Aurel Vlaicu University of Arad, Romania
Med Salim Bouhlel	University of Sfax, Tunisia
Fatma Bouhlel	University of Sfax, Tunisia
Lydia Bouzar-Benlabiod	Ecole nationale supérieure d'informatique, Algeria
Mehdi Elarbi	Institut Supérieur de Biotechnologie de Sfax, Tunisia
Simon Gay	Université de Rouen Normandie, France
Deepak Gupta	Maharaja Agrasen Institute of Technology, India
Firkhan Ali Hamid Ali	Universiti Tun Hussein Onn Malaysia, Malaysia
Aboul Ella Hassanien	Cairo University, Egypt
Dan Istrate	University of Technology of Compiègne, France

Christophe Kolskir	Hauts-de-France Polytechnic University, France
Efthyvoulos Kyriacou	Frederick University, Cyprus
Christele Lecomte	University of Rouen Normandy, France
Christos Liambas	Aristotle University of Thessaloniki, Greece
Antonella Longo	University of Salento, Italy
Oleksandr Makarenko	National Technical University of Ukraine (KPI), Ukraine
Francesco Masulli	University of Genova, Italy
Klaus Miesenberger	University of Linz, Austria
Lyudmila Mihaylova	University of Sheffield, UK
Gianmario Motta	Universita di Pavia, Italy
Fathallah Nouboud	University of Quebec at Trois-Rivières, Canada
Kais Ouni	Ecole Nationale d'Ingénieurs de Carthage, Tunisia
George Papadopoulos	University of Cyprus, Cyprus
Nearchos Paspallis	UCLan Cyprus, Cyprus
Edwige Pissaloux	University of Rouen Normandy, France
Ridha Azizi	ISETSO, Tunisia
Katerine Romeo	Université de Rouen Normandie, France
Khaled Rouabah	LMSE Laboratory, Slovenia
Stefano Rovetta	Università di Genova, Italy
Su Ruan	Université de Rouen Normandie, France
Stuart Rubin	Space and Naval Warfare Systems Center, USA
Khalil Sayidmarie	University of Mosul, Iraq
Frédéric Serin	Le Havre University, France
Souhir Tounsi	University of Sfax, Tunisia
Jolanda Tromp	State University of New York, USA
Miguel Carrasco	Universidad Adolfo Ibañez, Chile
Ramiro Velazquez	Universidad Panamericana, Mexico
Yu Yuan	IBM Research, China

Contents

Active Aging

Instrumented Activity Dice for Assessing Limitations of Physical Performance: A Pilot Study

Seethu M. Christopher(✉) and Rico Möckel

Maastricht University, Maastricht, The Netherlands
{seethu.christopher,rico.mockel}@maastrichtuniversity.nl

Abstract. Assessment tests can be frustrating for participants and - due to a meticulous documentation load - arduous for experimentalists. Consequently, research has been done to make assessments more fun for the participants by integrating these assessments into serious games, and less demanding for the experimentalists by automating observations through computer vision or wearable sensors. However, children and elderly participants become anxious and behave differently while being observed by a camera or when asked to wear sensor-suits. Hence, we investigate a different methodology to assess the physical status of a participant - an instrumented game dice with integrated sensors. Prior research has established that throws are a measure of physical capabilities. A participant in the context of a serious game throws the instrumented dice and we demonstrate that the variables extracted from the interaction with the dice provide us with an indication about the participant's wrist abilities.

Keywords: Serious games · Physical interaction · Intelligent toys · Human movement · Smart assessment tool

1 Introduction

Physical assessments are a "cornerstone of public health" [1]. Substantial advances have been made in developing affordable and easy-to-administer field tests for assessing physical performance, especially those needed in activities of daily living (ADL) [2]. The seated medicine ball throw (SMBT) for instance is an inexpensive, safe and repeatable measure of upper body power [3]. Seated shot-put (SSP) is another field test that is frequently used for assessing upper body performance [4]. Harris et al. used the SMBT test to measure the upper body power in older adults [3] while Davis et al. used it with kindergarten children [5]. During these tests, the participants are asked to throw a medicine ball or a shot put as far as possible and the researcher manually measures the distance using a tape. The throwing activities also provide a challenging stimulus to improve the balance of the participants [6].

Without the use of technology, such tests for the assessment of well-being and physical performance can be a tedious process since the researchers must perform the assessment and careful documentation. Moreover, with the steady growth of elderly population

E. Pissaloux et al. (Eds.): IHAW 2021, CCIS 1538, pp. 3–17, 2021.
https://doi.org/10.1007/978-3-030-94209-0_1

over the world, new practices for assessment of the elderly need to be adopted. It is estimated that in 2050 there will be three times more people over the age 85 than there are today [7]. Past research for automated assessments of physical performance focused on three different assessment approaches: Most work focusses on (1) the replacement of observations through a caregiver/researcher by a camera with automated video analysis [8–12], and (2) the attachment of sensors to persons' bodies [13–27]. (3) Our work falls into a third category for which so far only little literature can be found: the integration of sensors into game devices [28, 29].

There exists some limited research on using sensors like IMUs (Inertial Measurement Unit) on objects in sports to find the kinematic variables or capacity of the person executing certain movements [30]. Särkkä et al. talks about using IMU on a javelin to find the perfect angle so as to get the most efficient throw [31] while Grimpampi et al. describes the most effective angle for a baseball throw [32]. Burkett et al. investigated the kinematic data of seated throwing techniques [33]. This was done by applying 31 reflective markers on relevant anatomical positions, and an IMU with a marker on the thrown object, while for collecting data, a six-camera system was used to track the markers during the movement.

In this paper we study how the physical status of a person might be assessed by integrating an inertial measurement unit into an activity dice, thus creating an inexpensive everyday tool for assessments. To the best of our knowledge, such an automated assessment with activity dice has not yet been proposed in the literature. Our long-term goal is to incorporate the dice in serious games [34] or target throwing activities [35], thus training the physical abilities while physical status and well-being are continuously and automatically assessed without human intervention, without placing sensors on the person's body, and without the use of camera devices. Such a cost effective device would be beneficial for early intervention, as the tool can notify the caregivers if a change in physical status is noticed. Following this, time consuming and costly assessments and examinations can be further carried out, if necessary. The instrumented dice can be integrated into various games as our caregiver partners are currently doing it with non-instrumented dice. For now, in this work we explore which data pertaining to the wrist can be obtained from the dice. We show that we can extract the following information purely from the instrumented activity dice: (1) the initial velocity with which the dice was thrown, (2) the time of flight, and (3) the number of turns of the dice. We show how from these features, we can differentiate between throws performed with a fully functional wrist versus a wrist restricted in complete movement.

2 Materials and Methods

This section details the subject details, the activity dice used, the experimental setup and methods used in this study.

2.1 Subject Recruitment

Eight male and six female university students in undergraduate and graduate programs with no physical impairment were recruited to participate in the study. All participants were informed of the experimental procedure along with all associated risks and signed an informed consent following the guidelines of the ERCIC Maastricht University Ethics committee, which had approved the study (ERCIC_094_28_08_2018). Participants were instructed about the possibility of withdrawing their consent for the study at any given time without providing any further reasons or facing any consequences, both orally and in written form. Participants were also instructed about their data rights in the GDPR framework. The anthropometric values for each participant were measured prior to any testing (Table 1).

Table 1. Anthropometric values of all participants

Variable	Mean (SD)
Age (years)	27.4 (2.9)
Sitting height (m)[a]	0.91 (0.06)
Arm length (m)[b]	0.74 (0.06)
Elbow to hand length (m)[c]	0.46 (0.03)

[a] Sitting height is defined as the distance from the chair's surface to the vertex of the head.
[b] Arm length is defined as the distance from the shoulder to the middle of the hand (palm) of the right arm.
[c] Elbow to hand length is defined as the distance from the elbow to the middle of the hand (palm) of the right arm.

Fig. 1. Left: dice. Right: sensors placed inside the dice

2.2 Instrumented Activity Dice

To create the instrumented activity dice, we integrated a Raspberry Pi 3 embedded computer and inertial measurement unit (IMU), the BNO055 from Bosch Sensortec, into an off-the-shelf foam dice from Wehrfritz [36]. The sampling frequency of the IMU was set at 100 MHz. We used the fusion mode of operation for the IMU. This mode outputs orientation data in addition to the raw sensors values and guarantees higher data accuracy for the sensor values. The off-the shelf foam dice is shown in Fig. 1.

The off-the-shelf foam dice can be bought as a play device for activities with children and elderly. With an edge length of 20 cm it can be easily grasped and thrown. We chose this dice after consultations with elderly and caregivers. The dice itself can be used for different types of games with the children and elderly in the context of serious games. As a result, the dice itself might also be a good motivator to get elderly to be active. We integrated the Raspberry Pi embedded computer into the dice to read the accelerometer data provided by the IMU and to send this data via WLAN to a standard PC. The Raspberry Pi also records the IMU data so that it could be analyzed offline after a game and the instrumented dice can be used safely without a wireless data connection. Figure 2 shows the system overview and the overview of the data flow in the system.

The acceleration data is visualized and analyzed on the PC. A typical trajectory of the acceleration data as being generated during a throw is shown in Fig. 3. For all accelerometer analysis we used the average of the three axes of the accelerometer. As shown in Fig. 3, the trajectories can be divided into 3 phases: (1) before throw phase, when the dice is still being touched and accelerated by the human player, (2) thrown phase, when the dice is flying without physical contact, and (3) hit and roll phase where the dice makes contact with the ground. The moment the dice leaves hand can be clearly extracted from the accelerometer data automatically by the software since

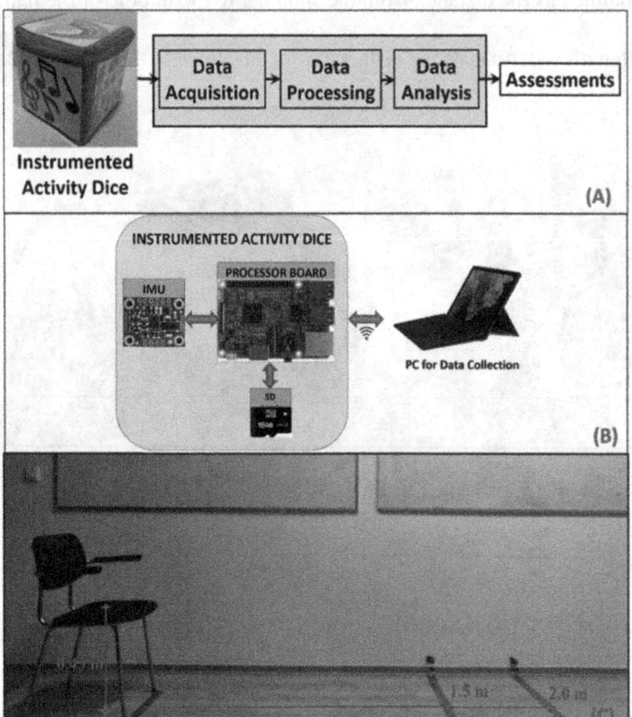

Fig. 2. (A) Overview of the data flow. (B) Overview of the computational hardware. (C) Experimental setup. Position of the chair and targets marked.

the accelerometer provides an output of zero [37]. The moment when ground impact is generated due to the dice hitting the ground is also marked in the data. From these two moments, the time of flight, which is the duration in which the dice was in the air, can be calculated.

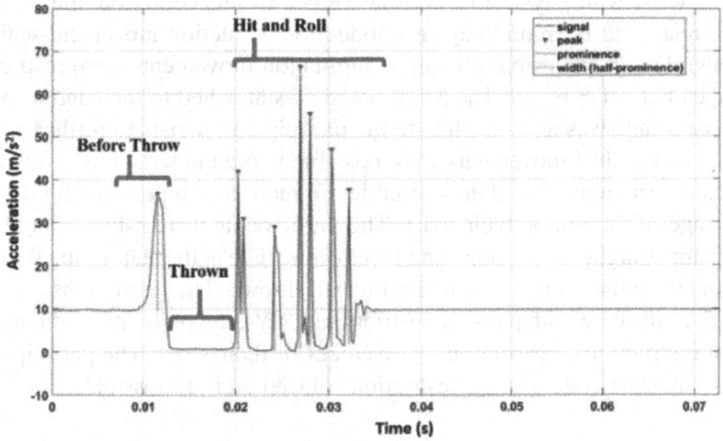

Fig. 3. Accelerometer plot (averaged over the three accelerometer axes) from the dice with the different phases marked. The blue triangles mark distinct peaks in the data. (Color figure online)

2.3 Experimental Set up

During the experimental sessions, participants were asked to throw the dice while sitting on a chair with a height of 45 cm. A camera, Logitech HD1040, was kept at a distance of 3 m from the chair, facing the chair from the side to record the throws performed by the participants for later analysis if needed. The camera was recording video data at 24 fps. A seated position was chosen to restrict any contribution from the lower part of the participant's body in the throw. Furthermore, the seated position is favored to mimic the conditions of those elderly who cannot stand safely or do not have full control of their lower limbs. The chair's front legs were marked on the floor to make sure that the chair's locations stayed the same for all participants. Participants self-selected a comfortable seating configuration before each session by performing a test throw at the beginning. Once participants felt comfortable, participants were asked to maintain the same seated position for the whole session, if possible. Figure 2 illustrates the seating arrangement and the targets marked on the floor.

At the beginning of each throw, the dice was handed to the participant by the researcher. Afterwards, participants were asked to throw the dice when they were ready. At the end of each throw, the researcher picked the dice up and gave the dice back to the participant for the next throw. After the release of the dice from the participant's hands, the height of the hands was measured manually.

The participants were asked to perform 4 different throws under 3 different conditions. The 3 different conditions were 1) Free Wrist (FW): In this condition, the participants' wrists were free to move and was not restricted in any way; 2) Restricted Wrist without any physical restrictions (NM – Non-physical Mode): In this condition, participants were asked to try not to move their wrist as much as possible while throwing; 3) Restricted wrist with physical restrictions (RW): In this condition, the participants' wrists were restricted for motion against abduction-adduction movement with a wrist brace and the flexion extension, pronation-supination movements were restricted with a hand shaped cut MDF board. The MDF board was attached to the hand using Velcro bands. A sports tape was also attached to the participants' wrists to further ensure that no abnormal anatomical movements were possible while the wrist brace was attached. The physical restrictions were done to mimic the motion of a person who do not have complete range of motion on their wrist. The participants were asked to hold the dice with their palm straight on two opposing faces of the dice at the start of the throw and to always throw from the center of their chest for all throws. The restrictions are shown in figure Fig. 5. In the case with physical restrictions (RW), the participants did not receive any explicit instructions regarding the movement of their wrist. The participants were free to move their wrist despite the restrictions placed on it, if possible.

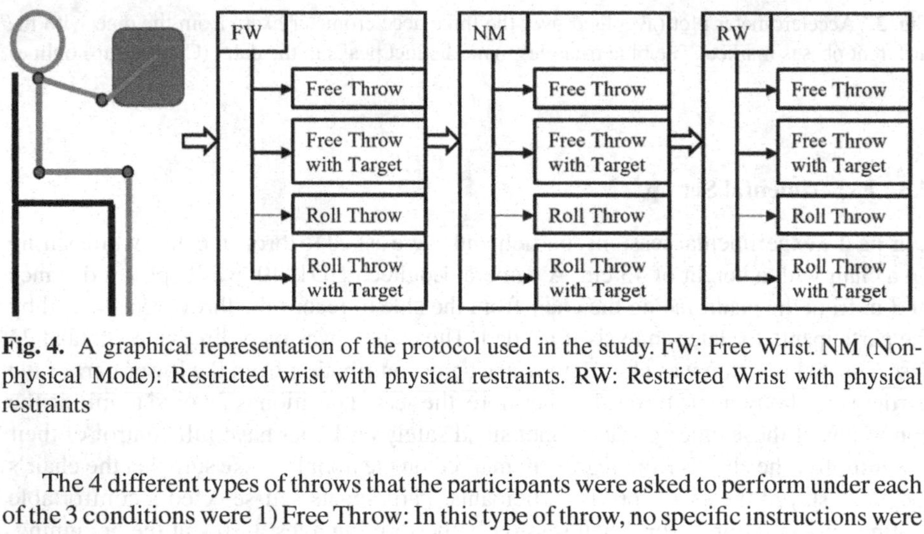

Fig. 4. A graphical representation of the protocol used in the study. FW: Free Wrist. NM (Non-physical Mode): Restricted wrist with physical restraints. RW: Restricted Wrist with physical restraints

The 4 different types of throws that the participants were asked to perform under each of the 3 conditions were 1) Free Throw: In this type of throw, no specific instructions were given to the participants regarding the use of force, wrist range and/or motivation required for the throw. The participants were asked to throw as naturally as possible within the conditions stated as to the starting position of the dice. 2) Free Throw with Target: This is the same type of throw as before except for the condition that the participants were asked to try to hit the target marked at 1.5 m away from the leg of the chair they were seated in. They were asked to throw as naturally as possible within the conditions stated as to the target and the starting position of the dice. 3) Roll Throw: In this type of throw, the participants were asked to try to roll the dice as much as possible for the throw. 4) Roll Throw with Target: The participants were asked to try to hit the target marked at

1.5 m away from the leg of the chair they were seated in while at the same time trying to roll the dice as much as possible.

So, in total each participant performed 12 throws in 1 session. This protocol was followed to ensure to capture the role of the wrist in the throwing motion and investigate whether this information could be captured by the variables extracted from the instrumented dice. A graphical representation of the protocol used in the study is depicted in Fig. 4.

At the end of the session, the participants were asked 2 questions. The questions were asked to assure that the restrains placed on the wrist were indeed restricting the movement of the wrist and to also see whether similar results could be obtained just by asking the participants to not move their wrist and without placing any physical restrictions on them. The questions were:

Q1: Do you think you moved your wrist during the throws performed in the second condition, where you were asked not to move your wrist without any physical restrictions placed on the wrist?
Q2: Did you move your wrist during the throws performed in the third condition, when there was a physical restriction placed on your wrist?

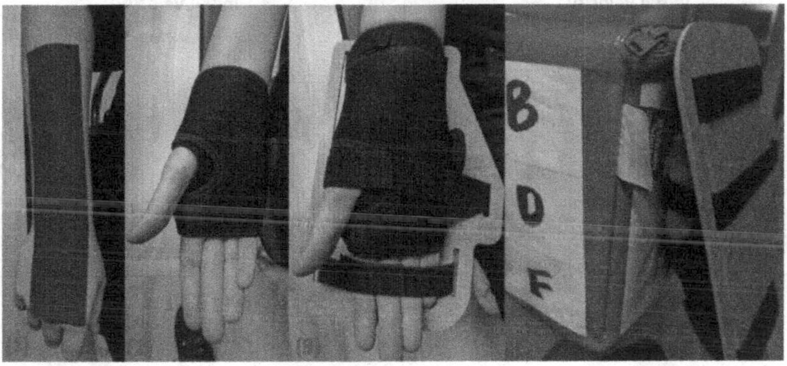

Fig. 5. Restrictions placed on the wrist (1) Sports tape attached to wrist. (2) Wrist Brace attached to wrist. (3) MDF board attached to wrist. (4) Participant with the restrictions attached holding the dice.

2.4 Variables Extracted from the Instrumented Activity Dice

To characterize the physical performance of the person throwing the dice and the type of throw we extracted 3 variables from data provided by the IMU within the instrumented dice:

1. We extracted the time of flight, t_f, because it characterizes how long the dice is in the air during a throw and we wanted to explore if the restrictions on the movement of the wrist have any effect on the time of flight achieved during a throw.

2. We extracted the initial velocity, v_0, the dice has when leaving the hand of the throwing person. v_0 can be used as an estimate of how much strength the person initiating the throw has used [38–40]. Thus v_0 provides an estimate about whether the strength of the person will be impaired by the restrictions on the movement of the wrist.
3. Finally, we extracted the number of rotations/turns of the dice while the dice was thrown as this information might also provide a measure of the physical performance of the wrist of the person initiating the throw [41, 42]. The number of rotations/turns provides an estimate about the range of motion achievable at the wrist.

3 Results

This section outlines the results for all the variables we extracted from the dice, namely: time of flight, initial velocity, and number of turns/rolls.

3.1 Time of Flight

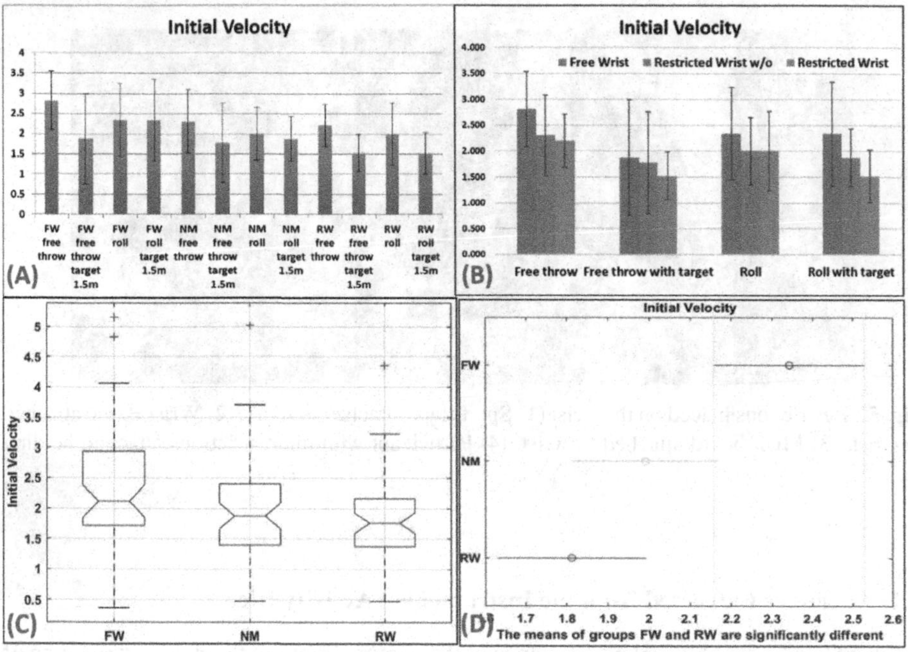

Fig. 6. (A) Initial Velocity for each type of throw. (B) Initial Velocity grouped together based on type of throw. (C) Means of the different groups for Initial Velocity. (D) ANOVA graph of means of different groups for Initial Velocity.

ANOVA test (single factor ANOVA [43]) was performed for the time of flight measurements calculated from the dice for different types of throw in various combinations.

The p-value for variation between the types of throws for time of flight variable, when we group the type of throw based on the different degrees of restriction for the wrist separately i.e., all the throws with FW, all the throws with NM, and all the throws with RW, is 0.1369. The p-value for variation between groups for time of flight variable, when we group the roll and non-roll throws, i.e., all the non-roll throws with FW, all the roll throws with FW, all the non-roll throws with NM, all the roll throws with NM, all the non-roll throws with RW, and all the roll throws with RW is 0.284. The p-value for variation between groups for time of flight variable, when we consider all the roll throws with FW, all the roll throws with NM, and all the roll throws with RW is 0.733. None of the combinations of throws showed statistical significance.

3.2 Initial Velocity

Figure 6 illustrates the initial velocity values, mean and standard deviation values for the different types of throws. ANOVA test (single factor ANOVA [43]) was performed for the initial measurements calculated from the dice for different types of throws in various combinations. The p-value for variation between the types of throws for initial velocity variable, when we consider all the types of throws, but group the type of throws based on the different degrees of restriction for the wrist separately i.e., all the throws with FW, all the throws with NM, and all the throws with RW, is 0.0032. The p-value for variation between groups for initial velocity variable, when we consider all the non-roll throws with FW, all the roll throws with FW, all the non-roll throws with NM, all the roll throws with NM, all the non-roll throws with RW, and all the roll throws with RW is 0.039. The p-value for variation between groups for initial velocity variable, when we consider all the roll throws with FW, all the roll throws with NM, and all the roll throws with RW is 0.022. The first combination showed highly statistical significance and the rest of the combination of throws showed statistical significance.

3.3 Number of Turns

Figure 7 illustrates the number of turns values, mean and standard deviation values for different types of throws. ANOVA test (single factor ANOVA [43]) was performed for the number of turns measurements calculated from the dice for different types of throws in various combinations. The p-value for variation between the types of throws for number of turns variable, when we consider all the types of throws, but group the type of throw based on the different degrees of restriction for the wrist separately i.e., all the throws with FW, all the throws with NM, and all the throws with RW, is 0.0003. The p-value for variation between groups for number of turns variable, when we consider all the non-roll throws with FW, all the roll throws with FW, all the non-roll throws with NM, all the roll throws with NM, all the non-roll throws with RW, and all the roll throws with RW is 2.42×10^{-14}. The p-value for variation between groups for number of turns variable, when we consider all the roll throws with FW, all the roll throws with NM, and all the roll throws with RW is 0.0002. All the combination of throws showed highly statistical significance.

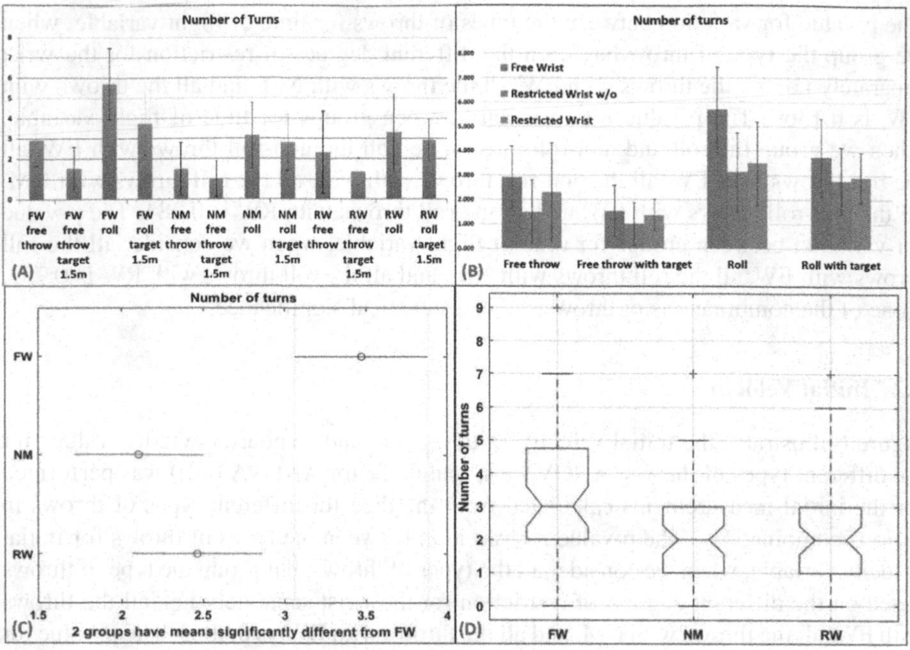

Fig. 7. (A) Number of turns for each type of throw. (B) Number of turns grouped together based on type of throw. (C) Means of the different groups for Number of turns. (D) ANOVA graph of means of different groups for number of turns.

3.4 Questionnaire

71.43% of the participants answered that they did not move their wrist when they were asked to not move their wrist without placing any physical restrictions on the wrist. 83.33% of the participants answered that they could not move their wrist after having a physical restriction placed on the wrist.

4 Discussion

The presented experimental results demonstrate that data like the time of flight, initial velocity, and the number of turns of the thrown activity dice can be automatically extracted from the IMU integrated inside the activity dice. The rotational behavior of the dice can be automatically characterized from IMU data by measuring the number of dice rotations during the throw, data that would be difficult to obtain through computer vision using a standard camera or through a wearable sensor. This data is valuable as research indicates that the number of turns that the dice can be rotated in a throw gives an indication about gross and fine motor skills of the person executing the throw [44].

Our results indicate that the number of turns is a predictor of high statistical significance for indicating the range of motion at the wrist. The range of motion at the wrist is important for giving the dice a twist for the rolling motion. Figure 7 shows that the number of turns is always higher for throws performed with a free wrist. Our statistical analysis also shows that the number of turns can differentiate between roll movements when the wrist is free to execute the throw versus when there is a restriction placed on the wrist, whether it be physical or otherwise. Hence the number of turns provides an indication about the active range of motion at the wrist of the person executing the throw. This would be an indication of the physical performance of the person performing the throw. Our statistical results show that the number of turns achieved when there is a physical restriction placed on the wrist is 20% higher than when the participants were asked to restrict the movement of the wrist themselves. This could be because the participants were free to move their wrists despite a physical restriction being placed on the wrist and they were not told to restrict their wrist movements.

The statistical tests on the value of the initial velocity, which is an indication of the energy provided to the throw, show that there is a high statistical difference between the throws performed with a restriction placed on the wrist versus the throws performed with a free wrist. This indicates that the initial velocity can be used for an assessment about the active range of motion possible at the wrist. Restricted wrists severely impact the strength achievable for a throw. Figure 6 shows that the initial velocity is always higher when there are no restrictions placed on the wrist. Our results show that the initial velocity can also be used as an indicator of the range of motion possible at the wrist of the person executing the throw. Our statistical results show that the initial velocity achieved when there is a physical restriction placed on the wrist is 6.5% lower than when the participants were asked to restrict the movement of the wrist themselves. This further shows that the movement at the wrist was impaired by the placement of the physical restriction as opposed to just asking the participant to not move their wrist, as indicated by the participants in the questionnaire also.

Our results show that the time of flight extracted from the dice has no contribution to the active involvement of the wrist for the throw performed. This indicates that the wrist does not affect the time of flight of a throw.

It is promising to see that the measures extracted from the dice can be used to distinguish between the various throws performed using a free wrist versus restricted wrist, giving an estimate about the physical performance of the person performing the throw, especially the range of motion of the person's wrist. It is also interesting to see that with the dice, it is easy to distinguish if a person is able to perform certain types of throws, i.e., a rolling throw, free throw or a throw aimed at a target. The presented results indicate that the dice can provide a clear indication about the limitations of the range of motion of the person performing the throws. Thus the dice could be used to examine if there is any change in the status of the range of motion of a person. This is especially useful for the elderly as the activity dice can be used for continuous measurements to evaluate whether a person's functioning is deteriorating or improving over time. As a result, the presented instrumented activity dice has the potential to become a low-cost solution that can be used for everyday automated assessments of physical abilities of elderly. An added advantage is that early interventions are made possible with this device. Time consuming and costly assessments need only be done when there is an indication about the status change of the physical performance, in this case the range of motion of wrist.

There are a variety of games with dice that elderly and caregivers can play without additional training and the instrumented activity dice can be used in any home environment. No technology barriers for elderly are created. Data extraction from the dice can be automated to reduce documentation load for caregivers. In comparison to any camera equipment, the usage of the presented instrumented activity dice does not generate any privacy concerns since no image or voice recordings, from which elderly or caregivers could be identified, are required. In contrast to high-precision motion tracking and wearable sensor technology, our instrumented activity dice do not require the placement of any sensors on elderly or caregivers that can lead to unnatural behavior and anxiety. During the observation of classical game situations, we found that elderly typically quickly forget that sensors are placed inside the dice.

A key challenge in measuring the physical status and well-being of a person with activity dice lies in the fact that the thrown dice does not provide direct measures of a person's body motion. While an external camera can continuously track the joints and joint angles of a person (given that there are no occlusions) and wearable sensors can directly measure body motion and joint angles, the instrumented activity dice only allows for indirect measures of physical performance. However, our experimental results indicate that the assessment of the limitations of the range of motion achievable at the wrist become possible despite the limited set of independent measures. The advantage of our proposed activity dice lies in their low costs (less than 500€) and in their ability to be easily integrated into serious games.

5 Conclusion and Future Work

The presented study aims to determine if information on a person's physical abilities can be automatically estimated by asking the person to throw an instrumented activity dice. The automated assessment does not rely on attaching sensors to the person's body and does not require any camera recordings. Instead, we modified an off-the-shelf activity dice into an instrumented dice by integrating an embedded computer and Inertial Measurement Unit (IMU). We demonstrate how measurements like the time of flight, initial velocity, and number of turns of the instrumented activity dice during the throw can be automatically extracted from the IMU recordings. Statistical results from a study with 14 participants show that the initial throw velocity and the number of turns of the dice are strong indicators allowing to detect limitations in a person's wrist movement.

Our long term goal is to integrate our dice into serious games for the elderly where the automated measurements from the dice integrated sensors can also be used for predicting the onset of adverse health [45]. The work aims at the development of a low-cost alternative to physical assessments that require manual documentation and generate high workload for caregivers. Furthermore, our unobtrusive design allows us to get data in a realistic way, as the elderly are not cognizant of the assessments taking place, which will help them act in a natural way. Thus, future work involves extracting information about the throws performed by elderly using our instrumented activity dice during the serious games with the elderly.

Acknowledgements. We thank Ms. Rosel Cleef-Stassen (head of the social and therapeutic services at the "Seniorenzentrum Breberen" in Germany) and Ms. Kathrin Polfers (from the "Familienzentrum Lindenbaum" in Germany) for advice.

References

1. Branch, L.G., Meyers, A.R.: Assessing physical function in the elderly. Clin. Geriatr. Med. **3**(1), 29–51 (1987). https://doi.org/10.1016/S0749-0690(18)30825-5
2. Katz, S.: Assessing self-maintenance: activities of daily living, mobility, and instrumental activities of daily living. J. Am. Geriatr. Soc. **31**(12), 721–727 (1983)
3. Harris, C., Wattles, A.P., DeBeliso, M., Sevene-Adams, P.G., Berning, J.M., Adams, K.J.: The seated medicine ball throw as a test of upper body power in older adults. J. Strength Cond. Res. **25**(8), 2344–2348 (2011). https://doi.org/10.1519/JSC.0b013e3181ecd27b
4. Mayhew, J., Bemben, M., Rohrs, D., Ware, J., Bemben, D.: Seated shot put as a measure of upper-body power in college males. J. Hum. Mov. Stud. **21**(3), 137–148 (1991)
5. Davis, K.L., Kang, M., Boswell, B.B., DuBose, K.D., Altman, S.R., Binkley, H.M.: Validity and reliability of the medicine ball throw for kindergarten children. J. Strength Cond. Res. **22**(6), 1958–1963 (2008). https://doi.org/10.1519/JSC.0b013e3181821b20
6. LaPier, T.L.K., Bain, C., Moses, S., Dunkle, S.E.: Balance training through ball throwing activities. Phys. Occup. Ther. Geriatr. **14**(3), 23–40 (1996). https://doi.org/10.1080/J148v14n03_02
7. NIH (2019) Turning Discovery into Health. https://www.nih.gov/news-events/news-releases/worlds-older-population-grows-dramatically. Accessed 25 Mar 2019
8. Ball, C., Puffett, A.: The assessment of cognitive function in the elderly using videoconferencing. J. Telemed. Telec. **4**(1_suppl), 36–38 (1998)
9. Jansen, B., Rebel, S., Deklerck, R., Mets, T., Schelkens, P.: Detection of activity pattern changes among elderly with 3D camera technology. In: 2008 Optical and Digital Image Processing, p 70000O. International Society for Optics and Photonics (2008)
10. Montero-Odasso, M., et al.: Gait velocity in senior people an easy test for detecting mobility impairment in community elderly. J. Nutr. Health Aging **8**(5), 340–343 (2004)
11. Skrba, Z., et al.: Objective real-time assessment of walking and turning in elderly adults. In: 2009 Annual International Conference of the IEEE Engineering in Medicine and Biology Society, pp. 807–810. IEEE (2009)
12. Stone, E.E., Skubic, M.: Evaluation of an inexpensive depth camera for passive in-home fall risk assessment. In: 2011 5th International Conference on Pervasive Computing Technologies for Healthcare (PervasiveHealth) and Workshops, pp. 71–77. IEEE (2011)
13. Ghasemzadeh, H., Jafari, R., Prabhakaran, B.: A body sensor network with electromyogram and inertial sensors: multimodal interpretation of muscular activities. IEEE Trans. Inf. Technol. Biomed. **14**(2), 198–206 (2010)
14. Yamamoto, K., Ishii, M., Noborisaka, H., Hyodo, K.: Stand alone wearable power assisting suit-sensing and control systems. In: RO-MAN 2004. 13th IEEE International Workshop on Robot and Human Interactive Communication (IEEE Catalog No. 04TH8759), pp. 661–666. IEEE (2004)
15. Mengüç, Y., et al.: Wearable soft sensing suit for human gait measurement. Int. J. Robot. Res. **33**(14), 1748–1764 (2014)
16. Zhang, T., Wang, J., Xu, L., Liu, P.: Fall detection by wearable sensor and one-class SVM algorithm. In: Huang, D.S., Li, K., Irwin, G.W. (eds.) Intelligent Computing in Signal Processing and Pattern Recognition. Lecture Notes in Control and Information Sciences, vol. 345, pp. 858–863. Springer, Heidelberg (2006). https://doi.org/10.1007/978-3-540-37258-5_104

17. Urbauer, P., Frohner, M., David, V., Sauermann, S.: Wearable activity trackers supporting elderly living independently: a standards based approach for data integration to health information systems. In: Proceedings of the 8th International Conference on Software Development and Technologies for Enhancing Accessibility and Fighting Info-Exclusion, pp. 302–309. ACM (2018)
18. Guk, K., et al.: Evolution of wearable devices with real-time disease monitoring for personalized healthcare. Nanomaterials **9**(6), 813 (2019)
19. Al-khafajiy, M., et al.: Remote health monitoring of elderly through wearable sensors. Multimed. Tools Appl. **78**(17), 24681–24706 (2019). https://doi.org/10.1007/s11042-018-7134-7
20. Sarria-Ereño, A., Méndez-Zorrilla, A., García-Zapirain, B., Gialelis, J.: Wearable sensor-based system to promote physical activity among elderly people. In: 2015 IEEE International Symposium on Signal Processing and Information Technology (ISSPIT), 7–10 December 2015, pp. 100–104 (2015). https://doi.org/10.1109/ISSPIT.2015.7394248
21. Kim, J., Campbell, A.S., de Ávila, B.E.-F., Wang, J.: Wearable biosensors for healthcare monitoring. Nat. Biotechnol. **37**(4), 389–406 (2019). https://doi.org/10.1038/s41587-019-0045-y
22. Dohr, A., Modre-Opsrian, R., Drobics, M., Hayn, D., Schreier, G.: The internet of things for ambient assisted living. In: 2010 Seventh International Conference on Information Technology: New Generations, pp. 804–809. IEEE (2010)
23. Zhou, Y., Vongsa, D., Zhou, Y., Cheng, Z., Jing, L.: A healthcare system for detection and analysis of daily activity based on wearable sensor and smartphone. In: 2015 IEEE 12th International Conference on Ubiquitous Intelligence and Computing and 2015 IEEE 12th International Conference on Autonomic and Trusted Computing and 2015 IEEE 15th International Conference on Scalable Computing and Communications and Its Associated Workshops (UIC-ATC-ScalCom), pp. 1109–1114. IEEE (2015)
24. Pham, M., Mengistu, Y., Do, H.M., Sheng, W.: Cloud-based smart home environment (CoSHE) for home healthcare. In: 2016 IEEE International Conference on Automation Science and Engineering (CASE), pp. 483–488. IEEE (2016)
25. Paradiso, R., Loriga, G., Taccini, N.: A wearable health care system based on knitted integrated sensors. IEEE Trans. Inf. Technol. Biomed. **9**(3), 337–344 (2005)
26. Seneviratne, S., et al.: A survey of wearable devices and challenges. IEEE Commun. Surv. Tutor. **19**(4), 2573–2620 (2017)
27. Kamišalić, A., Fister, I., Turkanović, M., Karakatič, S.: Sensors and functionalities of non-invasive wrist-wearable devices: a review. Sensors **18**(6), 1714 (2018)
28. Christopher, S.M., et al.: A digital wooden tabletop maze for estimation of cognitive capabilities in children. In: Salichs, M., et al. (eds.) ICSR 2019. LNCS, vol. 11876, pp. 622–632. Springer, Cham (2019). https://doi.org/10.1007/978-3-030-35888-4_58
29. Royers, T.: De Tovertafel. Denkbeeld **28**(1), 25 (2016)
30. Ren, X., Ding, W., Crouter, S.E., Mu, Y., Xie, R.: Activity recognition and intensity estimation in youth from accelerometer data aided by machine learning. Appl. Intell. **45**(2), 512–529 (2016). https://doi.org/10.1007/s10489-016-0773-3
31. Särkkä, O., Nieminen, T., Suuriniemi, S., Kettunen, L.: Augmented inertial measurements for analysis of javelin throwing mechanics. Sports Eng. **19**(4), 219–227 (2016). https://doi.org/10.1007/s12283-016-0194-x
32. Grimpampi, E., Masci, I., Pesce, C., Vannozzi, G.: Quantitative assessment of developmental levels in overarm throwing using wearable inertial sensing technology AU – Grimpampi, Eleni. J. Sports Sci. **34**(18), 1759–1765 (2016). https://doi.org/10.1080/02640414.2015.1137341

33. Burkett, B., et al.: Kinematic analyses of seated throwing activities with and without an assistive pole. Sports Eng. **20**(2), 163–170 (2016). https://doi.org/10.1007/s12283-016-0221-y
34. Michael, D.R., Chen, S.L.: Serious games: Games That Educate, Train, and Inform. Muska & Lipman/Premier-Trade (2005)
35. Gallagher, S.M., Keenan, M.: Independent use of activity materials by the elderly in a residential setting. J. Appl. Behav. Anal. **33**(3), 325–328 (2000)
36. Wehrfritz (2019). https://wehrfritz.com/de_DE/. Accessed 10 Apr 2019
37. Raasch, B.: Accelerometers and free-fall detection (2007). https://www.embedded.com/design/system-integration/4028129/Accelerometers-and-free-fall-detection-protects-data-and-drives. Accessed 28 Mar 2018
38. Debicki, D.B., Gribble, P.L., Watts, S., Hore, J.: Wrist muscle activation, interaction torque and mechanical properties in unskilled throws of different speeds. Exp. Brain Res. **208**(1), 115–125 (2011). https://doi.org/10.1007/s00221-010-2465-2
39. Debicki, D.B., Gribble, P.L., Watts, S., Hore, J.: Kinematics of wrist joint flexion in overarm throws made by skilled subjects. Exp. Brain Res. **154**(3), 382–394 (2004). https://doi.org/10.1007/s00221-003-1673-4
40. Derbyshire, D.: Physical factors influencing the throwing action in netball and cricket players. University of Stellenbosch, Stellenbosch (2007)
41. Matsuo, T., Nakamoto, H., Kageyama, M.: Comparison of properties of a pitched-ball rotation measured by three different methods. ISBS Proc. Arch. **35**(1), 115 (2017)
42. Matsuo, T., Jinji, T., Hirayama, D., Nasu, D., Ozaki, H., Kumagawa, D.: Middle finger and ball movements around ball release during baseball fastball pitching. Sports Biomech. **17**(2), 180–191 (2018)
43. Girden, E.R.: ANOVA: Repeated Measures, vol 84. Sage (1992)
44. Williams, K., Haywood, K., Vansant, A.: Changes in throwing by older adults: a longitudinal investigation. Res. Q. Exerc. Sport **69**(1), 1–10 (1998). https://doi.org/10.1080/02701367.1998.10607661
45. Joseph, B., Toosizadeh, N., Orouji Jokar, T., Heusser, M.R., Mohler, J., Najafi, B.: Upper-extremity function predicts adverse health outcomes among older adults hospitalized for ground-level falls. Gerontology **63**(4), 299–307 (2017). https://doi.org/10.1159/000453593

WisdomOfAge: Designing a Platform for Active and Healthy Ageing of Senior Experts in Engineering

Bogdan Gherman[1], Laurentiu Nae[2], Adrian Pisla[1], Eduard Oprea[2], Calin Vaida[1], and Doina Pisla[1](✉)

[1] Technical University of Cluj-Napoca, Memorandumului 28, Cluj-Napoca, Romania
doina.pisla@mep.utcluj.ro
[2] Digital Twin, Bd. Mircea Voda 24, Bucharest, Romania

Abstract. The European population is undoubtedly ageing at an accelerating pace and by 2050; the number the elderly people will increase with almost 50% compared with 2019 numbers. Under the current legislation, the retirement age within most EU countries is 65, when many people are still able to perform within their profession at a decent level due to their knowledge and vast experience. The paper focuses on the design of a digital platform through which the retired seniors are able share their expertise with the younger generations, thus providing a useful, safe, and friendly environment that also addresses current challenges generated by the COVID-19 pandemics. The paper presents the analysis of the most important user needs and challenges that come with the age, sets the main pillars to be considered in the development of the application, both related to the overall architecture and main functions, and the user interface characteristics. A modular user focused design of the digital platform is proposed, by emphasizing its main functions, namely, to provide the means of a seamless interaction and an improved user experience. Artificial intelligence agents will be integrated to improve the matchmaking process by relying on the overall experience during training sessions.

Keywords: Active and healthy ageing · Learning management system · Software design · Elderly people needs

1 Introduction

Ageing in the 21st century is very different from continent to continent, to different regions and different social groups. The technological culture and the lifestyle are superposing on the genetically structure of a population.

Studies [1] have clearly shown that ageing population has an increasing trend (more than 20% globally), with associated physical and mental multimorbidities, especially for people aged over 60. This impacts not only the patients, but also their families, public health systems and the overall economy in an accelerated rate.

E. Pissaloux et al. (Eds.): IHAW 2021, CCIS 1538, pp. 18–30, 2021.
https://doi.org/10.1007/978-3-030-94209-0_2

Lately there are a lot of efforts and progresses advocating a healthier lifestyle, better nutrition schedules and a balanced life between work, family and leisure. An active lifestyle of the elderly, especially after retirement has proved to be highly beneficial, since "there was significant improvement in perceived health, reduction in social isolation, improvement in frailty status and reduction of falls at 3 months", [2]. WHO [3] defines healthy ageing as "the process of developing and maintaining the functional ability that enables wellbeing in older age", having as main target the ability of the elderly to meet the basic needs, have the required mobility, build relationships, learn and provide contributions to society.

The current research targets two different age groups: elderly people (EP), representing a high and increasing percentage within the total population in the European Union (EU), and the young people (YP), as the ones at the beginning of their career. There is no age issue here, but rather the access to resources and the technological approach. While the EP are trying to survive, the YP need to develop, both groups requiring resources in the process. The generational differences can be summarized as: Perspective vs. Enthusiasm or Patience vs. Speed, meaning that while the EP do see and understand the context, knowing what to expect at every step and mastering the technologies, but rather conservative, while the YP compensate with abundant energy poured into the everyday activities, but rather unfamiliar or unaware about the technologies. So, the problem is that we face with two groups of "technological analphabets" and the generally developed solutions are not addressed to the real problem but to the "considered" problem. Besides this, the importance of training for a rapid switch towards industry 4.0 is clearly shown in [4]. Both large companies and SMEs employees could benefit from the shared experience of the EP, so why not develop an environment that cand bring them together, for the benefit of both?

The EU Eurostat report [5] has considered three distinguished groups of EP which can be addressed and represented by the statistically defined characteristics:

- Group one (G1), aged 65–74;
- Group two (G2), aged 75–84;
- Group three (G3), aged over 85.

The G1 is a relatively fit group of people, being prone to an active life, with well-established habits and hobbies that they are willing to continue. Most of the times, if they are in good health, a strong desire to contribute to the society is still noticed. They are or like to be involved in everyday life and be supportive for their families, friend, neighbors, or former workmates. Their changes of status from one day to another is not easily accepted and might be even damaging for the body, soul, and mind.

The G2 group consists by people who are already accommodated with the retirement conditions, being less fit than G1 and more dependent on the healthcare system, family, and friends (as support group), but generally can be self-supportive, keep contact regularly with their family and friends, take care about their health conditions, and still maintain a social life.

The G3 group consists of people in the most difficult conditions. There is a lot of frailty, the expectations are very low, the body failures are common, daily healthcare is required, the general strength is low, from the family and friends the number of support people is dramatically decreasing, depression often occurs, and the available resources are constant or diminishing in parallel with an increase of the needs.

The digital age components must be addressed differently to the mentioned three groups. Based on the analyzed situation and because almost always the solutions are addressed to specific cases, in real life it may be considered that is happening like this, but without any structuration analysis or systematic research on needs and solutions, not only customization but also integration is difficult. Therefore, a lot of digital solutions directly addressing the patients, the clinics, pharmacies or NGO's and governmental bodies, with different levels or kinds of certifications, but hard to be appreciated or to be compared may be found on the market. Sometimes the added value is not sufficiently explained, so the EP do not understand the real benefit of the technology, to which they could otherwise adapt. The result is that the EPs are facing the digital solutions as foreign bodies, technologically incompatible, hard to understand, looking only to be bought and then remain practically useless.

The rest of the paper is organized as follows: Sect. 2 focuses on the EP needs and how the proposed platform can provide a solution; Sect. 3 illustrates the design of the platform, focusing on a modular architecture, implementing artificial intelligence agents and EP specific user interface elements; Sect. 3 summarizes the conclusions of this work.

2 Specific Needs of the Elderly

The most basic needs and concerns of ageing adults can be summarized as follows: financial (limited resources, a need which can be exacerbated by increasing expenses due to medical treatments), medical (both physical and psychological) and social communication (attacks of loneliness, difficulty in communication). COVID-19 crisis has made things even worse, sending millions of EP in a deep social isolation, relying mostly on digital solutions for satisfying both basic needs required for survival and the need for connectivity. Out of the main needs, this paper focuses mostly on social interaction, but with strong influence upon the financial and medical ones.

Bruggencate et al. in [6] has identified four themes that help characterizing the elderly communities: diversity, proximity, meaning of relationship and reciprocity, which we can use to characterize the EP needs and their owners. Indeed, there are huge differences among individuals about all specific needs, which leads to a diversified audience. Background, training and personal experience play a huge role and anticipating the true dimension of the targeted market segment is almost impossible. It is mainly a matter of expectation, much more than the measurable, objective reasons that lead to one or another type of social interaction.

The social network tends to shrink as people get older, mainly due to retirement, loss of social role (people tend to depend less on them) or loss of health. Rarely, but not uncommon, this may be the reason of their conscious decision. Sometimes, the most important relationships are developed with neighbors, which provide support, counseling and safety, aspects seriously hampered by the COVID-19 crisis.

The functions of relationships are strongly connected to social support and networking. The EP interconnectivity should provide emotional, physical, and informational support, while social connections should provide a meaningful life, as a powerful source of positivity and purposefulness. A well-connected aged person is usually a healthy and active individual interested in more than survivability and security, who still believes that life still has a lot to offer and wants to engage in various activities with persons just like him/her. These people go to the local club for physical interaction with others and the lack of it usually has a strong negative imprint on their health. And COVID-19 has hit them hard!

The healthy and social active elder is not only interested of receiving, but also in providing support for all those who need it. It is their way of being useful and contribute to the society. It is a proof that he/she is not just frail or vulnerable, but capable of giving back to the society something meaningful. After all, this is related to wellbeing and a strong psychological and physical health, being the most important proof of an independent individual who does not want to put too much pressure on their friends and families to ensure their daily needs, something that contributes in a large way to their satisfaction with life. Figure 1 summarizes the discussion regarding the basic needs of the EP, where meeting all three of them is seen as the desired scope, which leads to an increased life quality.

Fig. 1. The basic needs of the elderly.

A viable solution to the current needs and challenges imposed by the COVID-19 pandemics is the development of social network digital platforms. Provided that seniors can handle digital devices (PCs, phones, or PC tablets), these platforms can connect the EP and become a tool to secure most of their needs: supply (food, drugs, etc.), information (instructions, tips, local news, etc.) and perhaps the most important social networking. Several such digital platforms have been developed, some of them dedicated to the EP education within the digital world, like seniorsgodigital.eu [7], which is set to provide digital skills for the EP through a digital Learning Management System (LMS).

Another solution is the SONOPA Project [8], which targeted the wellbeing of the EP within the four dimensions: social, nutrition, hobbies and mobility using a sensory system to monitor and register the activities of the user. A matchmaking algorithm is developed to help connect user with similar hobbies or habits. The KOMP project [9] is digital platform intended to help the users connect using photos, messages, make video calls, adapted to the EP specific needs: large fonts, simplified interface, and a self-explanatory user manual.

Other digital platforms are built to be integrated with the household devices (TV, PC tablets), and which can be used to play games or socialize. Coelho et al. in [10] an application similar with Facebook, to be used with a smart TV, having multiple features for remote connection, photo sharing and voice or gestures interaction modalities. SMILE [11] combines IPTV services with social networking and home-based sensors (e.g., microphones, cameras) to detect the EP activity and propose customized therapies or specific hobbies as health remedies.

In [12] a digital platform implementing a machine learning algorithm performing automatic message destination address finding and message sending for the EP is presented. In [13] the authors have presented a web application implementing speech recognition. Using YouTube, voice commands are sent to make video phone calls, to create, watch or upload videos. A social media application is mentioned in [14], promoting the active ageing of the EP online/offline interaction. A user profile is created and recreational and cultural activities, depending on their interests are proposed.

All these digital platforms target mainly the Social Interaction and in a lesser extend the Medical Needs of the elders. There is one aspect that is usually left out: the sudden decrease of the activity level, usually following the retirement, which is almost impossible to be replaced within a short time. People are still connected (at least emotionally) to their workplace and cutting suddenly all ties is painful, sometimes leading to a deep depression [15].

A solution, which might provide a solid answer to all previously mentioned needs (not only Social and Medical ones, but also the Financial needs, within the COVID-19 restrictions) would be to develop on-line digital platforms that enable training/mentoring activities between the EP (as trainers/mentors) and the young and unexperienced employees (as trainees/mentees). In this scenario, a win-win situation is targeted: the mentors with plenty of experience, gained over tens of years at their workplace and with plenty of spare time relate to aspirational employees who could learn and even practice through such a platform. Such an example is presented in [16] (ProMe), which is an on-line platform developed with the purpose of providing work opportunities in the lives of the EP post-retirement. Great emphasis is placed on user preferences and a matchmaking process between the mentors and mentees using an efficient machine learning algorithm. Rating possibilities are also offered to the user, to describe the provided service quality. The ProMe features include a Search portal, Content posting, Calendar, Alerts and Video Conference. Although ProMe seemed very promising, it did not reach commercialization status. Besides the business-related aspects that have led to the failure the ProMe commercialization, we believe that the lack of specific targeted groups (i.e., market segmentation) of EP and/or YP has played an important role. Other disadvantages include low interaction, low specificity, lack of motivation, all of which negatively impacts the exploitation of such systems.

3 WisdomOfAge: A Seniors' Learning Management System

To improve the results of previously developed digital platforms, this paper proposes a Learning Management System fitted to have as mentors the EP with a very specific profile (e.g. mechanical engineers for the beginning), integrating Artificial Intelligence agents for a successful matchmaking, and developing the means for a high level of interaction. WisdomOfAge is **an environment** through which the EP will be able to transfer their knowledge and experience towards the YP, usually the employees of small or large industrial companies in the need of counseling, advice, technical solutions, work organization or project-oriented solutions. The WisdomOfAge LMS provides various and customizable tools necessary to build quality mentoring relationships between companies and their 50+ mentors and advisors. Within WisdomOfAge, a technical oriented LMS is proposed, targeting, at least for the beginning, training activities within Digital Product Development. WisdomOfAge will be operated by Digital Twin (DTW) [17], a company with a lot of experience in the on-line training services provided to industrial partner companies, in the framework of Industry 4.0, aiming to extend its range of services, by providing personalized mentoring, coaching, and training through senior experts for industrial companies.

The G1 and G2 are by far the largest groups within the 65+ EP and most of them still lead an active life. Out of these, around 300.000 EP are still involved in educational processes at various levels according to [5], back in 2019, showing that their intellectual abilities are still very good and that they are willing to spend around 30 h/week for this activity (again according to [5]).

The specific EP profile targeted for the WisdomOfAge LMS has at least the following characteristics:

- Good technical background (e.g., engineers, technicians, professors) who miss the professional life involvement.
- EP with abilities in complementary fields: teaching (to help unexperienced EP to prepare the content for the LMS), translating (English will be the official language), ICT who again can help the EP specialists in preparing the required content.
- A great desire to share their long time acquired experience with the younger generations.

Figure 2 presents the Unified Modelling Language (UML) use-case diagram, as the way the main actors within WisdomOfAge interact with each other. They are the EP engineers, usually helped by the auxiliary EP working as translators/interpreters (language should not be a barrier in the experience sharing process), ICT specialists and the teaching specialists to develop content and communicate with the trainees, on one hand and the students (large and SMEs companies' employees or university students) as Clients on the other, willing to pay for this service. The EP engineers will be enrolled following a careful selection process performed by DTW, who operates WisdomOfAge. EP will perform the training activities as a service for which they will be paid, based on a contract. DTW will also search for Clients interested in expanding their knowledge in engineering. Based on the registered profile, developed content and Client's requirements, a matchmaking process between the trainers and trainees will be performed within WisdomOfAge. The UML shortly presents the business strategy developed by DTW, aimed to ensure the WisdomOfAge long term financial sustainability.

3.1 The WisdomOfAge LMS Architecture

Based on the application requirements defined in Fig. 2, a software architecture has been proposed and presented in Fig. 3. The three layers of WisdomOfAge are:

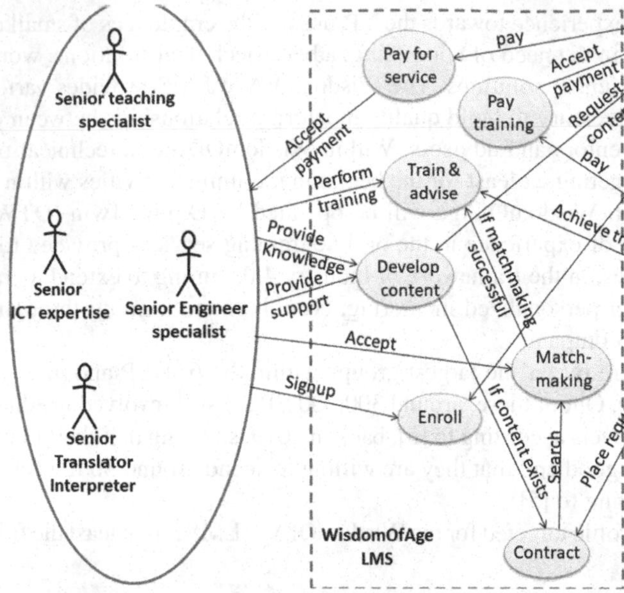

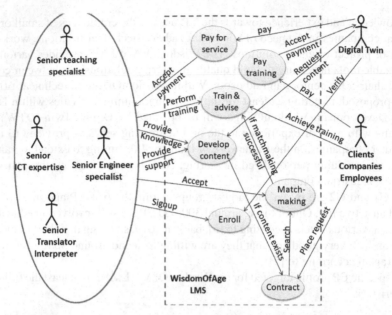

Fig. 2. The UML use-case diagram of the WisdomOfAge LMS.

- **Infrastructure layer** which consists of two modules: Knowledge Module and Matchmaking Module. The Knowledge Module consists in the teaching content developed by the trainer. As previously mentioned, the content will be initially developed for mechanical engineering CAD-CAE-CAM software packages, but it will be extended to other fields as well (electronics, ICT, etc.). In case the trainers need additional help in presenting the content (mostly updating the presentation style), other actors may be involved (employed by DTW). The Matchmaking Module will be achieved using Artificial Intelligence (AI) agents and will perform two types of matchmaking: T-C (Trainer-Client) or **primary matchmaking** and the T-T (Trainer-Trainer) or **secondary matchmaking** which leads to a team of trainers, usually having complementary abilities.
- **Platform layer** consists of the Client Module and Teaching Module. The Client Module is mainly a database of clients and EP trainers with its specific management interface which records all requests from the Clients (payers) in terms of content or consultations on specific matters of interest. The Teaching Module is an EP database with various competences, enrolled for performing training activities or consultations. It has its own management and signup interface for seniors.
- **Interface layer** has two components: Client and Trainer interface because the consortium knows some seniors do not have the required abilities to handle a complex UI. This layer introduces the two parties to each other and delivers the required content and information in an efficient and pleasant way. Besides the training possibilities, organized within a certain frame and in a more rigid manner, WisdomOfAge also offers the possibility for private consultations on request, for specific situations.

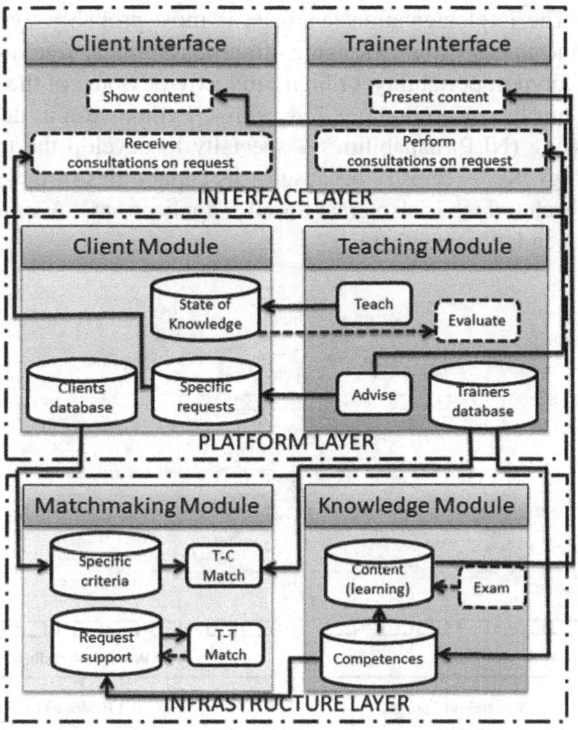

Fig. 3. The WisdomOfAge LMS architecture.

Regarding the **Matchmaking module**, AI agents with double role are developed:

- Perform the **matchmaking** between the trainers and trainees based on various criteria: trainer's experience and specialization, trainer's rating in certain areas, trainer's developed content (a dynamic feature); the trainee required experience, specific issues (if any), the trainee personal development level and the allocated budget. The AI matchmaking module targets an automated matching between trainers and trainees, permanently improved, so that as the Trainers database and Clients database are increasing in size (and data), better services are offered for the clients.
- **Monitor the Trainers** activity in a strict relation with the Clients (companies' employees), during training activities. Besides the actual rating, which sometimes is highly subjective, a short questionnaire is submitted by the trainees after each session, yielding a more realistic evaluation of the whole activity. A similar questionnaire is submitted by the trainer as well, to describe the overall activity.

A possible Artificial Neural Network (ANN) architecture is presented in Fig. 4. It analyses the profiles expressed in words, standard (selection-based) or non-standard (written text) and predicts the matching probability (a regression algorithm would be suitable). A dataset of 5.000 profiles will be used for initial training. It will be a data-driven deep learning approach and the Gated Recurrent Unit is mostly probable to be implemented. The implementation language is most probably Python because of several reasons: the in-built libraries, integration possibilities, free and open source, easy to create prototypes, portability, or high productivity. Some of the best libraries in Python, used for machine learning are: TensorFlow Python (useful due to its Natural Language Processing (NLP) capabilities – specially to develop the trainers' profiles or word embedding), Keras (mostly because of its capabilities of developing fast and precise NN), PyTorch (which is also great for NLP applications). A similar architecture can be used for secondary matchmaking.

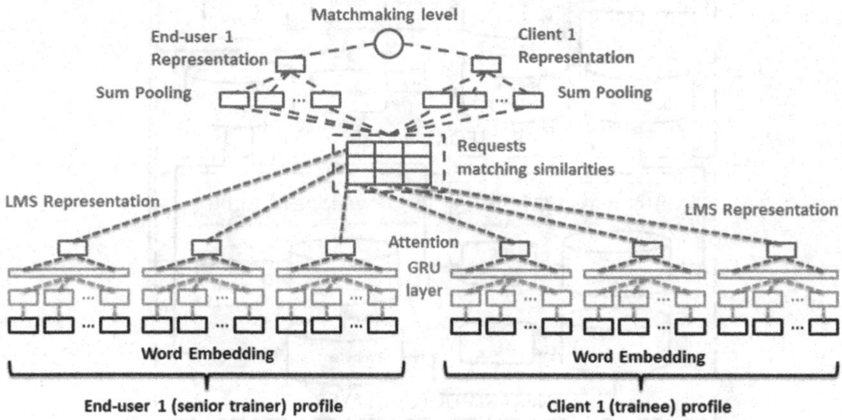

Fig. 4. The WisdomOfAge LMS ANN architecture.

3.2 The WisdomOfAge LMS User Interface

Due to the natural age impairments and the diversity of the trainers (background experience and ICT skills), designing the User Interface (UI) of WisdomOfAge is a challenging and difficult task. Generally, older adults suffer from a declining in the **perceptual, psychomotor, cognitive, and physical capabilities** [18]. About 50% of EP, especially men, suffer from hearing loss after the age of 65 [19], while most people over the age of 40 notice visual problems [20]. Among the most common causes of visual impairment for the EP are presbyopia, cataracts, macular degeneration, primary open angle glaucoma and diabetic retinopathy. The UI design alone cannot mitigate the effects of the visual impairment, but proper considerations, such as: use of contrasting colors, large objects, for example, can improve the overall experience. Physical impairments may lead to haptic deterioration or motion range limitations, which become more important when using touch screen devices (mobile), by reducing the capability of performing various gestures like tapping, pinching, dragging. Cognitive issues are also common with EP, the main manifestation being related to their ability to carry out demanding processes [21]. The cognitive decline, within WisdomOfAge, will be most obvious when the EP will have to learn the functions and processes required to operate the LMS, like the correct sequence of actions to upload content or to prepare it, prepare for the final test, etc.). However, within WisdomOfAge we are looking for experienced trainers who are willing and able to share their experience, despite their age and inherent health issues, which is why we are only considering the ICT skills (or lack of them) within the LMS design. The most important characteristics of the WisdomOfAge UI, can be summarized as in Table 1:

Table 1. Main characteristics of the WisdomOfAge UI for a positive user experience.

UI characteristic	Details
Attractiveness/Simplicity	A simple design, reducing the number of steps/operations to achieve the required tasks is desirable. Also, a nice balance of geometry and colors would increase WisdomOfAge user friendliness
Consistency	Same colors, objects' geometry, fonts (types and size) would improve readability and reduce the user confusion
Intuitiveness/Clarity	Simple and unambiguous icons and symbols, using well-known styles, meaningful labels (familiar for the user) would increase clarity and intuitiveness. A well-established set of questionnaires during testing, can be used as a measure of intuitiveness, targeting to quantify both the required effort to reach the goals and the learning curve (how easy it is to remember the steps)
Responsiveness	Feedback provided after each taken action (e.g. buttons pressed) and informing the user with regard to what is happening at each moment increases user self-confidence and trust in WisdomOfAge
Anticipation	The means to prevent the user to perform inappropriate tasks by implementing a strict control (e.g., disabling objects/menus until necessary) should be provided
Indulgence	Dead-ends should be avoided and ways to go back to previous steps in case of bad decisions should be provided within WisdomOfAge
Efficiency	Continuous optimization, based on user feedback should target the improvement of multitasking capabilities and/or the faster performance of certain tasks
Featuring	Explicit visual content for and easy understanding within the decision-making processes should be provided. Contextual menus where necessary and examples should be used. Online tools and templates for content development should be also provided

Figure 5 presents a hierarchization of the specific EP challenges and needs, based on an initial informal evaluation performed within our research center. Visual (32.8%) and cognitive (31.1%) impairments have showed up as the most important, which means that a great emphasis will be placed on designing a UI that is able to palliate these aspects.

A correlation matrix between the hierarchized EP challenges and the main characteristics of the WisdomOfAge UI is presented in Fig. 6, using the House of Quality within the Qualica QFD [22]. A correlation coefficient has been attributed between the

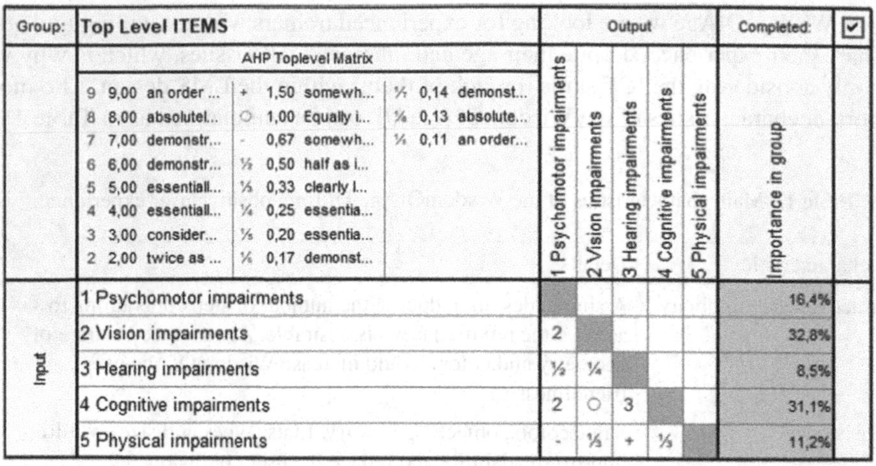

Fig. 5. The analytical hierarchy process of the EP challenges using the Qualica QFD software.

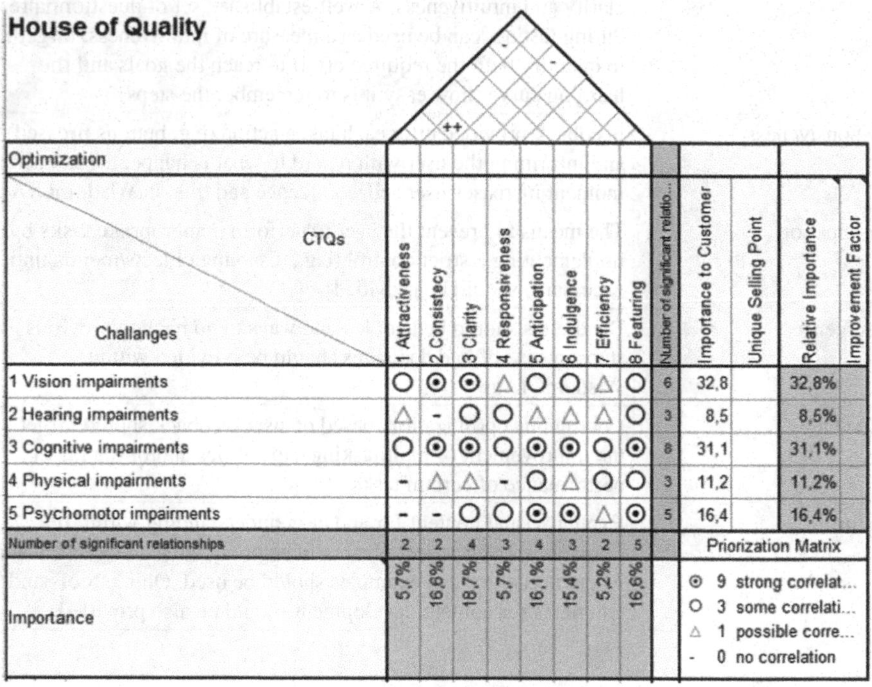

House of Quality
++
Optimization
CTQs
Challanges
1 Attractiveness
2 Consistecy
3 Clarity
4 Responsiveness
5 Anticipation
6 Indulgence
7 Efficiency
8 Featuring
Number of significant relatio...
Importance to Customer
Unique Selling Point
Relative Importance
Improvement Factor
1 Vision impairments
2 Hearing impairments
3 Cognitive impairments
4 Physical impairments
5 Psychomotor impairments
6 32,8 32,8%
3 8,5 8,5%
8 31,1 31,1%
3 11,2 11,2%
5 16,4 16,4%
Number of significant relationships
2 2 4 3 4 3 2 5
Priorization Matrix
Importance
5,7% 16,6% 18,7% 5,7% 16,1% 15,4% 5,2% 16,6%
9 strong correlat...
3 some correlati...
1 possible corre...
0 no correlation

Fig. 6. The correlation matrix between the EP challenges and the UI characteristics.

EP challenges and the UI characteristics, using the following scale: 9 points for strong correlation, 3 for minor correlation, 1 for a possible correlation and 0 for no correlation at all. In addition, we have noticed a positive effect between Consistency and Clarity (indicated by the "++" symbol within the roof of the House of Quality) and a possible negative effect between the Attractiveness and Efficiency, and Clarity and Featuring (where Clarity also means Simplicity). The results show that most stress should be placed upon a clean and simple UI (18.7%), but also highly consistent and provide important features to guide and explain how the UI should be used for best user experience (16.6%).

3.3 Conclusions

The paper presents the most important elements in the design of a learning management system where the trainers are mostly retired engineers. With a modular architecture, integrating AI agents, the WisdomOfAge digital platform can be easily improved and updated following validation tests and user feedback. The proposed ANN network provides multiple benefits: automated matchmaking between trainers and trainees and performs a close monitoring of the trainers' activity for the benefits of the Clients. The study regarding the EP challenges have shown that certain UI characteristics and functions should be mostly considered (clarity, consistency and featuring) for the alleviate the cognitive and visual impairments, that appear to be the most encountered impairments among the EP. The presented study will be a reference in the development of the WisdomOfAge LMS, targeting the following advantages for the EP: preserve an active professional or quasi-professional life, a feeling of purpose, interaction with YP, a feeling of satisfaction by social contribution and improved relations with their peers.

Future work focuses on designing the EP initial tests, followed by the implementation of the proposed design into a functional Learning Management System. Simultaneously, the YP users' interface will be developed, based on their specific needs.

Acknowledgement. This work was supported by a grant of the Romanian Ministry of Research and Innovation, CCCDI - UEFISCDI and of the AAL Programme with co-funding from the European Union's Horizon 2020 research and innovation programme project number AAL-CP-AAL-2020-7-83-CP-WisdomOfAge within PNCDI III.

References

1. Naja, S., Mohei, M., Makhlouf, E.D., Chehab, M.: An ageing world of the 21st century: a literature review. Int. J. Commun. Med. Public Health **4**(12), 4363–4369 (2017)
2. Merchant, R.A., Tsoi, C.T., Tan, W.M., Lau, W., Sandrasageran, S., Arai, H.: Community-based peer-led intervention for healthy ageing and evaluation of the 'HAPPY' program. J. Nutr. Health Aging **25**, 520–527 (2021)
3. World Health Organization Homepage. https://www.who.int/westernpacific. Accessed 25 June 2021
4. Clarizia, F., De Santo, M., Lombardi, M., Santaniello, D.: E-learning and industry 4.0: a chatbot for training employees. In: Yang, X., Sherratt, S., Dey, N., Joshi, A. (eds.) Proceedings of Fifth International Congress on Information and Communication Technology. AISC, vol. 1184, pp. 445–453. Springer, Singapore (2021). https://doi.org/10.1007/978-981-15-5859-7_44
5. Eurostat Homepage. https://ec.europa.eu/eurostat. Ageing Europe – looking at the lives of older people in the eu, 2020 report. Accessed 25 June 2021

6. Bruggencate, T., Luijkx, K., Sturm, J.: Social needs of older people: a systematic literature review. Ageing Soc. **38**(9), 1745–1770 (2018)
7. SENIORSGODIGITAL Hompage. http://seniorsgodigital.eu/. Accessed 24 June 2021
8. Bilbao, A., Almeida, A., López-de-Ipiña, D.: Promotion of active ageing combining sensor and social network data. J. Biomed. Inform. **64**, 108–115 (2016)
9. KOMP Homepage. https://www.noisolation.com/global/komp/. Accessed 24 June 2021
10. Coelho, J., Rito, F., Duarte, C.: "You, me & TV"—fighting social isolation of older adults with Facebook, TV and multimodality. Int. J. Hum Comput Stud. **98**, 38–50 (2017)
11. Gusev, M., Patel, S., Tasic, J.: Stimulating intellectual activity with adaptive environment (SMILE). In: Zdravkova, K., Eleftherakis, G., Kefalas, P. (eds.) The 8th Balkan Conference in Informatics, pp. 1–4. Association for Computing Machinery (2017)
12. Kobayashi, T., et al.: Social media mediation system for elderly people: message exchange learning type switching method. In: Guerrero, J. (eds.) International Conference on Network-Based Information Systems (NBiS), pp. 286–291. Conference Publishing Services (CPS) (2016)
13. Marcelino, I., Laza, R., Pereira, A.: SSN: senior social network for improving quality of life. Int. J. Distrib. Sens. Netw. **12**(7), 2150734 (2016)
14. Ha, T.V., Hoang, D.B.: An assistive healthcare platform for both social and service networking for engaging elderly people. In: 2017 23rd Asia-Pacific Conference on Communications (APCC), pp. 1–6 (2017)
15. Storeng, S.H., Sund, E.R., Krokstad, S.: Prevalence, clustering and combined effects of lifestyle behaviours and their association with health after retirement age in a prospective cohort study, the Nord-Trøndelag Health Study, Norway. BMC Public Health **20**(1), 900 (2020)
16. Kostopoulos, G., Neureiter, K., Papatoiu, D., Tscheligi, M., Chrysoulas, C.: ProMe: a mentoring platform for older adults using machine learning techniques for supporting the "live and learn" concept. Mob. Inf. Syst. **2018**, 9723268 (2018)
17. Digital Twin SRL Homepage. https://www.digitaltwin.ro/. Accessed 25 June 2021
18. Chang, J.J., Zahari, N.S., Chew, Y.H.: The design of social media mobile application interface for the elderly. In: IEEE Conference on Open Systems (ICOS), pp. 104–108. IEEE (2018)
19. Lawrence, B.J., Jayakody, D., Bennett, R., Eikelboom, R., Gasson, N., Friedland, P.: Hearing loss and depression in older adults: a systematic review and meta-analysis. Gerontologist **60**(3), e137–e154 (2020)
20. Swenor, B., Lee, M., Varadaraj, V., Whitson, H., Ramulu, P.: Aging with vision loss: a framework for assessing the impact of visual impairment on older adults. Gerontologist **60**(6), 989–995 (2020)
21. Wildenbos, G.A., Peute, L., Jaspers, M.: Aging barriers influencing mobile health usability for older adults: a literature based framework (MOLD-US). Int. J. Med. Inform. **114**, 66–75 (2018)
22. Qualica GmbH Homepage. https://www.qualica.net/. Accessed 30 June 2021

Application of a Comprehensive and Extendable Package of Personalizable Digital Services in Supporting Healthy Ageing

Marcin Adamski[1], Maciej Bogdański[2], Mikołaj Buchwald[2], Ludo Cuypers[3], Kinga Ćwiklińska[2], Michał Kosiedowski[2](✉), Marcin Wieczorek[2], and Sergiusz Zieliński[2]

[1] Grinfinity Sp. z o.o., Pl. Wladyslawa Andersa 7, 61-894 Poznan, Poland
[2] Poznan Supercomputing and Networking Center, ul. Jana Pawla II 10, 61-139 Poznan, Poland
kat@man.poznan.pl
[3] Commeto Bvba, Veldhovenstraat 40, 3945 Ham, Belgium

Abstract. It is by now a long-established fact that the European population is ageing. While this trend results largely from positive phenomena, it does come with a set of societal challenges. One of these challenges is making sure that the quality of life experienced by the growing population of elderly citizens remains as high as possible. The PELOSHA project aims to tackle this challenge by developing a comprehensive, personalizable and extensible solution aiding the wellbeing and remote care of older adults. The solution consists of a set of tools targeting various areas of the senior's wellbeing, orchestrated by unified mobile applications dedicated for end users. Work performed on the solution included user involvement every step of the way. The design and development of the platform and its user interface take into account the user needs obtained via interviews. The resulting system undergoes validation in a series of pilot deployments in 3 countries.

Keywords: Seniors · Ageing · AAL · Wellbeing · Package

1 Introduction

PELOSHA is a comprehensive solution aiding the wellbeing and remote care of older adults. The solution consists of a set of tools targeting various areas of the senior's wellbeing, orchestrated by unified mobile applications dedicated for end users.

The main target group for PELOSHA are seniors in assisted living facilities and their caregivers. The seniors start out with different sets of services depending on their age and condition. Afterwards, they continue to utilise the system while aging and the set of services evolves according to their changing needs, from preserving a good quality of life to managing the difficulties that will arise with the passing of time. The marketing claim of the PELOSHA platform focuses on the positive ways it influences the life of the user - "Assist me in living an active and happy life".

This paper describes the problem background, the idea behind the PELOSHA project, as well as the design of the technological platform.

E. Pissaloux et al. (Eds.): IHAW 2021, CCIS 1538, pp. 31–36, 2021.
https://doi.org/10.1007/978-3-030-94209-0_3

2 Problem Background

It is by now a long-established fact that the European population is ageing. Data by Eurostat from 2020 [1] shows that older people, defined as those aged 65 or more, made up 20.3% of the EU population in 2019. This ratio is projected to increase to 29.4% by 2050, and within this group, a growing part will be the people aged 75 or more. Furthermore, it is important to note that the old-age dependency ratio for the EU-27 was 25.9% in 2001, 34.1% in 2019, and is projected to reach 56.7% by 2050, meaning there will be fewer than two persons of working age for each older person (aged 65 or more). One of the challenges that arise from this trend is making sure that the quality of life experienced by the growing population of elderly citizens remains as high as possible.

A very promising route that is being explored in order to tackle this challenge is the usage of ICT technologies for alleviating the impacts of adverse symptoms related to ageing. Contrary to popular belief, low uptake of modern technology by seniors might not be a big barrier for this application. Our experience from the AAL Fit4Work project [2] has shown that seniors, at least the ones in the Exit phase of their life (so still professionally active), are willing to use ICT-based services, especially ones that offer support for their health and wellbeing. Eurostat's data on information and communication technologies (ICTs) [3] shows that in 2014 more than one third (38%) of the elderly population in the EU used the internet on a regular basis, which means there were at this time around 36.5 million elderly people in the EU who used the Internet on a regular basis and this number is bound to increase.

3 Proposed Solution

PELOSHA is a comprehensive solution aiding the wellbeing and remote care of older adults. The solution consists of a set of tools targeting various areas of the senior's wellbeing, orchestrated by unified mobile applications dedicated for end users.

The technologies and devices comprising the base of the various PELOSHA services are organised into independent modules. A module is a logical entity able to provide recommendations based on the operation of dedicated hardware (sensors) and software (rules for interpreting the measurements from the sensors). Therefore, from the point of view of the whole platform, a module is an autonomous unit capable of providing a specific recommendation-based service.

The general concept of the PELOSHA platform from the senior's point of view is presented in Fig. 1. The utilization of PELOSHA services is managed by the PELOSHA Assistant – an intermediary component between the user and the different modules integrated within the PELOSHA platform. The Assistant initially determines the general needs of the user based on their age, a set of preliminary measurements from the available sensors and/or a simple questionnaire. Afterwards, the Assistant queries the available PELOSHA modules about the current status of the user and their surroundings. Upon receiving an answer that is unsatisfactory in the context of the previously established personalized goals, the Assistant sends a follow-up request to the module, asking for recommendations for the user. The Assistant is also able to ask the modules for more specific data or to request that they perform a specific function (e.g. display guidance for an exercise).

The modules, on the other hand, initiate communication with the Assistant whenever the need to send a recommendation arises, e.g. a measured value exceeds a certain threshold. It is the Assistant's role to decide which recommendations obtained from the modules should be presented to the user as a notification, as well as how to combine the data received from different modules. The purpose of the Assistant is to provide the user with a single entry point to the modular PELOSHA services that assists them in maintaining a healthy, active and happy lifestyle in a seamless and proactive way.

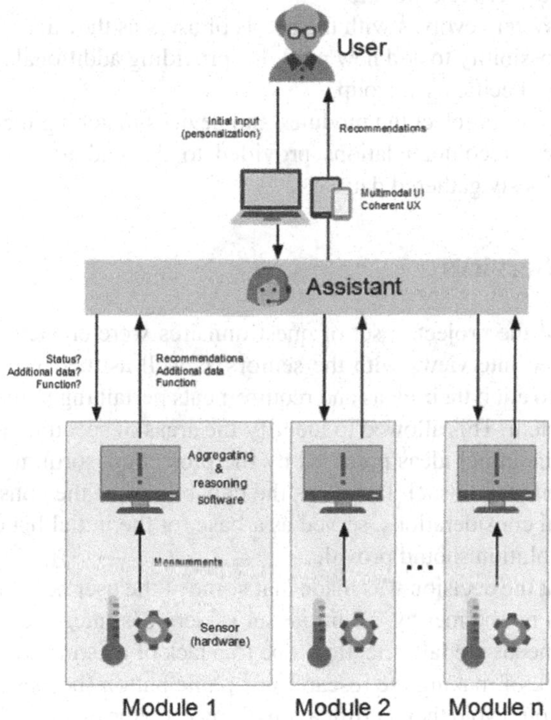

Fig. 1. Generic diagram of the PELOSHA platform from a senior's point of view

The caregivers interact with the different PELOSHA modules using the Caregiver Dashboard. The Dashboard presents the caregiver with aggregated data concerning all their charges. They are also able to view detailed data gathered for a specific person. The caregiver receives a notification in the Dashboard when an event requiring their attention occurs, e.g. a measured value exceeds a certain threshold. Thanks to the Caregiver Dashboard, caregivers are able to keep better track of their charges, without getting overwhelmed by the amount of gathered information.

The platform takes advantage of the synergy between the integrated solutions due to a novel combination of both: the capabilities provided by individual modules, and a set of crucial characteristics of the platform. Some of those characteristics are unique to PELOSHA, while others can be found in other AAL solutions targeted at tackling the challenge of supporting healthy ageing by providing a package of integrated services, such as DAPAS [4], INCARE [5], LIFANA [6], POSTHCARD [7], vINCI [8], or VITAAL [9].

In particular, the PELOSHA solution combines the following characteristics:

- comprehensiveness,
- uniformity of user experience,
- connectedness - data coming from different modules is analysed in parallel,
- sharing of devices between modules,
- flexibility - the system evolves with the needs of users as they age,
- extensibility - possibility to add new modules providing additional services,
- dedication to the specific user group,
- customizability - users select the modules and devices matching their needs/budget,
- personalizability - recommendations provided to the end user are influenced by analysis of previously gathered data.

4 Integrated Services

In the beginning of the project, a set of questionnaires were created and used to conduct semi-structured interviews with the seniors as well as their formal and informal caregivers, meant to elicit their ideas and requirements pertaining to the functionality of the PELOSHA system. This allowed to identify the areas of specific interest for the end user base among the initial ideas prepared by the project consortium. This set of areas of interest, confronted with such factors as the capabilities of the consortium, scope of the project, or legal considerations, served as a base for the initial list of functionalities that the prepared solution should provide.

This means that the decision was made that some of the user needs expressed during the interviews will not be met by the initial set of services integrated with the system. Examples of such needs are fall detection (due to a lack of existing solutions possible to integrate at the time of making the research) or panic button (because integration with existing systems would void their certification). However, the extensibility characteristic of the PELOSHA mentioned before means that those services can be integrated into the platform at a later time, when e.g. a fall detection solution maker is interested in making it available through PELOSHA.

As a result, the modules currently integrated into the PELOSHA platform include:

Health - allows to collect data on seniors' health (e.g. blood pressure, weight, body temperature), and provides access to this data for the caregivers. This helps maintain the continuity of care and improves the peace of mind of both the senior and the caregiver.

Reminders - gives caregivers the ability to add any event (e.g. reminder to perform a measurement) to the senior's calendar. The senior then receives a notification on the event at the specified time, allowing them to keep track wellbeing-related calendar.

Night Activity - the module collects electrical data from the distribution board via current transformers on each phase wire. The data is then analysed in order to determine which appliances have been active at what times. Finally, the data is transformed into human night-time activity patterns, which can be useful for detecting early symptoms of cognitive impairment (sundown syndrome).

Air Quality - the module monitors the state of the environment and recommends the appropriate actions to the user. This improves the indoor air quality, which results in better health conditions for the user. For outdoor air quality, recommendations about good and bad times for going out can be given.

Training - the general concept of the module is similar to a virtual personal trainer, with visualisation of an animated 3D trainer character and several virtual training spaces. The user appears in the virtual room as a stylized avatar following the user's movements thanks to full body motion capture. After an exercise set, the module evaluates the user's movements and performance, and a report is generated on the accuracy with which the user was following the instructions of the virtual trainer.

Activity - the module uses data gathered with the use of a smartband to provide a measure of physical activity of the user, including information on the type of user's movement, on the overall intensity of actions performed by the user during a given day, and on meeting the daily activity goal that is defined by the users themselves, given their BMI.

Staying in Touch - the module is created in order for an elderly person's needs to be automated logistically. It gives a possibility to ask for help with a help button. This button redirects to friends, family and professional caregivers, allowing the senior to signal their need of help in practical issues and improving their mental state by providing the feeling of safety.

5 Final Remarks

In this paper we discussed the construction of the PELOSHA platform. This platform is the approach of the project consortium at contributing to the increasing challenge of supporting good quality of life of the growing European population of seniors. The PELOSHA platform, while having its own vision of enabling a future marketable, extensible and customizable AAL solution, implements several features common to other solutions in the area that have been already developed or are currently under development. These include e.g. the comprehensiveness, connectedness, flexibility and personalizability of the platform. It must be noted that the PELOSHA solution has been extensively based in the identified needs of the target end users and the process leading to the creation of the platform prototype was characterized by a high degree of user inclusion, in order to increase the certainty concerning its usefulness.

As we have reached the moment in which the project has been able to successfully develop the envisaged prototype of the platform, end users will remain at the centre of our attention in the next step. This relates particularly to the already ongoing phase of pilot testing of the created solution. The developed platform undergoes testing in a pilot deployment in 3 countries, meant to validate its operation and, most importantly, confirm the correctness of the elected approach to the idea of integrating AAL services and offering them to the end users. This testing phase should enable us to deliver the final porotype of the developed platform at the end of the project. This prototype, in our opinion, constitutes the basis of providing a minimum viable product (MVP). This MVP could get extended in the future with further functionalities that were not included during the project, but might carry a potential of increased value to the target users and/or customers. Potential examples of such extensions include modules providing new services, like fall detection, or further development of the capabilities of the Assistant module, allowing it to make an even bigger use of the data coming from different sources in order to provide ever more informed recommendations. Adding such extensions should however, follow the first practical deployments of the developed solution.

Acknowledgements. The research presented herewith has been conducted within the PELOSHA project which is co-financed through the AAL Joint Program, managed by AAL Association and supported financially by the European Commission within call no. AAL-2017 AAL packages/Integrated solutions.

The project is also co-financed by national funding agencies in Poland, Belgium, Switzerland, and Hungary.

References

1. Ageing Europe—Looking at the lives of older people in the EU—2020 edition. Publications Office of the European Union, Luxembourg (2020)
2. Cvetković, B., et al.: Management of physical, mental and environmental stress at the workplace. In: 2017 International Conference on Intelligent Environments (IE), pp. 76–83. IEEE, Seoul (2017)
3. People in the EU: who are we and how do we live? Publications Office of the European Union, Luxembourg (2015)
4. DAPAS project webpage. https://dapas-project.eu/. Accessed 28 July 2021
5. INCARE project webpage. http://www.aal-incare.eu/. Accessed 28 July 2021
6. LIFANA project webpage. https://www.lifana.eu/. Accessed 28 July 2021
7. POSTHCARD project webpage. http://posthcard.eu/. Accessed 28 July 2021
8. vINCI project webpage. https://vinci.ici.ro/. Accessed 28 July 2021
9. VITAAL project webpage. https://vitaal.fit/. Accessed 28 July 2021

Assistive Devices and Systems

Co-designing Software and Co-building Inclusive Territories: Experimentation on a Campus as a Decisive Space for Empowerment

Franck Bodin[1(✉)] and Marie-Lavande Laidebeur[1,2(✉)]

[1] TVES Research Unit, University of Lille, Lille, France
{franck.bodin,marie-Lavande.laidebeur}@univ-lille.fr
[2] LIR3S, University of Burgundy, Dijon, France

Abstract. The mobilization of all expertises (scientists, IT developers, users with various profiles) and the co-design of a digital application on the "Cité Scientifique" campus (University of Lille) aims at the co-construction of an innovative digital tool for datavisualization and interactive mapping as a vector for optimizing spaces, mobility, equality, and inclusion of all populations. The design process, like the ITC tool itself, must increase and combine the skills of groups as individuals, and improve their interactions with spaces. The final goal is to allow the dissemination of the tool within civil society with a constantly increasing demand and users awaiting solutions. GEVU (Global Evaluation and Visualization of Uses) is a multimodal assistive ICT device to empower people. It is the outcome of a new participatory method with end users. Everybody, especially people with sensory, cognitive, motor, balance and spatial impairments, can use the software. The specifications allow to: generate an «Accessibility Performance Audit» in a guided and simplified way according to the four major types of impairments (visual, motor, mental and auditory); map the accessibility levels and barriers; find technical solutions and evaluate the costs of the installations and prioritize the actions to be carried out in the short, medium and long term; generate accessibility reports in relation to legal and usage indices.

Keywords: Data visualization and inclusive society · Space diagnostic system · Space optimization

Accessibility refers to the geographical scales, to the administrative, experienced and perceives spaces, and also to the diversity of territories stakes: diversity of actors, diversity of users and diversity of temporalities. This complex system products big data, complicated decision circuits and a lack of understanding. How to make data efficient? How to connect usage expertise, construction expertise, empowerment and inclusion? Digital tools are one of the most powerful vectors of changes, if it is based on a principle of sharing information and collective intelligence. The co-construction design invents new digital technologies to form databases viewable, readable, scalable and performative. The evolution of technologies is upsetting the modes of territorial visualization and offers new perspectives both for understanding and for action. The project is deployed

E. Pissaloux et al. (Eds.): IHAW 2021, CCIS 1538, pp. 39–44, 2021.
https://doi.org/10.1007/978-3-030-94209-0_4

on the campus "Cité scientifique" (University of Lille), miniature territory representative of the diversity of practices and facilities. As in many campus, user feedback reveals difficulties. This verdict concerns both people with impairments and people without impairments. But disabled people find difficult to keep up with their studies. The campus, a pilot site, hosts over 25,000 people. At a decisive and vulnerable time in their lives, young people come to live, study and undertake research. Student life is a crucial phase for accessing financial autonomy (through education and professional integration) and becoming a fully-fledged citizen (growing aware of diversity, accessing knowledge, developing team projects). The project also aims to train future professionals to inclusive planning.

1 Co-design an Innovative Digital Tool to Optimize Spaces and Social Inclusion

Co-design and work with users, with or without disabilities, will provide information about the degree of accessibility. It will indicate routes according to the capacities. The implementation of software and a web application will materialize twenty years of research in the area of digital development of territorial diagnosis and mobility facilitation. The interface GEVU (Global Evaluation and Visualization of Uses) will include: dynamic and participatory mapping, space audits, virtual visits with visualization of barriers, and decision support for administrators. The device can carry out and integrate surveys, visualize territorial data. This unique and centralizing service will promote the sharing and dissemination of information between actors, decision makers and users. It will assess the level of accessibility, propose technical solutions, estimate costs, pool solutions. This software will offer concise information to solve problems related to use and management. First dedicated to accessibility, this tool aims to support one of the three pillars of sustainable development, which is often less explored compared to economic and environmental stakes: the social pillar. The project is intended to design a diagnostic and assessment tool to visualize all the elements from the pathway to the furniture passing through the buildings, the services, the rooms, to co-construct a spatial and social framework accessible to all. The software will optimize the mobility chain. This visualization and management application will prioritize actions and carry out transformations. It will offer an interactive support integrating the information updated by the users, and will provide the competent authorities with the means to take actions. GEVU propose a new navigation solution, adapted through personalized user profiles (impairments, injuries, pregnancy, transport of bulky objects). At the end, the project creates stimulation around the production of collective reflections to promote. The co-construction fosters accessibility to higher education, citizenship and contributes to equal opportunities in the professional sphere and in civil society. The project trains students in the inclusive sustainable perspective in order to apply it in their future professional and business practices. It also makes a scientific contribution to the challenges of an inclusive society.

2 Providing Concrete Solutions to Improve the Mobility of All Users: Fundamental, Operational and Experimental Research

Is it people who are disabled or is the environment that is disabling? At the beginning of the 21st century, it became clear that space and buildings did not allow optimized accessibility and left the most vulnerable population. How to contribute to give equal access to education, goods and services? How to foster a democracy conducive to inclusion and the exercise of its rights of access to knowledge and to spatial justice? These questions imply inventing analytical participatory methodologies to raise accessibility indices from standards and comfort of use and to grasp the revolution resulting from digital innovations. In 1975, the first French law imposed handicap accessibility in public construction. Laws and decrees were initially perceived as constraints, with an additional cost. At the same time, the social demand for the legitimate right of access to citizenship has grown. The reversal of perspective, seeing accessibility as a lever for optimization, opens up new potentialities. The markets are turning towards generalized accessibility, which is reinvented as economic development, fluidity, mobility, quality of use. Communities and businesses are seizing it: for buildings (home automation, information and energy management), for transport (GPS, voice commands), for businesses. The acceleration of digital progress offers possibilities. The initial hypothesis has been validated: improving the accessibility of vulnerable people contributes to the accessibility of the entire population.

We are studying how digital technologies are reconfiguring our relationship to the territory. In this sense, we join Tewfic Hammoudi on city 2.0 and citizen skills [6]. Rather than "smart cities", our team prefers to speak of "connected territories" to mark the principle of human responsibility with regard to the use of technology, and equal access to all types of environment that have become interdependent (urban and rural). We rely on the one hand on the potential of data visualization, and, on the other hand on participatory innovations. The vision of structural accessibility, disruption and the frontier of disability has been replaced by the concepts of "universal accessibility" or "inclusion". The latter goes beyond the scale of the individual disabilities. It questions the role of the environment and education. It is no longer just a question of integrating vulnerable populations as a social act, even a disabling constraint, but of contributing to the benefit of all and to an inclusive democracy. User expertise becomes an angle of analysis to optimize space. This turning point in the humanities took place in the 1980s, starting with Canadian research, at the forefront of the subject, then in the United States and Japan. At the beginning of the 2000s, the concept found applications in facilities and training. They stimulated elected officials to act through the obligation of diagnosis and the search for technical solutions. They also updated the lack of tools to meet the need for inclusive accommodation. The UN International Convention on the Rights of Persons with Disabilities marks international awareness (2006, ratified by France in 2010). We are therefore at a crucial point, where scientific issues meet societal and economic issues.

The project mixes scientific analysis, user expertise and concrete implementation in action together. They innovate through the interaction of these three axes, as Patrick Fougeyrollas, a pioneer researcher: "access is a quality of the various elements of the environment, namely amenities (architectural and urban), technologies (equipment and consumer goods), public infrastructure (networks of transport and communication, public services), community spaces and interpersonal relationships (social networks, attitudes and social representations) and services (social, health, cultural, educational, leisure and sports, etc.)" [5]. Susanne Iwarsson and Agneta Stahl [7] define accessibility as an "umbrella" concept, covering numerous parameters in the life course of populations. Therefore, accessibility has an important scope, of a character anchored in practice, on social and material spaces. In 2019, after a restrictive vision imposed by the legislator, the aging of the population and access deficits, "handicap" standards become an essential diagnostic support for the High Quality of Use (HQU) advocated by Régis Herbin. From the poorly accepted and controlled normative constraint, we move on to the desire for optimized planning, an element of territorial economic development. This process is called "human-evotionary design concept" Franck Bodin [2]. The field of accessibility takes on a dimension parallel to space: the co-development of the individual and the collective.

3 A Participatory Method: Researchers, Practitioners, Students, and Staff Working Together

The inclusive research approach is defined by the co-construction of all the stages of production by all stakeholders in a specific territory. This principle stimulates interactions between actors/system/values/actions. Research becomes an operator of cooperation and translation of languages. Since the 1960s, experiments and social demand have emerged from new concepts for implementing social and political changes: consultation, cooperation, participation. In 1969, Sherry Ainstein defined a ladder of citizen participation in eight stages. But this scale always leaves a border between the decision-makers and the users, between the "bottom" and the "up". Co-design and co-construction goes beyond this paradigm. They designate a process of producing transformations by promoting real interactions between actors and with the environment. Stakeholders with different expertise engage together to product new tools and new ideas. Researchers create the conditions for meeting and dialogue with a team of web developers, students, and practitioners. This year, more than 90 students have already been involved in all levels in geography, urbanism and sociology. Both disabled and valid users took part in fieldwork, workshops, interviews, observations, and diagnostics. The results of this investigation provide very rich material, currently under analysis, for research and the app. The co-building process is on going, looking at ergonomics, architecture, software features, and considering solutions. This dimension is fully integrated into the diagnostics, since it reveals the difficulties, constraints and barriers that hinder studies and the campus experience.

The concept of "handimension" has proven to be effective. It consists of going through the situation, taking into account, by the body and the conciousness, the difficulties of certain users. This method completes quantitative surveys. Handimension goes through experience to become aware of the challenges of inclusion. Handimension consists of resizing the space with regard to the different forms of disabilities and implementing the principles of non-discriminating accessible accommodation. During these in-situ courses and workshops, issues and needs will be identified, categorized and analyzed as vectors of recognition of unfulfilled rights and disruption of access.

Disabled people are formulated with users. They make up the field diagnostic indices from the perspective of users' perception and needs, vectors of reclaiming spaces built for the benefit of the comfort of use of disabled and non-disabled citizens.

As a consequence, diversity of active partners are associated with the project: the TVES Research Unit, the University of Lille, Municipality of Villeneuve d'Ascq, Office of Student Life and Handicap, the Handifac Association, dedicated to supporting people with disabilities. The project was awarded by the FIRAH (International Foundation for Applied Research on Handicap) for the applied research part and by the BPI, I-Site and the Start Airr system of the Haut de France Region. The valuation of results is carried out with SATT Nord (Société d'Acceleration et de Transfert de Technologie) and ALACRITE France. Gulivers Campus also benefits from the support of CCAH (National Committee for Disability Action Coordination), companies (AG2R and Pro BTP). Since 2014, we have carried out comparative approaches with North American tools for cartography, spatial analysis and town planning with the University of Laval in Quebec (Quebec/Canada), CIRRIS (Interdisciplinary Center for Research in Rehabilitation and Social Integration-Quebec/Canada). Thanks to this collaborative process approach, the project was selected as "POC" (Proof Of Concept) by Lille 2020, World Capital of Design.

4 Results and Prioritary Perspectives

Built in the 1970s, the campus represents a huge site and an aging complex originally designed for cars, which, paradoxically, hinders mobility for everyone. This territory, which is particularly difficult to understand, is described as a labyrinth by the users. This is the case for many campuses in France and Europe. There is a need to create physical, human and digital links in terms of development and between users. The investigation showed the absence of accessible sanitary facilities or the possibility of access to the floors. This situation forces some students to stop their studies. Designing accessibility tools is therefore an emergency. Two phenomena intersect and have a series of significant effects on spatial and social organization: the aging of the population and the massive arrival of students with disabilities on campuses in France. Accessibility criteria are becoming a priority for public and private action. Between 2000 and 2050, the proportion of the world's population over the age of 60 will double from around 11% to 22% (WHO). In France, the second phenomenon directly concerns the university with the massive influx of students with disabilities. It results from the mainstream schooling policy and new accessibility legislation (1975–2005). A survey of Higher Education and Research Ministry shows that French universities had only 4,842 students enrolled and declared to be disabled during the year 1999–2000. In 2018–2019, they are 30,905, an exponential increase of 538% in less than 20 years [8]. To this can be added people whose mobility is temporarily reduced due to an injury, pregnancies, heavy objects, strollers: accessibility concerns everyone.

An experience and solutions booklet is in the process of being published. He will present the results of the research, largely in interviews, in order to provide testimony on the obstacle course imposed by the university space today. The other part has an operational vocation in order to disseminate the solutions, in the form of files according to the division by university area. Managers and users of other universities will therefore be able to consult this booklet to participate in the movement to make higher education accessible. The features of the software are emerging: The diagnostics interface for tablets, based on standards and use indices, is operational. It creates an "Accessibility Performance Audit" with visual outputs of positive and negative points for each type of impairment (diagrams and colors systems).

To conclude, we have identified three axes for the future. They have emerged during the project. The first is principle of humanism for higher education missions. It is one of the most important stages to build an inclusive society, and it must act in accordance with fundamental principles: equal access to knowledge and autonomy. The second is principle of reality and alignment with access initiatives. Educational access laws are starting to have the desired effect, and many people with disabilities are arriving at university. Campuses are not prepared to respond to a strong and urgent social demand. The third is principle of transmission: training future professionals in accessibility and datavisualization remains a major challenge. GEVU relies on a methodology combining theoretical analysis, simulations, and co-building with the users concerned. Students confirm that this allows them to gain an awareness and grasp of the issues at hand.

References

1. Arnstein, S.R.: A ladder of citizen participation. J. Am. Inst. Plann. **35**(4), 216–224 (1969)
2. Bodin, F.: Populations, Handicaps et Villes Durables: perspectives internationals et pratique nationale. In: Hommes et Terres du Nord, pp. 2–10. Société de Géographie de Lille, Lille (2003)
3. Bodin, F., Laidebeur, M.L.: Des territoires à venir, Chercher, innover, co-construire, Innovapresse, Paris (2018)
4. Fougeyrollas, P., et al.: Disability, environment, social participation and human rights: from the concept of access to its measurement. J. Hum. Dev. Disabil. Soc. Change 5–28 (2015)
5. Herbin, R., Gardou, Ch. (eds.): Handicap, une encyclopédie des saviors. Erès, Paris (2014)
6. Hammoudi, T.: De l'urbs oppodium à la datapolis. In: Sciences du Design, 2016/1 (n°3), pp. 42–49. PUF, Paris (2016)
7. Iwarsson, S., Stahl, A.: Accessibility, usability and universal design - positioning and definition of concepts describing person-environment relationships. Disabil. Rehabil. **25**(2), 57–66 (2003)
8. Ministère de l'Enseignement et de la Recherche et de l'Innovation, État de l'Enseignement supérieur, de la Recherche et de l'Innovation en France, Paris (2020)

CARIOT+ Care Coach – An Ambient Assisted Living Ecosystem for Supporting Open Data and Open Science Projects

Stefan Wagner(✉)

Department of Electrical and Computer Engineering, Aarhus University, Finlandsgade 22, 8200 Aarhus N, Denmark
sw@ece.au.dk

Abstract. Europe faces a demographic shift towards a population with more elderly and less working age people. This necessitates the development of relevant technology-based care services, utilizing ambient assisted living (AAL) concepts and technologies. AAL products often rely on third-party vendor services and cloud hosting, storing and retrieving measurements from these using application programming interfaces (API). This strategy is prone to breaking changes when the third-party vendor changes interfaces or licensing agreements, and can also present legal, privacy, and security problems for healthcare organizations. Using open and independent components represents an alternative approach, allowing the systems to work autonomously together with third-party systems, thereby securing data privacy and security, and allowing for easy replacement of components and services from third-party vendors. Technology, components, and services that support open standards and open data approaches allows for reuse in new systems, and for hosting them in the most relevant settings. The aim of this technical paper is to present the CARIOT+ Care Coach ecosystem for supporting open data and open science. The technical components forming the ecosystem are presented based on experiences gained during three AAL programme projects, the CAMI project, the HELP ME BRUSH project, and the ORASTAR project. The center piece is the CARIOT gateway which is designed for easy collection of ambient sensor data in the home setting, allowing third-party systems full control of the data flow and storage. The paper presents the preliminary experiences gained during the projects and discusses future relevant developments, including how third-party organizations can build on the CARIOT+ Care Coach ecosystem. Finally, the paper discusses how other projects can use the ecosystem to build new and open ambient assisted living systems in the future.

Keywords: Ambient assisted living · Telemedicine · eHealth · Pervasive health · Assisted devices · Human system interaction · Silo systems · Open science · Open data · Oral care · Healthcare · Micro service · CARIOT · CAMI · ORASTAR

E. Pissaloux et al. (Eds.): IHAW 2021, CCIS 1538, pp. 45–59, 2021.
https://doi.org/10.1007/978-3-030-94209-0_5

1 Introduction

Europe is undergoing a demographic shift where the rising population of elderly is straining healthcare systems and institutions across Europe. There are more than 75 million people above 65 years of age living in Europe [1], and it is projected, that by 2060 the total number of people at 65+ will constitute up to 35% of the European Union's population [2]. With old age comes increased morbidity and increased healthcare expenditures [1, 2]. European countries have in the last decades felt an increasing financial pressure due to chronic disease epidemics including: cardiovascular disease (CVD), cancer, diabetes, chronic obstructive lung disease (COPD), and chronic kidney disease (CKD), musculoskeletal diseases, and dementia. Already, chronic diseases affect more than 80% of people aged 65+ in most of the developed world, and is causing up to 90% of all deaths in Europe, with numbers foreseen to rise further in the next two decades [3]. An estimated 80% of healthcare costs are spent on chronic diseases in Europe, corresponding to an estimated cost of more than EUR 700 billion in the European Union alone, estimated to increase further as incidence rates increases further in the coming years [3].

Ambient assisted living systems have been hailed as a part of the solution and continue to provide increasingly more advanced services aiming at increasing the efficiency and effectiveness of caregivers and promoting additional self-care and patient autonomy [4]. The European Commission has been a major proponent for supporting this change, including via the AAL programme, a research program focusing on AAL as the solution to the demographic shift, strongly supporting open data and science.

There are already countless relevant platforms and components available that may be reused in new AAL products and ecosystems [4]. Some of these are based on open source and/or open standards, supporting open data and open science. However, many relevant products which are popular in the AAL community, and used widely in AAL programme projects, are tied to a third-party cloud service, where data security cannot be ensured by the healthcare provider organization themselves, thus potentially violating the GDPR rules of private and public healthcare service provider organizations. As an example, FitBit activity trackers have been used in several AAL projects. FitBit devices feature a functional semi-open API, allowing AAL ecosystem IT architects to tap into activity data (steps, sleep, heart rate) using basic REST based communication protocols accessing Fitbit's cloud services. However, systems based on Fitbit and similar services are often at the mercy of the product vendors (in this example, the US company Fitbit Ltd.), who can, at any time, and without warning, change their API or revoke access to the API altogether, leaving all systems using Fitbit devices vulnerable to future events outside of the control of the end-user organization. Same goes with Google Wear based devices using the Google Fit API, Apple wearables featuring the Apple HealthKit, and similar products from other vendors, including from Samsung and Huawei. What seems tempting and easy to adapt at first, can turn out to be a major problem in the future, during the implementation or operating phases, not only in terms of integration problems with changing API's and security tokens, but also in conflict with regional & national data security & privacy regulations. For instance, the storage of certain types of health data outside of Europe is not legal according to GDPR regulations, and some organizations even require that all data are kept locally within the ensuing organization with full accountability and ownership of data. Arguably, it is thus highly relevant to ensure that components being selected for existing and new AAL ecosystems, are not relying on third party servers, where data, privacy, and ethical regulations cannot be guaranteed. Thus, this paper calls for policy and decision makers to require components to be transparent, and to make support for open API's mandatory when designing new AAL systems and ecosystems.

The CARIOT+ Care Coach ecosystem presented in this paper is an example of an ecosystem consisting of individually independent components, that may be used either stand-alone or in combination with each other, as well as with third-party components. The CARIOT+ Care Coach ecosystem is based on work done in three AAL projects, the CAMI project, which developed a range of independent but mutually compatible ambient assisted living products and system components for supporting elderly with one or more chronic diseases, including the CAMINO telemedicine gateway (which was later developed into the CARIOT gateway product), and the HELP ME BRUSH and ORASTAR projects, which both have focus on supporting oral care, in the nursing home setting and the home care settings respectively.

The aim of this technical paper is to present the CARIOT+ Care Coach ecosystem for supporting open data and open science.

2 Methods

A study on end-user and technical design needs based on the synthesis of data from three AAL projects CAMI [5], HELP ME BRUSH [15], and ORASTAR [16] projects spanning four European countries, was performed. It involved mixed methods including workshops, interviews, field studies with observations at nursing homes, private homes, and hospitals, questionnaire studies with healthcare professionals: doctors, nurses, caregivers, dentists and dentists' assistants, as well as patients and informal caregivers. This was combined with technical design considerations and discussions with legal representatives and decision makers. The synthesized collated findings from the end-user and technical design studies led to a range of research challenges being identified, which were later used to create formal requirements for building the CARIOT+ Care Coach ecosystem. The resulting individual components are presented in this technical paper in order to provide an overview for third party developers seeking to use the full ecosystem or components thereof, in order to support open science and reuse.

3 Results

In the following sections, the ensuing CARIOT+ Care Coach ecosystem is described including its individual components. It is important to note, that the components can work independently of each other, allowing for open innovation. Thus, both the CARIOT gateway, as well as the apps presented in the following: the BeSAFE smart phone and smart watch apps, the CAMINO user interface, the OpenTele clinician and patient apps, and the REDCap clinical database can all be used as part of other ecosystems relying on open API's for integration, securing HIPAA and GDPR regulations are respected, and securing full control and transparency to the clinical partners, thus securing support for open data and open science. Next all user interface components can be replaced with new components, or they can get their data from other gateways and even become part of third-party ecosystems. Finally, the CARIOT gateway is not tied to any specific type of medico devices as long as they comply with the Bluetooth BLE (GATT) or Bluetooth ISO/IEEE 11073 PHD standard, although each device needs to be supported by relevant drivers. Likewise, the BeSAFE app can run on any Android based device (Google Wear for the BeSAFE Wear smart watch app).

We start with presenting the CAMINO Home Platform, which constitutes a major part of the CARIOT+ Care Coach ecosystem, originally developed as part of the CAMI project and later used for the HELP ME BRUSH & ORASTAR projects, as it enables the link from the home of the end-user with the rest of the ecosystem. A range of applications & devices are supported by the ecosystem, some of which will be presented.

3.1 The CAMINO Home Platform

The CAMINO Home Platform (Fig. 1) was jointly developed by the Danish company Aliviate and Aarhus University. It is conceptually based on the existing open-source project OpenCare and the Common Ambient Assisted Living Home Platform (CAALPH) developed as part of the CareStore project [6], and further modified to suit the CARIOT+ Care Coach ecosystem's requirements. OpenCare has been used for more than 10,000 nursing home end-user touch screen solutions marketed by several commercial vendors utilizing alternative user interface and back-end server functionality.The CAMINO Home Platform consists of a core engine running in a.NET environment, either Windows.NET or Linux Mono, which controls the execution of a range of independent micro-services, running either as separate processes or services, or running in a virtual machine process, either as virtualized components, or in a full virtual machine. The CAMINO Home Platform core controls the lifecycle of all the services and delivers a graphical environment for launching graphical user interface services. The individual micro-services may be implemented in either.NET, Java, Python, native C or C++. This is possible through the use of remote procedure calls for inter-micro-service communication. The CAMINO platform supports the automated discovery of other devices deployed in the home setting, such as the CAMI, CAMINI and CARIOT gateways, using service discovery based on the Bonjour & Avahi technologies, based on the Zero Configuration standard. These allow for the automatic detection of other hardware nodes in the network, including for instance one or more CARIOT gateways deployed in the home, thus enabling them to discover each other and synchronize.

Below, we present a selection of the graphical user interface applications that are running as micro-services within the framework. First, the Home Screen application (shown in Fig. 2), which is the starting point of the interactive system, in the shape of a touch screen launch menu for all registered user interface applications installed in the ecosystem. It is also possible to activate applications automatically (e.g., from an incoming call), or if an event is triggered by a sensor, e.g., a fall detection device, which could launch an audio sound alert asking for the user to confirm that he or she has not fallen.

Next, the "Health application" (Fig. 3), which can present healthcare data from either a local event data storage, from either the CAMI Cloud, OpenTele or REDCap. In fact, due to its open design, any data source can be used. The "Health application" is adapted for these diverse data sources and can easily be modified to include third-party components.

The Robot Control Center app (Fig. 4), which provides control over installed robots in the home setting. This application requires manual installation and configuration of all service robots.

Besides these, the Appointment, Calendar and Task applications provide basic calendar and task display and management to the user, including reminder services. All of these applications integrate seamlessly into the CAMINO Ecosystem, but may also run as stand-alone applications, or as part of other ecosystems.

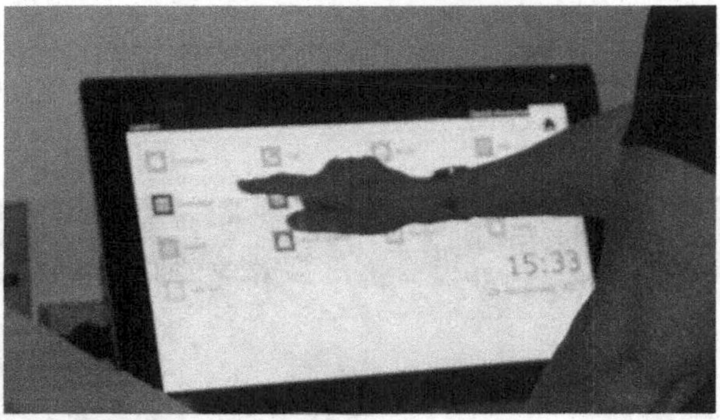

Fig. 1. The CARIOT+ CareCoach platform running on a touch screen device in the home of an end-user with the CAMINO user interface. The screen is an "always on device", which allows the user easy access for launching apps and getting information. A pattern adapted by several commercial AAL vendors, and used in more than 10,000 deployments.

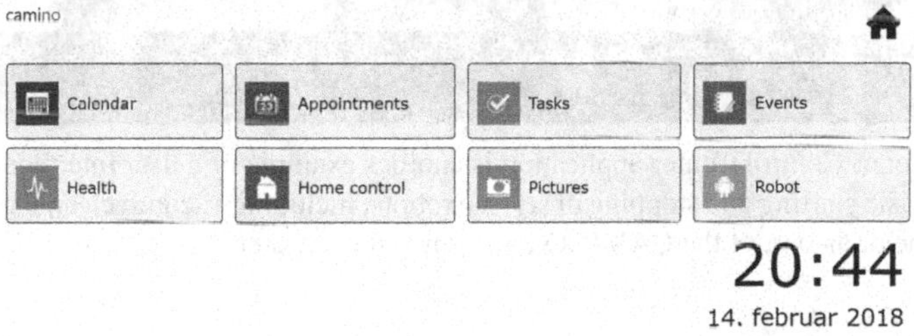

Fig. 2. The "CAMINO home screen" application represents the starting point of the user interface (same user interface as shown in an end-user setting in Fig. 1). From here, all installed applications featuring a graphical user interface may be launched. They will run as micro-services using inter process communication.

3.2 CareCoach User Interface

The CareCoach User Interface is a basic version of the CAMINO user interface. It especially targets end-users who prefers or requires (e.g., due to cognitive impairment) a minimalistic user interface that is extremely easy to navigate and use. It operates using

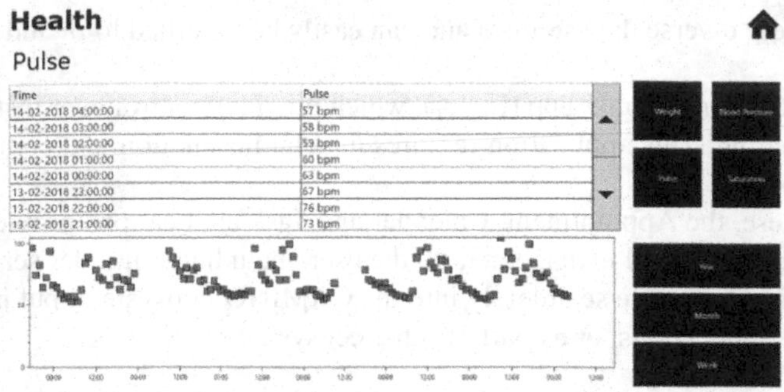

Fig. 3. The "Health" application also runs as a separate process acting as a micro-service. It can either communicate with local data services, or with cloud-based data stores. It can run stand-alone, or as part of the CAMINO platform & ecosystem, launched either from the home screen, or when a new measurement is received.

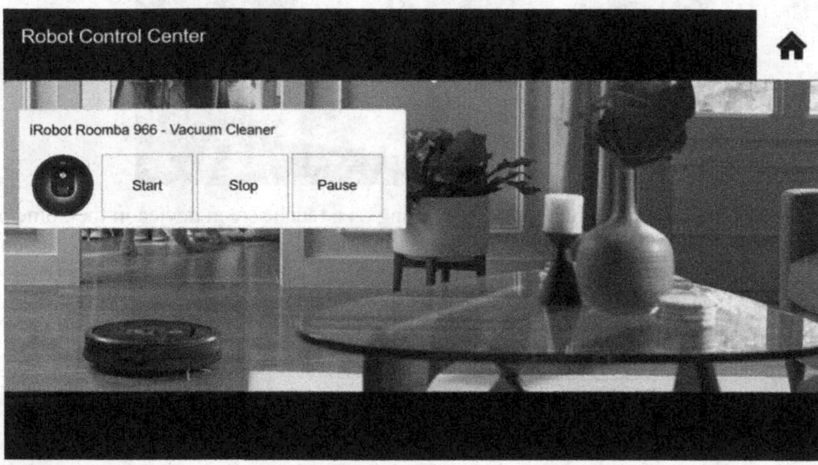

Fig. 4. The Robot Control Center application is another example of a user interface application. It is used for basic starting and stopping of service robots, including vacuum cleaners. It can either run stand-alone or as part of the CAMINO Platform and ecosystem.

microservices and receives data configured for the user, and facilitates limited end-user interoperability. As shown in Fig. 5, the system can be used to sample the mood of the user when an occupancy detects the user arriving in the area every morning, which is useful in many AAL and telemedicine scenarios. As shown in Fig. 6, it can also be used to present relevant sensor data arriving, e.g., that a blood pressure was received. It can also include localized decision support, prompting a warning if a measurement is beyond normal. Finally, when no relevant info is shown, the screen can either turn black, or shift between a range of pictures previously uploaded by the end-user or by relatives (Fig. 7).

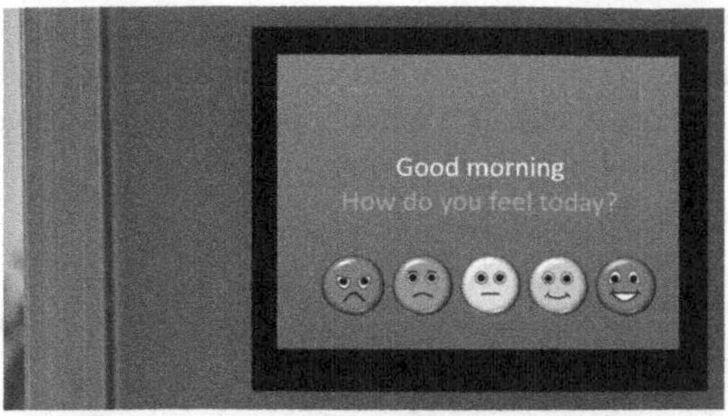

Fig. 5. A mood indicator in CareCoach

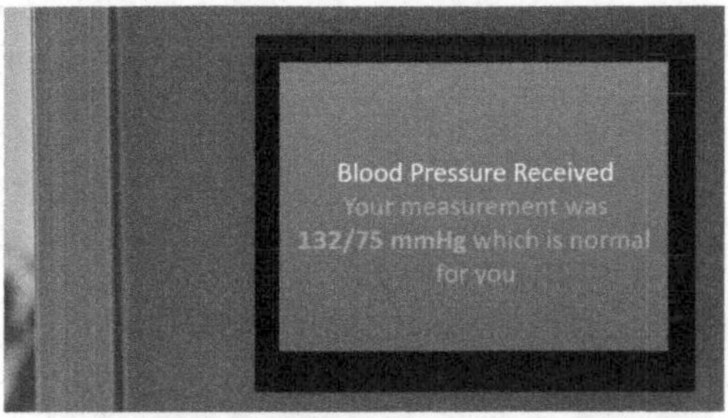

Fig. 6. Receiving various medico data and providing relevant information.

Fig. 7. The system turns into a wall picture viewer when not in use.

3.3 The REDCap Platform

The REDCap platform (Fig. 8) is a "secure web application for building and managing online surveys and databases" [11]. REDCap can be used to collect "any type of data in any environment" specializing in healthcare data. It supports both "online and offline data capture for research studies and operations", including having an HTTP-based REST API, which for example is used by the CARIOT gateway for reporting measurements. REDCap was originally developed by Vanderbilt University and since 2006 maintained by the REDCap consortium. REDCap is free to install and use on a research or clinical end-user organizations own server, it is however not open source, and the strict licensing rule implies, that only healthcare and research organizations are allowed to use it free of charge. Thus, REDCap is not useful for commercial projects not involving a clinical and/or a research partner. It is highly suited for supporting strict HIPAA and GDPR regulations, especially those concerning clinical projects, which have higher ethical and legal requirements than "wellbeing" projects.

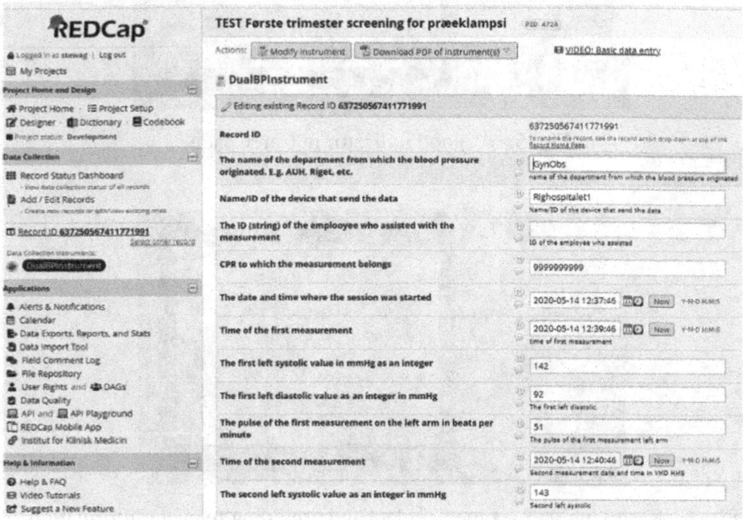

Fig. 8. REDCap is a database with API & a web-based user interface. It is used to collect clinical research data. An important feature is that each member organization can install the server and database in their own hosting environment, & thus comply with HIPAA & GDPR rules, and any national, regional, and local restrictions.

3.4 The OpenTele Platform

The OpenTele platform is a telemedicine ecosystem based on open-source technology [7, 8]. The 4S organization who is responsible for the further development of OpenTele defines it as: "a complete telemedical platform for handling patient-recorded outcome data and measurements from personal health devices. The platform comprises a server part and a tablet and/or smartphone app installed which is either provided to the patient or installed on the patient's own device if possible. From the OpenTele app, the citizen can answer questionnaires, perform measurements, and via a video link communicate with the general practitioner or hospital staff. The server also features a web site where a clinician can login, manage, and communicate with patients, as well as review collected data" [7] as shown in Fig. 9.

OpenTele is both open source and component-based, and thus very adaptable and extendable for new applications [8]. It is built using the Java programming language for the server side, and HTML5 and JavaScript for the web clients (Fig. 9). The database is based on the popular MySQL database server, while a REST interface is provided for integration with third party systems using JSON (Java Script Object Notation) encoding [7]. Besides the OpenTele Android app for patients, a code library (named 4SDC) for integrating with a range of IEEE 11073 telemedicine medico devices has been developed [7, 8].

OpenTele has been deployed to more than 10,000 telemedicine patients and has been adopted by more than 20 organizations around the world, including private companies, hospitals, and care institutions [8]. OpenTele is in many ways unique in the sense that no other widely deployed open-source telemedicine system exists, where the source code can be downloaded and modified by any third-party company or research organization, thus being a proponent of open data, open science, and open innovation. It continues to be used for clinical applications, including with back-end integration to electronic patient record systems. OpenTele has also been adapted to become part of the CARIOT+ Care Coach ecosystem where it can be used both as backend web site for clinicians, but also as a patient user interface. Integration is achieved using OpenTele's REST interface using the OpenTeleNet API, as an example of the open data approach of CARIOT+.

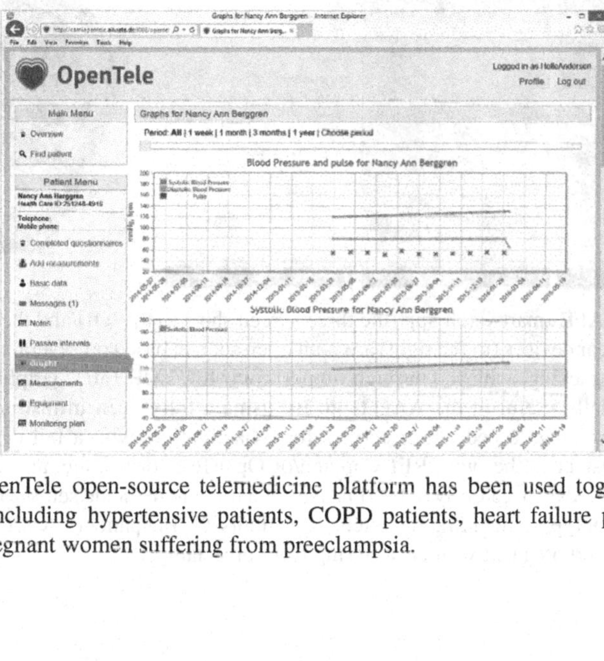

Fig. 9. The OpenTele open-source telemedicine platform has been used together with many patient types, including hypertensive patients, COPD patients, heart failure patients, diabetes patients, and pregnant women suffering from preeclampsia.

3.5 The BeSAFE and BeSAFE Wear Apps

The BeSAFE app for smartphones and the BeSAFE Wear app for smart watches (Fig. 10) were developed by Aarhus University and Aarhus University Hospital for facilitating clinical telemedicine research into patient activity, rehabilitation, and fall detection where sensor fusion, combining environmental (ambient) sensors with wearable sensors were needed, and where it was not legal to use Fitbi, Google Fit, nor Apple HealthKit (or similar) cloud-based services. Thus, the BeSAFE apps provides basic activity tracking, including pedometer (based on Android's step counter virtual sensor service), location tracking (BLE proximity), as well as fall detection. The BeSAFE apps can send data via either HTTP(S) REST or MQTT formatted using JSON following the HEUCOD recommendation, a tentative open standard for "Healthcare Equipment Usage and Context Data" systems [21].

The BeSAFE apps allows clinicians at Aarhus University Hospital to do independent research, sending data directly to a REDCap database. Both apps are open source, and can be adopted for third-party ecosystem and other scenarios of use.

Both BeSAFE apps are open source, and build on open-source software by James Montemagno. They are completely free of any bindings to for-profit companies, and can be used as a research platform.

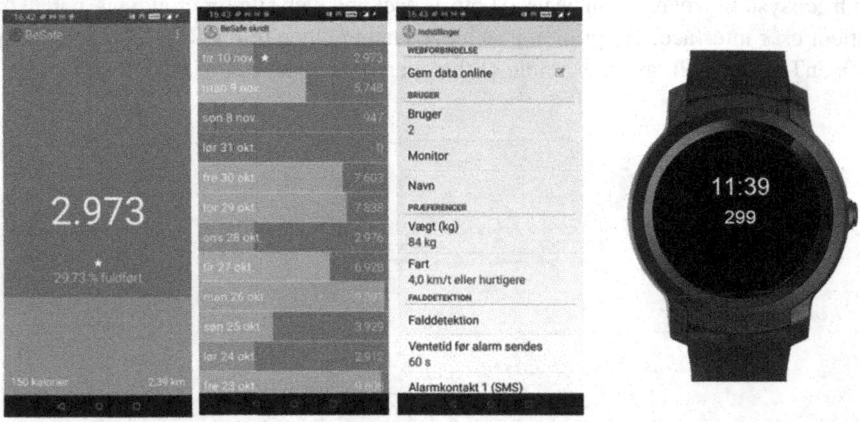

Fig. 10. The BeSAFE smartwatch app (the three screen shots to the left) and the BeSAFE Wear app for Google Wear devices (to the right) are both open source, based on several research papers. Low-cost activity tracking, achieved through support for below EUR 150 smartphones and smartwatches, is especially useful in the AAL field. By using a fully open infrastructure, it is easy to combine services, e.g., a pedometer service for rehabilitation, with a fall detection service. BeSAFE can be used together with REDCap and/or OpenTele for storage, and with CAMINO, OpenTele and the CARIOT gateway to become part of a full telemedicine setup which can be useful for many patient types, including hypertensive patients, COPD patients, heart failure patients, diabetes patients, and pregnant women suffering from preeclampsia.

3.6 The CARIOT Gateway

The CARIOT gateway (Fig. 11), is developed by the Danish IoT company Aliviate, Aarhus University, and the University of Minho, and brought to market by the Danish AAL service company Medica Connect as the CARIOT BRUSH product. However, it can be licensed by any third-party company looking for full control of a multipurpose gateway product with source code access. It enables non-internet connected healthcare and care devices such as blood pressure, saturation, and weight devices used for traditional telemedicine and telehealth applications to become internet-of-things (IoT) enabled [9]. This includes: support for the open source "the Things Network" IoT Cloud platform, as well as support for commercial IoT platforms such as Loriot.

This integration is achieved using a combination of 2G, 3G, 4G, LoraWAN, BLE, and/or WiFi communication channels, depending on the specific usage-scenario and the needs of the end-users. The widely used medico devices for telemedicine and telehealth are already supported, including IEEE 11073 PHD and BLE GATT based devices, and the CARIOT platform can easily be expanded with additional healthcare and acre devices as required.

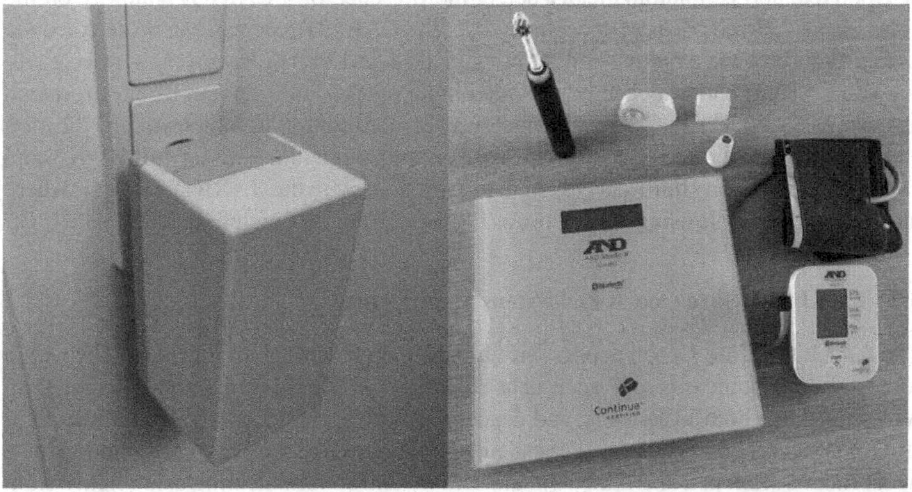

Fig. 11. The CARIOT gateway is marketed by Danish company Medica Connect, but both hardware and software stacks can be licensed to third-parties. It is essentially a platform rather than just a gateway, and can both communicate with local medico and ambient sensor devices, store the data, provide end-user warnings and signaling (via light and sound interfaces), as well as perform long-range communicate using Lora, GSM (2G), 3G/4G/5G, and WiFi. The software stack is flexible, and besides Lora and IP communication, HTTP/HTTPS/REST/MQTT is supported out of the box to any end-point. Some models have support for ZigBee, while BLE and Bluetooth is fully supported. As shown on the illustration, we have used the gateway with toothbrushes, blood pressure and weight devices, as well as presence and occupancy sensors.

Besides telehealth and telemedicine devices and services, the CARIOT gateway supports a range of telecare and personalized medicine devices and services. These include traditional telecare and ambient assisted living services such as fall detection and prevention, generalized support for tracking user activity-levels and activities of daily living using both wearables and ambient sensors. Furthermore, the CARIOT platform has support for interfacing with ZigBee sensors, and thus more than 3,000 different sensors.

The CARIOT gateway can in the CARIOT+ Care Coach ecosystem be substituted by other data capture gateways, including the CAMI gateway platform developed by the Swiss company Eclexsys, and the CAMINI gateway developed by Danish company Aliviate, both of which are running the open source AdCAMI service developed by Aliviate, for supporting telemedicine devices, such as blood pressure, oximeter, weight, temperature and more. Other commercial sensor gateways exist, including the Qualcomm 2Net gateway. However, the Qualcomm 2Net gateway relies on the use of closed silo cloud solutions, with a REST API providing access using a subscription-based business model.

The CARIOT gateway features seamless service discovery on WiFi networks, using the Bonjour and Avahi frameworks, as well as zero-configuration deployment when using LoraWAN or 4G. The Bonjour zero-configuration service means a CAMINO or OpenTele app can automatically detect the presence of a CARIOT gateway on the network, and allow for easy connection. Also, the CARIOT gateway can be detected via Lora presence or via a unique and proprietary IP-based MQTT discovery service.

The CARIOT gateway can be provided in an open-source version free for research use, but its foremost strength is, that it allows absolute control of which storage location and technology is preferred by the end-user organization, allowing for full HIPAA and GDPR flexibility. Any third-party system can integrate with the CARIOT gateway, where integration is possible using either Lora or IP-based protocols, including REST & MQTT.

3.7 CARIOT+ Care Coach Ecosystem Architecture

The CARIOT+ Care Coach ecosystem utilizes a microservice architecture [12] with a focus on open standards and open data connections. Microservice architectures is in widespread use both in industry and academia [13]. In the Microservice architectural style, a system is composed of independent and fine-grained services, each running in its own process, often in a distributed system setting, and communicating using lightweight protocols such as HTTP or MQTT [13, 14]. Microservices and microservice architectures are intended to be simple and focus on accomplishing one task well, while retaining the ability to work independently of each other (within practical limitations), which also implies that they can be reused for different purposes [14]. Also, due to their heterogeneity, each service can be built using the most appropriate technologies for the task, making it possible to combine different open source and commercial products into a single system. As an example, the CARIOT+ ecosystem uses both C, Python, Java, HTML5, and C#, running on both servers, PC's, and embedded hardware. Furthermore, microservices natively support so called "continuous delivery" allowing frequent releases and fast feedback loops. As opposed to a Service-based architecture, where system vendors rely on third-party services, e.g., on a Fitbit cloud service, the Microservice architecture prescribes that the system owner has full control over all components in the system.

4 Discussion

The aim of this paper was to provide an overview of the various components identified during three AAL projects as useful for supporting an open ecosystem for ambient assisted living services for supporting open data and open science, and open innovation. The paper was made in order to inspire the AAL and other research communities and industry vendors to reuse existing frameworks when building new systems, including those presented in this paper, and to a higher degree rely on open standards-based microservices using open and standardized communication protocols, rather than closed silo solutions. In addition, by sharing our findings, we hope to receive suggestions from the community on other third-party platforms that would be useful for expanding on the CARIOT+ Care Coach Ecosystem.

While there is naturally some amount of manual technical plumbing involved, the CARIOT+ Care Coach ecosystem is fairly easy to configure and deploy, both on a cloud server, on a private networked server, or even as an in-home-only system, providing ultimate privacy settings. However, the technical difficulties in bringing heterogenic platforms and technologies together should not be underestimated.

Thus, we will not argue against the need for large monolithic care applications and services for some use cases, but with the CARIOT+ Care Coach ecosystem, we have shown the way for a dynamic, flexible, and highly adaptable ecosystem that will allow for the integration with other systems through the use of open standards and the microservice architecture pattern. However, more work is needed, in terms of creating a true standards-based common inter-communication language for these services. Here, the HL7 FHIR standard [20] appears highly relevant to employ combined with the emerging HEUCOD recommendation [21]. However, HL7 FHIR is only slowly maturing into relevancy for the AAL sector, and more work is arguably needed before it becomes an effective tool for use within the AAL community.

Finally, we acknowledge the work of previous consortia to develop similar open ecosystem architectures for ambient assisted living, including the UniversAAL and the Reaal platforms [4, 10, 17–19]. The integration from CARIOT+ with these platforms has not yet been achieved due to a range of dependencies that we were not able to satisfy, and plain difficulties in running the open-source code provided by these frameworks. Thus, we would recommend for the redesign of these platforms, and any similar platforms, to be divided into smaller services as. microservices, which would allow easier reuse of the platforms as part of new ecosystems, and we would call for creating dedicated and low-cost hardware, such as sensor gateways, which will make it fast to start integration efforts. In addition, we call upon added standardization support in the field. While there are many standards for device integration and healthcare data integration, the CARIOT+ Care Coach ecosystem currently has to rely on industry standards including MQTT and HTTP to create an effective middleware. A tentative recommendation is being developed as part of the HEUCOD project, called the HEUCOD recommendation [21], which is currently supported by the CARIOT+ Care Coach ecosystem, but which need to be further disseminated and developed in order to attract proper industry interest.

5 Conclusion

This paper has provided an overview of the CARIOT+ Care Coach ecosystem. The paper presented the various components used, and detailed how they could be used together, either as part of the ecosystem or to help build other systems, or even become part of third-party ecosystems, completely independent of CARIOT+.

However, as argued in the paper, the main quality of the approach of the CARIOT+ Care Coach ecosystem lies in the extensive support for open science and open data, as the ecosystem does not rely on cloud services from third party vendors which could be in conflict with legal and ethical regulations and requirements in the partner country, but rather support REDCap and OpenTele, which combined represents some of the most used datastores for clinical research. Also, by ensuring full developer control of all components, including the interfaces, endpoints, and connection; projects using the CARIOT+ Care Coach ecosystem will not run the risk of sudden and unexpected breaking changes from a third-party vendor, nor the risk of breaching GDPR regulations.

Acknowledgments. Under the project numbers AAL-2014-1-087, AAL-2018-5-184, and AAL-2020-7-239 this work was supported by three grants from the Active and Assisted Living Programme (AAL) and Innovation Fund Denmark, as well as by a grant of the Danish Agency for Science, Technology and Innovation. Also, thank you to the CAMI, HELP ME BRUSH and ORASTAR consortium partners respectively and their national funding agencies. Also, thank you to our many commercial, research and end-user partners for making this work possible. Also, the project was supported by the HEUCOD project "Healthcare Equipment Usage and Context Data (HEUCOD)" under the "Smart Industry 4.0 Programme" from the Danish "Regionalfonden og Socialfonden".

References

1. European Union, Europe's population is getting older. How will this affect us and what should we do about it? IP/05/322, Brussels, 17 March 2005
2. European Union, The 2021 Ageing Report: Underlying Assumptions and Projection Methodologies. EUROPEAN ECONOMY, European Union (2021)
3. Locatelli, F., Covic, A., Macdougall, I.C., Wiecek, A.: ORAMA: a study to investigate EBPG impact on renal anaemia–design and baseline data. Life **9**, 10 (2008)
4. Memon, M., Wagner, S.R., Pedersen, C.F., Beevi, F.H.A., Hansen, F.O.: Ambient assisted living healthcare frameworks, platforms, standards, and quality attributes. Sensors **14**, 4312–4341 (2014)
5. CAMI consortium. http://www.camiproject.eu/. Accessed 27 Mar 2018
6. Wagner, S., Stenner, R.G., Memon, M., Beevi, F.H.A., Pedersen, C.F.: Common ambient assisted living home platform for seamless care. In: Proceedings of the 8th International Conference on Pervasive Computing Technologies for Healthcare, pp. 199–200, May 2014
7. 4S organization. OpenTele. http://4s-online.dk/wiki/doku.php?id=opentele:overview. Accessed 1 July 2021
8. Wagner, S.: Telemedicine with OpenTele. Medivate Publishing (2017)
9. Medica Connect webshop. http://medicaconnect.eu. Accessed 27 Mar 2018
10. Ferro, E., et al.: The universAAL platform for AAL (ambient assisted living). J. Intell. Syst. **24**(3), 301–319 (2015)
11. Harris, P.A., Taylor, R., Thielke, R., Payne, J., Gonzalez, N., Conde, J.G.: Research electronic data capture (REDCap) - a metadata-driven methodology and workflow process for providing translational research informatics support. J Biomed Inform. **42**(2), 377–381 (2009)
12. Yussupov, V., Breitenbücher, U., Krieger, C., Leymann, F., Soldani, J., Wurster, M.: Pattern-based modelling, integration, and deployment of microservice architectures. In: 2020 IEEE 24th International Enterprise Distributed Object Computing Conference (EDOC), pp. 40–50 (2020). https://doi.org/10.1109/EDOC49727.2020.00015
13. Newman, S.: Building Microservices: Designing Fine-Grained Systems. O'Reilly Media, Inc. (2015)
14. Lewis, J., Fowler, M.: Microservices: a definition of this new architectural term, July 2021. https://martinfowler.com/articles/microservices.html

15. AAL Programme – HELP ME BRUSH. http://www.aal-europe.eu/projects/help-me-brush. Accessed July 2021
16. AAL Programme – ORASTAR project. http://www.aal-europe.eu/projects/orastar/. Accessed July 2021
17. Marcos-Pablos, S., García-Peñalvo, F. J.: Technological ecosystems in care and assistance: a systematic literature review. Sens. **19**(3), 708 (2019)
18. Gonzalez-Usach, R., Julian, M., Esteve, M., Palau, C.: Federation of AAL & AHA systems through semantically interoperable framework. In: 2021 IEEE International Conference on Communications Workshops (ICC Workshops), pp. 1–6. IEEE, June 2021
19. Gambi, E., Montanini, L., Raffaeli, L., Spinsante, S., Lambrinos, L. Interoperability in IoT infrastructures for enhanced living environments. In: 2016 IEEE International Black Sea Conference on Communications and Networking (BlackSeaCom), pp. 1–5. IEEE, June 2016
20. Saripalle, R., Runyan, C., Russell, M.: Using HL7 FHIR to achieve interoperability in patient health record. J. Biomed. Inform. **94**, 103188 (2019)
21. Wagner, S.R.: HEUCOD draft recommendation (2020). https://pure.au.dk/portal/da/publications/heucod-draft-recommendation(5399d8e7-22d9-4b39-86f8-7ab9ebef4661).html. Accessed July 2021

Detection and Monitoring of the Destructive Impacts in the Social Networks Using Machine Learning Methods

Elena Doynikova(✉), Alexander Branitskiy, and Igor Kotenko

St. Petersburg Federal Research Center of the Russian Academy of Sciences (SPC RAS), St. Petersburg Institute for Informatics and Automation of the Russian Academy of Sciences, 14-th Liniya, 39, St. Petersburg 199178, Russia
{doynikova,branitskiy,ivkote}@comsec.spb.ru

Abstract. With the growing importance of the digital world, it becomes more and more important to ensure people's, especially young people's, security in the digital world as a whole and in the social networks, particularly. In this paper the authors introduce for the first time the developed full-cycle methodology for detection and monitoring of the presence of destructive impacts via their manifestation in young people profiles in the social network. The research uses information technology methods together with psychological methods. The paper describes the proposed methodology and the techniques included in it as well as the results of the experiments. The methodology should help to determine the features of destructive impacts for further development of recommendations for young people on how to identify and resist them.

Keywords: Destructive impact · Social network · Digital space · Young people · Detection · Monitoring · Machine learning

1 Introduction

Modern world started moving to the digital space before the COVID-19 pandemic but it enforced this process. In this space the social networks are important means of information propagation and communication, especially for young people. With the growing importance of the digital world, it becomes more and more important to ensure people's, especially young people's, security in the digital world as a whole and in the social networks, particularly. It can be done by understanding and learning of the destructive impacts, providing young people with the means of resisting the destructive impacts, and creation of healthy digital environments. The authors understand the destructive impacts as "impact that can provoke aggressive actions and aggressive behavior in relation to others or yourself" [2].

E. Pissaloux et al. (Eds.): IHAW 2021, CCIS 1538, pp. 60–65, 2021.
https://doi.org/10.1007/978-3-030-94209-0_6

In this research the authors started from the understanding and learning of the destructive impacts via their manifestation in young people profiles in the social network, researching the young people's vulnerability to such impacts, and developing the mechanisms for detection and monitoring of the presence of such impacts.

The research used information technology methods together with psychological methods. The research was conducted using the data from the Vkontakte social network [1] jointly with the results of the psychological tests.

The psychological tests allowed detecting changes in the individual's psychological portrait. Such changes can indicate vulnerability to the destructive impacts and presence of such impacts.

Information technology methods allowed forecasting the results of the psychological tests based on the information within young people profiles in the social network to monitor the presence of the destructive impacts as well as to analyse the individual's environment to outline the groups in the social network that propagate such impacts.

Previously the authors already published the selected research results, namely, in [2] the common idea of the approach to detection of destructive impacts was introduced, in [3,4] the technique for classifying the social network profiles according to the psychological scales using machine learning methods was described. In this paper the authors introduce for the first time the developed full-cycle methodology for detection and monitoring of presence of destructive impacts via their manifestation in young people profiles in the social network that integrates the previous contributions. The contribution of this paper is as follows:

- The developed full-cycle methodology for detection and monitoring of the presence of destructive impacts via their manifestation in young people profiles in the social network.
- The techniques applied on the separate stages of the methodology.

The novelty of the paper consists in the new methodology for detection and monitoring of the destructive impacts integrating the technique for the determination of the social network profiles' classes according to the psychological scale and the technique for the determination of the social network communities' classes according to the psychological scale.

The methodology should help to determine the features of destructive impacts for further development of recommendations for young people on how to identify and resist them.

The paper is organized as follows. Section 2 briefly analyzes the related research. In Sect. 3 the proposed methodology is introduced. Section 4 contains the discussion and conclusion.

2 Related Works

There are multiple papers considering impacts provided by the people, society, and information processes on the person in the period of adolescence. These impacts can be both positive and negative [5,7,8].

Negative impacts, such as aggression and destructiveness, are usually analysed considering the ideas of Erich Fromm [2,6,7,9]. They are also considered in [10].

In [9,11] it is noticed that information processes that can potentially lead to destructive behavior can be unfolded in the information streams that are shared between people and various social groups, for example, in the information streams of the Internet [2]. In [2] the authors supposed that the destructiveness can be reflected in the communication system, including Internet space.

Due to the size of the Internet space it is almost impossible to analyse it manually. Thus, to analyse information in the Internet space, and particularly in social networks, machine learning methods are used.

For example, in [12] the authors use convolutional neural networks to identify psychological disorders in services of social microblogs. In [13,14] the authors analyse the sentiments of Internet users based on the data extracted from short messages using a deep neural network. In [15] the authors build a system for recognizing the psychological profile and character traits of a person using his/her photos from the Facebook social network. In [16] the authors investigate the level of emotional impact produced on a person when looking at the content presented in digital images using a naïve Bayes classifier.

While a lot of research has been done in the social network's data analysis for different goals, they do not consider the detection and monitoring of the destructive impact manifestation in the social network's profiles.

3 The Proposed Methodology

The proposed methodology for detection and monitoring of presence of destructive impacts via their manifestation in young people's profiles in the social network incorporates the following stages:

1. Application of the technique for the determination of the class on the psychological scale for the social network profiles. If some deviation from normal values is detected for the profile, then it is sent for manual analysis.
2. Monitoring of the profiles and redefinition of their classes on the psychological scale. If a deviation from the normal values exceeds the predefined threshold then the features that lead to the deviation are outlined and sent for manual analysis. The social network communities related to the appropriate profiles are sent for automated analysis on stage three first.
3. Application of the technique for the classification of the social network communities related with the appropriate profile on the psychological scale. The communities that have a potentially destructive impact are added to the separate list and sent for manual analysis.

4. Determination and construction of constructive stimuli to eliminate destructive impacts.

On the first stage of the methodology (determination of the class on the psychological scale for the social network profiles) the following technique is applied:

- Form the dataset of the labeled profiles from the Vkontakte social network. For this goal the profiles of the Vkontakte social network were gathered. Then testing of the profile owners using Ammon's test was conducted [17]. This test was developed for the determination of constructive, destructive and deficient manifestations of six personality Ego-functions (namely, aggression, anxiety, external Ego-delimitation, internal Ego-delimitation, narcissism, and sexuality). Mapping of the test results with the gathered profiles allowed us to label the dataset.
- Apply the machine learning methods to determine the class on the Ammon's psychological scale automatically based on the information gathered from the users' profiles. The authors determined 100 features including the numerical parameters, a set of words and the parameters specified based on image processing. To train the software classifiers the obtained on the previous step labeled dataset was used.

On the second step of the technique the experiments were conducted for the 460 labeled profiles using a 10-block cross-validation, 90% of the dataset were used as the training sample and 10% - as the testing sample. The following classifiers were tested: the support vector machine (SVM), linear regression (LR), multilayer neural network (MNN) with the ReLU activation function and convolutional neural network (CNN). The MNN showed the best accuracy for the Ammon's test results forecasting: 59,94% [4].

On the second stage (monitoring of the profiles and redefinition of their classes on the psychological scale) the social network profiles are monitored for timely detection of possible manifestations of destructive impacts. For this goal the technique from stage one is applied. The information from the profiles is gathered with given intervals and reclassified using trained machine learning models.

On the third stage (classification of the social network communities related to the appropriate profile) outlined in the previous stage communities are classified on the psychological scale using the following technique:

- Form the dataset of the labeled communities from the Vkontakte social network. For this goal the communities were extracted from the profiles gathered on the previous stage. The first time the classes of the communities were determined considering the classes of users' profiles that are part of the appropriate community.
- Apply the machine learning methods to determine the community's class on the psychological scale automatically based on the information gathered from the communities (i.e. the text content of posts). To train the software classifiers the obtained on the previous step labeled dataset was used.

On the second step of the technique the experiments were conducted for the 250 labeled communities using a 10-block cross-validation, 90% of the dataset were used as the training sample and 10% - as the testing sample. The following classifiers were tested: bag of words, weighted bag of words, continuous bag of words, skip-gram and fastText - as basic classifiers, and max-wins, weighted voting and soft voting ensembles - as combining ensembles. The soft voting ensembles showed the best accuracy for the community class forecasting: 55,72% [4].

The communities that were classified as potentially destructive or the communities that are common for the profiles with a tendency to destructiveness are sent for manual analysis.

The communities that were returned from manual analysis with approved destructive content are added to the new dataset for further retraining of the classifiers.

Stage four (determination and construction of constructive stimuli to eliminate destructive impacts) provides recommendations for young people on how to identify and resist the destructive impacts. It is in the scope of further work.

4 Conclusion and Discussion

In the paper the methodology for detection and monitoring of the destructive impacts in social networks was proposed. The accuracy obtained for the techniques implementing the stages of the methodology is common for the tasks of this class but it requires further enhancement in future work.

First of all it should be noticed that destructiveness itself is a rather complex phenomenon, thus, searching for its features in the information space of social networks is not a trivial task. But manual implementation of this process by the experts is time-consuming and almost impossible because of the volumes of information in social networks. Thus, the joint application of information technology methods and psychological methods looks promising.

The manifestations of destructive impacts in the users' social network profiles do not necessarily indicate destructive impacts within the social network as soon as these impacts can be external. That is why the third stage of the methodology requires manual confirmation. Currently the authors form a dataset of communities obtained on the third stage for manual checking by the experts and plan to use it in future work to enhance the community classification technique.

Detecting deviations in users' profiles can help timely outline the profiles that require attention and possibly preserve young people's health. Besides, analysing information that leads to deviations can help determine the features of destructive impacts and better understand their nature.

In future work it is planned to develop recommendations for young people on how to identify and resist the destructive impacts.

Acknowledgement. The reported study was funded by RFBR, project number 18-29-22034 mk.

References

1. Social network Vkontakte. https://vk.com. Accessed 30 July 2021
2. Branitskiy, A., et al.: Determination of young generation's sensitivity to the destructive stimuli based on the information in social networks. J. Internet Serv. Inf. Secur. (JISIS) **9**(3), 1–20 (2019). https://doi.org/10.22667/JISIS.2019.08.31.001
3. Branitskiy, A., Doynikova, E., Kotenko, I.: Use of neural networks for forecasting of the exposure of social network users to destructive impacts. Inf. Control Syst. (1), 24–33 (2020). https://doi.org/10.31799/1684-8853-2020-1-24-33
4. Branitskiy, A., Doynikova, E., Kotenko, I.: Technique for classifying the social network profiles according to the psychological scales based on machine learning methods. J. Phys. Conf. Ser. **1864**, 012121 (2020). https://doi.org/10.1088/1742-6596/1864/1/012121
5. Zlokazov, K.: Perception of the extremist text by subjects with different levels of destructive attitudes. In: Politicheskaya lingvistika, no. 1 (2014)
6. Fromm, E.: The anatomy of human destructiveness, vol. 2337. Random House (1975)
7. Boduszek, D., Hyland, P.: The theoretical model of criminal social identity: psycho-social perspective. Int. J. Criminol. Sociol. Theory **4**(1), 604–615 (2011)
8. Shneyder, L.: Personal, gender and professional identity: theory and methods of diagnosis. Moscow State University of Psychology and Education (MSUPE) (2007)
9. Zlokazov, K.: Destructiveness and personal identity. In: Science year-book of the Institute of Philosophy and Law of the Ural Branch of RAS, vol. 14, no. 1. RAS Institute of Philosophy (2014)
10. Hamilton, M.A.: Verbal aggression: understanding the psychological antecedents and social consequences. J. Lang. Soc. Psychol. **31**(1), 5–12 (2012)
11. Rojkov, V.: Parameters of youth socialization destructiveness: methodological aspect. In: Izvestiya of Saratov University, vol. 11, no. 3, pp. 12–16 (2011). [in Russian]
12. Lin, H., et al.: User-level psychological stress detection from social media using deep neural network. In: Proceedings of the 22nd ACM International Conference on Multimedia, pp. 507–516. ACM, Orlando, Florida, USA (2014)
13. Dos Santos, C.N., De Bayser, M.G.: Deep convolutional neural networks for sentiment analysis of short texts. In: Proceedings of COLING 2014, the 25th International Conference on Computational Linguistics: Technical Papers, pp. 69–78 (2014)
14. Socher, R., Pennington, J., Huang, E.H., Ng, A.Y., Manning, C.D.: Semi-supervised recursive autoencoders for predicting sentiment distributions. In: Proceedings of the Conference on Empirical Methods in Natural Language Processing. Association for Computational Linguistics, pp. 151–161 (2011)
15. Segalin, C., et al.: What your Facebook profile picture reveals about your personality. In: Proceedings of the 2017 ACM on Multimedia Conference, pp. 460–468. ACM (2017)
16. Machajdik, J., Hanbury, A.: Affective image classification using features inspired by psychology and art theory. In: Proceedings of the 18th ACM International Conference on Multimedia, pp. 83–92. ACM (2010)
17. Ammon, G., Finke, G., Wolfrum, G.: Ich-Struktur-Test nach Ammon (ISTA). Swets, Zeitlinger, Frankfurt (1998)

GUIDed: An Augmented Reality Assisted-Living and Social Interaction Platform for Older Adults

Kale Strahinja Lazic[1](✉), Achilleas Achilleos[2], Stefan Parker[1], Christos Mettouris[3], Alexandros Yeratziotis[3], George A. Papadopoulos[3], Charalampos Theodorou[3], and Karol Pecyna[4]

[1] Kompetenznetzwerk Informationstechnologie zur Förderung der Integration von Menschen mit Behinderungen (KI-I), 4040 Linz, Austria
{strahinja.lazic,stefan.parker}@ki-i.at

[2] Frederick Research Center, 7 Filokyprou Street, 1036 Nicosia, Cyprus
com.aa@frederick.ac.cy

[3] Department of Computer Science, University of Cyprus, 2109 Nicosia, Cyprus
{mettour,ayerat01,george,ctheod07}@cs.ucy.ac.cy

[4] Harpo Sp. z o.o., 27 Grudnia 7, 61-737 Poznan, Poland
kpecyna@harpo.com.pl

Abstract. The demographic trend causes a rising pressure on health and care systems. Information and communications technology (ICT) provides many appliances that may support older people in prolonging independence while reducing the pressure on health and care systems. Research provides insights into the needs of older people as well as insights into the suitability and usability of ICT appliances for older people. As a result, this work presents the GUIDed system that aims at supporting the independence and quality of life of older people by using augmented reality as the central element of the user's interaction, whereby the paper's focus is placed on the technical development. The system is comprised of five services that are related to older people's daily activities or issues and social needs. These include the intake of medication, navigation, communication, smart home control and safety. Finally, a mobile application is included that allows older people to access all the services in an Augmented Reality (AR) interaction mode, while a conventional accessible user interface (UI) is also provided in the case an older adult prefers this as an interaction method.

Keywords: Augmented reality · Assisted-living · GUIDed services · Medication planner · Smart home · Social communication · Mobile application · Older adults

1 Introduction

The demographic trend predicts a rapidly aging population in advanced economies including the European Union, which comes from advances in health care, higher incomes, shrinking fertility, improved education and increased gender equality. One effect of the rapidly aging population is the rising pressure on health and care systems

E. Pissaloux et al. (Eds.): IHAW 2021, CCIS 1538, pp. 66–79, 2021.
https://doi.org/10.1007/978-3-030-94209-0_7

[1]. Therefore, the need for self-care of older people will continue rising. Information and communications technology (ICT) including smart home technology has the capability to decrease or in a few cases almost eliminate older people's dependency on caregivers [2]. However, some research [3–5] shows that older people tend to be fearful of adopting new technologies. Augmented Reality (AR), a technology that adds computer-generated objects to the real world, enhances and facilitates the possibilities of designing user-friendly services, which may lead to a reduction of fear and usability issues, especially among older people, when adopting a new technology. Some authors examined the acceptability of an AR-based virtual coach for home-based balance training with older people. Their results suggest that the participants in their study find the AR system encouraging and stimulating [6].

Rosales and Fernández-Ardèvol describe that older people enjoy using mobile applications such as WhatsApp, a medium for exchanging messages, images, audio or video[1], as they offer services that correspond to their needs while providing a good and intuitive user interface (UI). They summarize the older people's needs as: basic communication, security and safety, support of personal interests including social interaction, personal management such as pill management and entertainment [7].

The GUIDed AAL EU project aims at supporting these needs by offering five services accessible through a mobile application, while also providing the AR interaction mode as an alternative UI layer in order to reduce usability issues. The first service represents the "Medication Planner" service which supports users with taking pills by offering the capability to set appointments and receive reminders. The second service, "Smart City Navigation", helps its users to navigate to places they select. The third and fourth services, "Smart Home Control" and "Smart Home Safety", support older people's safety and control needs. Furthermore, a smart home system is established that facilitates the integration of many different smart home devices from different vendors. The fifth service, "Social Communication", helps the users stay connected to their family and friends offering a medium for video calls in order to counteract loneliness. Furthermore, the "call a stranger"-function offers the capability to get to know other users from the GUIDed community that also use this system.

The goal of this paper is to describe the development of the GUIDed system from the ICT perspective, which places AR as the key technological element that aims to reduce usability issues. This includes the examination of challenges faced and consequent solutions adapted. Previous research, the experience gained from previous ICT projects, literature reviews, technical documentations as well as insights from the development process itself served as the input for this article's examination.

The remainder of this article begins with describing related work examined in existing literature which provide recommendations that were followed in the design and development process. These include the engagement of older adults in the design and usability testing, and the consideration of best practices for design and development of mobile applications and web applications suitable for older adults. Then a synopsis of the GUIDed system's architecture is presented. Next, each service is described in more detail. Initially, the "Medication Planner" service is examined which shows the

[1] https://www.whatsapp.com/?lang=en.

implementation of a medication planner for pill taking. Secondly, the "Smart City Navigation" service is described. It includes the integration of a system called "Mapbox" for requesting routes by providing coordinates. Thirdly, the "Social Communication" service is presented. It shows how a communication between two users can be established over a peer-to-peer network using WebRTC[2]. Then, the last two services, "Smart Home Control" service and "Smart Home Safety" service, are examined. These services illustrate how cost-efficient and more open smart home systems can be designed by using mainly open-source systems. Finally, this article concludes with a summary of the work conducted for implementing and integrating the services and directions for future research.

2 Related Work

2.1 Related Projects and Systems

In terms of EU funded projects aiming to offer ICT solutions for enhancing and supporting the home living of older adults we have the following:

- The IOANNA (Integration of All stores Network & Navigation Assistant) project aims at developing ICT-based solutions for seniors for everyday facilitation in shopping management and navigation, focusing on assistive mobility and social engagement through crowdsourcing [15].
- The FrailSafe project aims to better understand frailty and its relation to other health conditions to develop a set of measures and tools, together with recommendations to reduce its onset [16].
- The MedGUIDE project offers an approach to social networking and e-learning focused on polypharmacy management, where seniors will be supported in their medication adherence via sensor technology and smart pillboxes [17].
- The Many-Me project builds a social interactive care system to help people with dementia, their relatives, informal and formal carers [18].

The above present the main projects and systems relevant to this work, while additional work is presented in the previous work of the authors that focused on the needs analysis and requirements for the definition of the GUIDed app and system using a co-design and participatory approach [13].

2.2 Lifestyle Problems Faced by Older Adults

Medication Reminders

Stuck et al. examined some of the most downloaded medication reminder applications concerning their suitability for the usage by older people. Their findings reveal issues including unintuitive navigation, poor visibility and a lack of transparency. Furthermore, the authors inferred guidelines for application design from their findings. These include

[2] https://webrtc.org/.

the inclusion of older people in the design and usability testing phases of the development process, as well es the compliance with standard age-specific design guidelines [8].

How Older People Struggle with Maps
In a recent research Yu and Chattopadhyay examined the accessibility of current mobile maps from the perspective of older people. They classified the issues encountered by older people into motor issues and non-motor issues. In this context, motor issues represent interaction problems where a user failed to successfully execute an intentional action such as tapping or swiping. Non-motor issues include for instance the unwilling ignorance of UI components due to inadequate visual saliency, ambiguous affordances or low information scent. They concluded that non-motor issues were more critical as they often resulted in frustration and resignation among users [9].

Social Needs of Older People
As loneliness tends to increase with age [10] communication applications such as WhatsApp or Viber have gained a strong popularity among older people. They enable them to stay connected to their family and friends that are not nearby. Bruggencate et al. examined the social needs of older adults. These include active involvement, respect for individuality, stimulating social contacts including close and peripheral relationships, and the sharing of knowledge [11].

Smart Home for Older Adults
Yusif et al. conducted a systematic review of empirical studies concerning the adoption of Assistive Technologies (AT) including smart home. Their findings suggest that older people are mostly concerned about privacy, costs of ATs, ease of use, suitability for daily use and the general benefit, which some older people assess to be low. However, their results also suggest that older people in general have a positive attitude towards ATs as they see it as a means to maintain independence [12].

2.3 Previous Research in the Context of GUIDed

Mettouris et al. describe the user-centered design approach with the focus on the co-creation aspect in the context of the GUIDed system. This includes the evaluation of high-fidelity (Hi-Fi) paper prototypes (i.e., the designs) for the GUIDed services. The hi-fi paper prototypes are based on the recommendations from the literature and the authors' goal was to validate them and the proposed additional AR UI. The Hi-Fi prototypes were tested by older adults and their caregivers using focus groups in four European countries, namely Austria, Cyprus, Norway and Poland. The results show that the users found the GUIDed system understandable and easy to use [13]. This represents an encouraging finding considering older participants' low technological literacy.

3 GUIDed System – Overall Architecture

The architecture of the GUIDed system is depicted in Fig. 1, which is described shortly as follows, whereas more details are described in the report from the GUIDed EU

AAL Project [14]. The architecture of the GUIDed system consists of three entities: the Android client for the users, the cloud instance for configuring, relaying and processing data and the Raspberry Pi 3B+ for the smart home services at the user's home. The cloud hosts a Drupal content management system (CMS) instance for configuring the five services and saving user data (Services 1–5), a spring boot application for handling smart home operations and smart home safety functions such as sending push notifications to specific users when an alarm is triggered (S1, S2), as well as a WebRTC signaling server to keep track of all connected and available GUIDed users and for establishing a communication channel between two users within the "Social Communication" service (S5). The GUIDed system exposes the services through REST APIs which enable the use and manipulation of information through the mobile application. The Drupal CMS, which is accessed over a web browser, allows users including older people to use a mouse, a keyboard, bigger user interfaces and clearer navigation structures that simplify the configuration process in contrast to using a mobile application.

4 Medication Planner Service

Compared to existing medication planner mobile applications that in almost all cases perform data management and data access on the mobile application and interaction through restrictive user interfaces, the "Medication Planner" service enables data management via the GUIDed CMS that offers usable and clear navigation interfaces, enables data access for the mobile application via the exposed REST API and allows interaction using either intuitive AR interfaces or standard UIs to serve all different older adults' requirements and needs.

Specifically, the primary user (i.e., older adult) or secondary user (e.g., family, caregiver) assisting the older adult can use the CMS accessible over a web browser to manage the drug and prescription data. This allows defining and managing medication, vitamins and supplement data using larger user interfaces, with clearer navigation and easier interaction, rather than administering data on the mobile application.

Moreover, Headless Drupal is used on the backend framework to expose the required REST APIs that provide remote access to the medication data from the mobile application. The mobile application provides the capability to the primary user to select the "Medication Planner" service using the tiles-view, which loads the camera view of the phone. The Android ARCore framework and the TensorFlow machine learning (ML) model are initialised, which allow detecting respectively either a 2D image of a pillbox or a 3D physical pillbox object. As soon as the 2D image or 3D physical pillbox object is detected the REST API is invoked, which returns the matrix with the medication information augmented on the camera view, including intake times and dosages of the prescriptions. Furthermore, it allows to tick the checkbox when the medication is taken (see Fig. 2). However, the checkbox is only enabled 15 min before and after the intake appointment. The user can also click on the maximize-button to expand the augmented matrix view and see the complete list of medication to be taken for the current day (see Fig. 3).

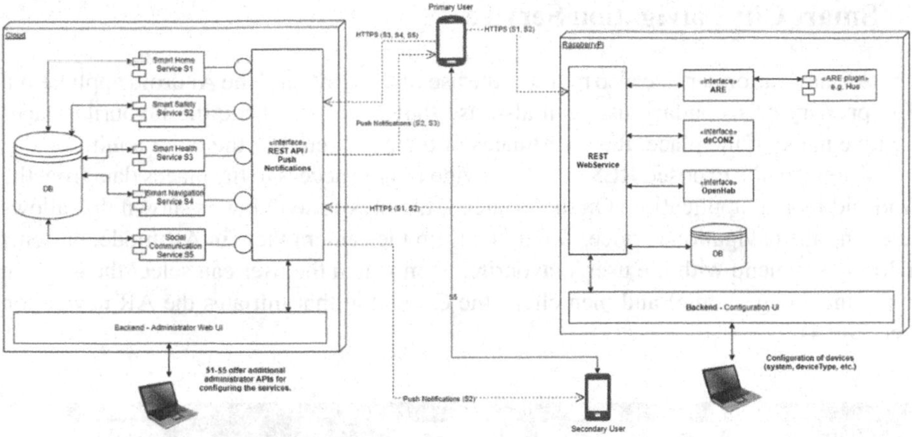

Fig. 1. High-level architecture for the GUIDed system

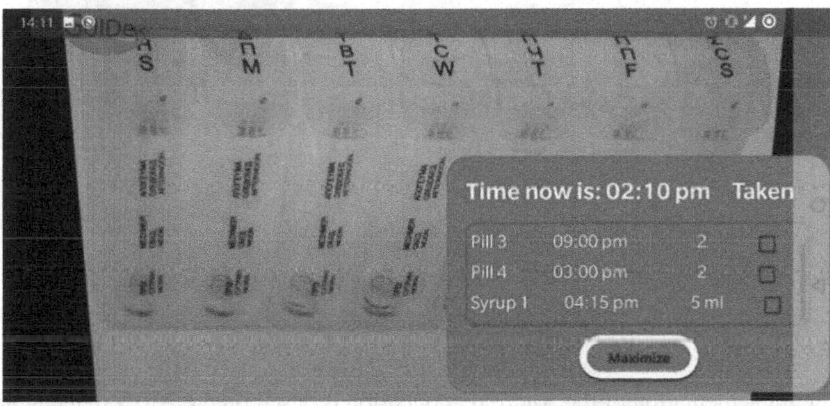

Fig. 2. AR medication planner pillbox detection - showing next intake information.

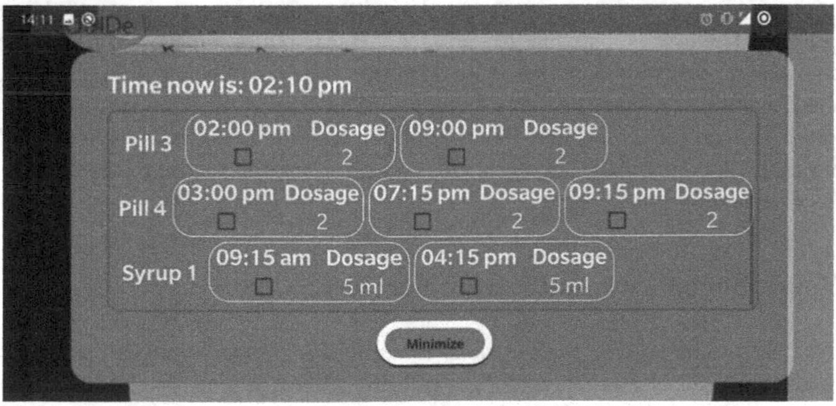

Fig. 3. AR medication planner pillbox detection – expanded view.

5 Smart City Navigation Service

The AR navigation service also requires the use of the CMS and the Android application. The primary or secondary user can also use the CMS to manage the favourite places (unique name of the place, the coordinates of the place, etc.) of the older adult.

Moreover, the exposed REST APIs provide remote access to the places data from the Android mobile application. On the frontend, the tiles-based view is shown that allows selecting the navigation service, which loads up the camera view in AR mode, presents a dropdown menu with the user's favourite, from which the user can select the location to navigate (e.g., home) and then clicks the Go button that initiates the AR navigation (see Fig. 4).

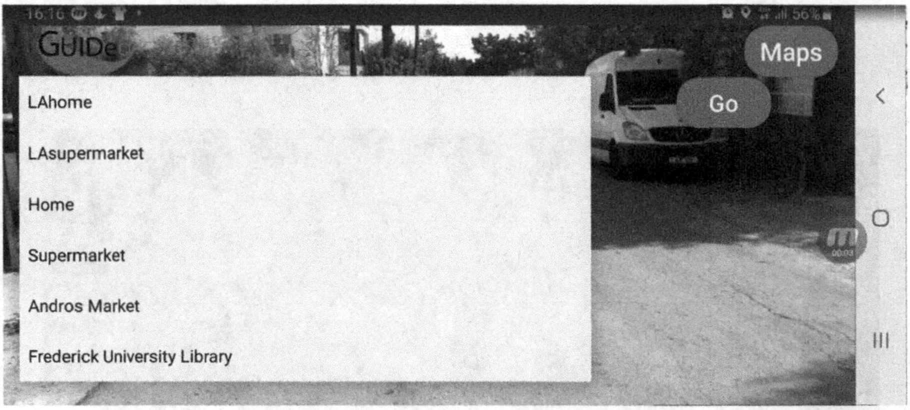

Fig. 4. Selecting the navigation place.

The implementation of the Android application is based on the ARCore technology and the Mapbox APIs, which enable to detect the current location of the user, getting navigation instructions and rendering this information as augmented visual cues (i.e., direction arrows), providing an augmented reality navigation experience to the users (see Fig. 5). The user is also able to click the "Maps"-button on the top right, in case the map-based navigation is preferred, to open the map view. The location of the user is detected, and the user can select any location on the map as the destination. The route is plotted, and the user clicks the "Start"-button to begin the map view navigation. This enable users that are technology-oriented and accustomed to the map view to use this mode of navigation.

6 Smart Social Communication Service

The Social Communication Service aims to address the issues of social isolation and loneliness that older adults experience, by offering a sense of real-life physical presence between the older adults and the communicating family members, healthcare providers, friends and even a stranger (explained further below). This is achieved by providing

Fig. 5. Navigating in augmented reality view.

a video calling service with a simple (yet functionally complete), minimalist design and easy-to-use UI, that is also appropriate for use by older adults. Using the service, older adults can remain in contact with family and friends while engaging in everyday activities, such as eating together, drawing with the grandchildren, knitting and much more.

The Social Communication Service differs from existing similar apps in the market in three fundamental aspects: 1) it targets older adults, making thereby the appropriate design decisions in terms of UI elements' size and colors, 2) the workflow of the service and the architecture of the various functionalities have been designed and developed having in mind HCI (Human Computer Interaction) related parameters like usability and ease-of-use, targeting at the same time older adults, and 3) it offers the "Meet Others" functionality, an innovation of GUIDed (please see paragraph below).

Besides conducting video calls, the service offers a secondary functionality called "Meet Others". This functionality enables primary users, through the push of a virtual button, to conduct video calls to another GUIDed primary user in a random fashion. The remote user belongs in the GUIDed community, i.e., he/she is a GUIDed user as well, and is randomly selected by the GUIDed system, provided that the preferred languages of the two users match, and that the remote user has agreed to the communication request at the moment of the call.

The GUIDed services, including the Social Communication Service were briefly described in [13]. In that paper, the architecture and technical information about the service were provided in detail. In this paper, the focus is on the "Meet Others" functionality as an innovation in this service and of the GUIDed system overall.

6.1 Architecture

The Social Communication Service was developed using the WebRTC framework. WebRTC is a free, open-source framework that enables Real-Time Communications with audio and/or video, by providing web browsers and mobile applications with the means for real-time communication via its APIs. The Social Communication Service includes two different architecture designs: a Client-Server architecture between Android devices (smartphone/tablets clients) and a signaling server that is used for setting up the connection between two communicating users, and a P2P (Peer-to-Peer) architecture between two Android devices for conducting the video call. It is important to note that the signaling server does not retain any information about the two clients during a video call, thus ensuring the user's privacy and data security. All WebRTC clients' data are deleted as soon as the signaling process is terminated. Apart from the signaling process, the server listens and handles any special case events e.g., client disconnection, client reset and client network changes. More on the Social Communication Service architecture and the WebRTC can be found in [13].

6.2 Workflow

The Social Communication Service can be divided into two main features, the video call process and the process of adding new contacts to a primary user. The former is mainly handled by the WebRTC API and the signaling server, as previously explained in Sect. 6.1. The latter takes place through an appropriate Web UI on the GUIDed web platform, where the primary user (active user) or a helping secondary user can add other GUIDed users as contacts to the active user, by initiating a pending contact request to another user. Users can check their pending contact requests and accept or decline each request. In addition, adding a new contact to a primary user can be done during a video call with a stranger in the "Meet Others" mode (more on this below).

Through the Android application, the user can enter the "Meet Others" mode by clicking a virtual button on the contact's list screen so that the process of finding a suitable candidate begins. Based on the user's preferred language, the algorithm run by the Signaling Server will respond with a random GUIDed user that meets the language requirement and is also currently online and available for a video call. Figure 6 shows the incoming call from the "Meet Others" process. When both users agree to the video call, it initiates. During the video call between the two strangers, there is an option to send a contact request to the communicating user. Then, a pop-up appears on the receiving user's screen notifying him/her of the contact request and providing an accept/decline option to immediately notify the sending user of the result. Figure 7 shows the workflow for the "Meet Others" functionality.

7 Smart Home Control Service and Smart Home Safety Service

The GUIDed services "Smart Home Control" and "Smart Home Safety" offer solutions to mitigate concerns related to ATs discussed in chapter two. Figure 8 summarizes the concerns and their respective solutions via a non-formal mind map. On the left side the model summarizes four issues for ATs: hard to use, high prices, vendor lock-in and privacy. The right side of the model proposes approaches to reduce or eliminate the issues. The links between issues and solutions are depicted as green arrows. These approaches were incorporated into the implementation of the services for the GUIDed system. In order to make the usage of the system easier, the GUIDed system relies continuously on

Fig. 6. "Meet Others" process: the receiving user's incoming call.

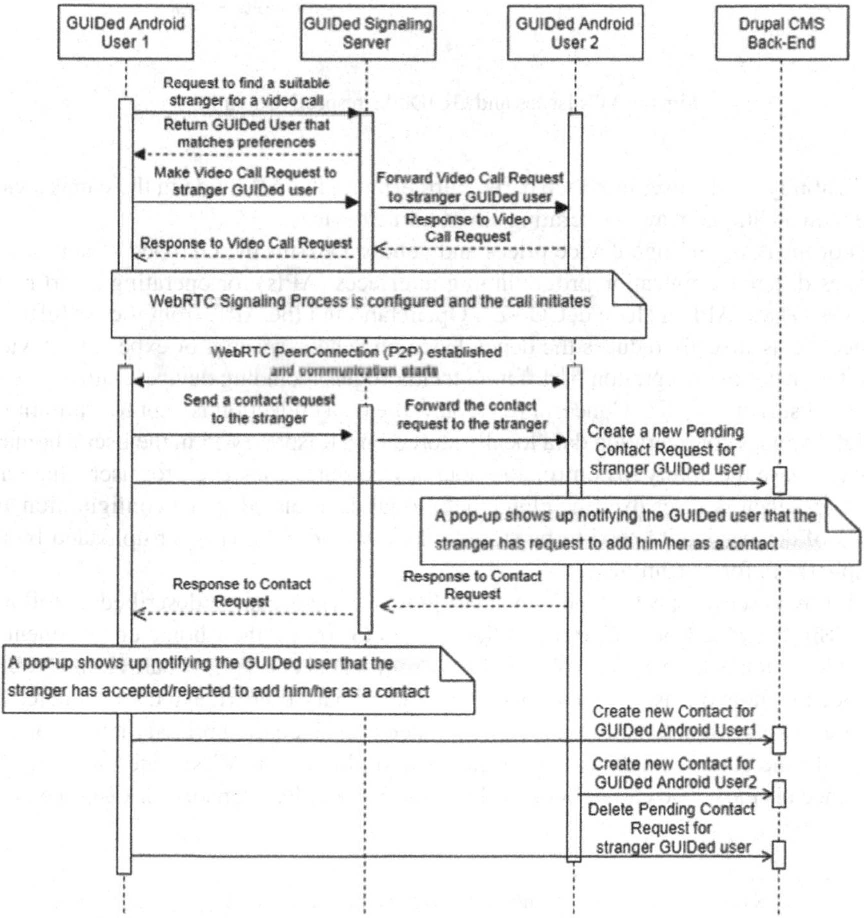

Fig. 7. Sequence diagram for the "Meet Others" functionality.

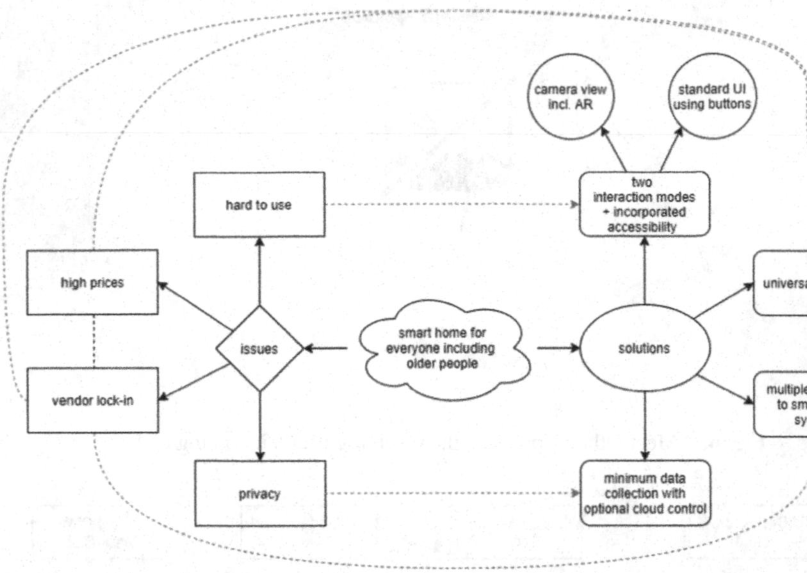

Fig. 8. AT's issues and GUIDed's respective solutions

accessibility for the user interface parts. Furthermore, the AR mode in the camera view offers an additional way of operating smart home devices.

For the issues of high device prices and vendor lock-ins the GUIDed system incorporates different application programming interfaces (APIs) for operating smart home devices. These APIs include deCONZ[3], OpenHab[4] and the ARE from the AsTeRICS[5] project. This strongly reduces the dependence on vendor-specific or expensive devices as it facilitates the integration of different technologies including devices with a specific protocol such as ZigBee. Concerning privacy, the data collection is kept to a minimum, which includes configuration data locally stored on a Raspberry Pi in the user's home in order to have the ability to control and read device states. However, for users that wish to control their devices over the cloud, additional data related to the configuration and states of devices would need to be stored which would be fetched or uploaded by the Raspberry Pi for synchronization.

From a user perspective the two smart home services can be described as follows. The "Smart Home Control" service allows users to control their home environment. It provides features such as control of lights or power sockets. The "Smart Home Safety" service monitors the users' homes and alerts the primary user when a threat is detected. Furthermore, push notifications are sent to linked users including primary and secondary users. In the current implementation the "Smart Home Safety" service can track the presence of smoke and carbon monoxide. Door or water leak sensors for example could

[3] https://www.dresden-elektronik.com/wireless/software/deconz.html.

[4] https://www.openhab.org/.

[5] https://www.asterics.eu/.

also be supported. Figure 9 shows the AR view for the services, whereas a user can also choose a standard UI to check and operate devices.

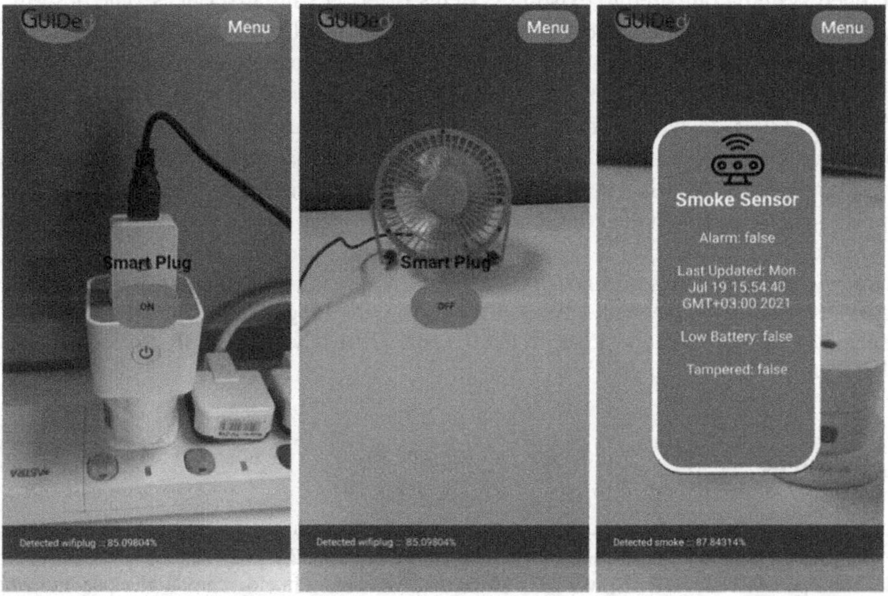

Fig. 9. Augmented reality: smart home control & safety

7.1 Architecture

The Raspberry Pi is the central hardware component responsible for the "Smart Home Control" and "Smart Home Safety" services, which together with a set of sensors and actuators need to be installed in the user's home. The Raspberry Pi connects over a REST API to the proprietary Drupal instance running remotely on the cloud, and to the third-party smart home systems deCONZ, OpenHab and ARE installed locally. Furthermore, a proprietary front-end application ("Configuration Client") is served by the Raspberry Pi. It enables the configuration of smart home devices (naming, room configuration, device type - e.g., light, smart home system - e.g., deCONZ).

8 Conclusion

This paper presented the GUIDed system including its five services from a technical perspective. The services were chosen to support the daily activities of older people supporting not only their independence but also incorporating their social needs. The development was conducted after and while considering recommendations from the literature including the results presented from the evaluation of the GUIDed Hi-Fi prototypes [13]. In terms of the usability aspect, the recommendations include for example the consideration of the navigation, transparency and visibility of UI objects, which is incorporated using design guidelines from the literature as well as the user feedback. Moreover, AR was incorporated as the integral part and the differentiating point of the GUIDed system compared to existing systems offering similar services. The described results of the development process represent the GUIDed prototype. Future work will test this prototype extensively as it will be installed in so-called living labs at the users' homes. The feedback will provide valuable insights that will allow a profound evaluation of the GUIDed system. To be more precise, the system will be examined on how well recommendations from the literature and user feedback were incorporated. Most importantly, the effect of AR on usability and user experience will be evaluated since this is the main goal and the contribution of the prototype built in this work.

Acknowledgements. This work is supported by the European Commission as part of the GUIDed EU project funded by the Active Assisted Living (AAL) Programme Call 2019–under grant agreement no aal-2019-6-190-CP, and by FFG (Austria), RIF (Cyprus), NCBR (Poland) and RCN (Norway).

References

1. Causa, O., Browne, J., Vindics, A.: Income redistribution across OECD countries: main findings and policy implications. OECD Econ. Policy Pap. **23**, 2–23 (2018)
2. Schultz, J.S., André, B., Sjøvold, E.: Managing innovation in eldercare: a glimpse into what and how public organizations are planning to deliver healthcare services for their future elderly. Int. J. Healthcare Manag. **9**(3), 169–180 (2016)
3. Tsuchiya, L.D., De Oliveira, G.A., De Bettio, R.W., Greghi, J.G., Freire, A.P.: A study on the needs of older adults for interactive smart home environments in Brazil. In: Proceedings of the 8th International Conference on Software Development and Technologies for Enhancing Accessibility and Fighting Info-exclusion, pp. 33–40. ACM, Thessaloniki, Greece (2018)
4. Lin, C.I., Tang, W.H., Kuo, F.Y.: Mommy tants to learn the computer: how middle-aged and elderly women in Taiwan learn ICT through social support. Adult Educ. Q. **62**(1), 73–90 (2012)
5. Papa, F., Cornacchia, M., Sapio, B., Nicolò, E.: Engaging technology-resistant elderly people: empirical evidence from an ICT-enabled social environment. Inform. Health Soc. Care **42**(1), 43–60 (2017)
6. Mostajeran, F., Steinicke, F., Ariza Nunez, O.J., Gatsios, D., Fotiadis, D.: Augmented reality for older adults: exploring acceptability of virtual coaches for home-based balance training in an aging population. In: Proceedings of the 2020 CHI Conference on Human Factors in Computing Systems, pp. 1–12. ACM, Honolulu, HI, USA (2020)
7. Rosales, A., Fernández-Ardèvol, M.: Smartphones, apps and older people's interests: from a generational perspective. In: Proceedings of the 18th International Conference on Human-Computer Interaction with Mobile Devices and Services, pp. 491–503. ACM, Florence, Italy (2016)
8. Stuck, R.E., Chong, A.W., Tracy, L.M., Rogers, W.A.: Medication management apps: usable by older adults? In: Proceedings of the Human Factors and Ergonomics Society Annual Meeting, pp. 1141–1144. SAGE Publications, Los Angeles, CA, USA (2017)
9. Yu, J.E., Chattopadhyay, D.: Maps are hard for me: identifying how older adults struggle with mobile maps. In: Proceedings of the 22nd International ACM SIGACCESS Conference on Computers and Accessibility, pp. 1–8. ACM, Virtual Event Greece (2020)

10. Victor, C.R., Bowling, A.: A longitudinal analysis of loneliness among older people in Great Britain. J. Psychol. **146**(3), 313–331 (2012)
11. Bruggencate, T.T., Luijkx, K.G., Sturm, J.: Social needs of older people: a systematic literature review. Ageing Soc. **38**(9), 1745–1770 (2018)
12. Yusif, S., Soar, J., Hafeez-Baig, A.: Older people, assistive technologies, and the barriers to adoption: a systematic review. Int. J. Med. Inform. **94**, 112–116 (2016)
13. Mettouris, C., et al.: GUIDed: assisted-living smart platform and social communication for older adults. In: Krieger, U.R., Eichler, G., Erfurth, C., Fahrnberger, G. (eds.) I4CS 2021. CCIS, vol. 1404, pp. 135–151. Springer, Cham (2021). https://doi.org/10.1007/978-3-030-75004-6_10
14. GUIDed EU AAL Project, KI-I, UCY, KARDE, HARPO, FRC, PLATUS: D3.1 Report on Platform Specification and Architecture. Ambient Assisted Living Joint Programme, 30 June 2020. https://www.guided-project.eu/wp-content/uploads/2020/07/GUIDed-D3.1_Report-on-platform-specification-and-architecture_OfflineVersion.pdf. Accessed 17 June 2021
15. IOANNA (Integration of All stores Network & Navigation Assistant) EU AAL Project. http://www.ioanna-project.eu/. Accessed 17 June 2021
16. Frailsafe: (Sensing and predictive treatment of frailty and associated co-morbidities using advanced personalized patient models and advanced interventions) H2020 Project. https://frailsafe-project.eu/. Accessed 17 June 2021
17. MedGUIDE EU AAL Project. http://www.aal-europe.eu/projects/medguide/. Accessed 17 June 2021
18. Many-Me (Social Interactive Care System to support the wellbeing of people living with dementia) EU AAL project. http://many-me.eu/. Accessed 17 June 2021

Brain Functions Support and mHealth

Brightening Up Brain Injuries: Design, Synthesis and Characterization of a PET Diagnostic Agent for Neuronal Trauma

Jessica Allingham[1(✉)], Wely B. Floriano[1], and Michael Campbell[1,2]

[1] Lakehead University, Thunder Bay, ON P7B 5E1, Canada
jallingh@lakeheadu.ca
[2] Thunder Bay Regional Health Research Institute, Thunder Bay, ON P7B 6V4, Canada

Abstract. Concussions are an increasingly significant issue today, however, there is still no single standard, objective criterion for diagnosing them. An objective test with high sensitivity and specificity for concussions would provide a substantial advance in concussion diagnostics, which can help in the prognosis, treatment, and medical decision-making regarding the disorder. This research looks to fill the void in concussion diagnostic techniques by synthesizing a specifically designed, small molecule [18] F-radiotracer capable of binding to a biomarker of neuronal trauma, thus allowing for the imaging of its upregulation using a PET scanner.

Keywords: Mild traumatic brain injury · Concussion · PET · S100B · Radiotracer

1 Introduction

A concussion is a traumatic brain injury resulting from the rapid acceleration or deceleration of brain tissue within the skull, which results in physical, chemical, and metabolic changes within the brain cells [1]. Globally, traumatic brain injuries (TBI) are a leading cause of death and disability in children and young adults [2]. Mild traumatic brain injuries (mTBI) like concussions, cause neuropathological, neurophysiological and neurocognitive changes to occur [3]. Despite the prevalence and severity of mild traumatic brain injuries (mTBI), there is still no single objective standard for diagnosing them. Presently, concussions are diagnosed using a variety of measures including neurological examination, neurophysical evaluation and neuroimaging. Many of the neurological and neurophysical tests are very subjective and can provide inconclusive results. Additionally, symptoms of concussions are often observed in the absence of significant structural damage [4] rendering neuroimaging techniques such as computerized tomography (CT) and magnetic resonance imaging (MRI) ineffective in mTBI diagnostics.

An objective test with high sensitivity and specificity for concussions would provide a substantial advance in concussion diagnostics, which can help in the prognosis, treatment, and medical decision-making regarding the disorder [5]. Early detection of concussions would be invaluable given that individuals with concussions are acutely at

E. Pissaloux et al. (Eds.): IHAW 2021, CCIS 1538, pp. 83–93, 2021.
https://doi.org/10.1007/978-3-030-94209-0_8

risk for bleeding and axonal injury [6, 7]. Research is being conducted to develop new neuroimaging techniques for neuronal trauma including functional MRI, diffusion tensor imaging, magnetic resonance spectroscopy, magnetoencephalographic (MEG) connectivity and positron emission tomography (PET) [8–19]. However, these techniques have not been applied clinically [20].

Investigations into molecular tests for concussions have also been conducted, in fact, research in the field of TBI biomarkers has increased significantly over the past 25 years [21–24]. Several biomarkers have been discovered that could provide diagnostic and prognostic information about traumatic brain injuries [25]. S100B is one of the most frequently assessed biomarkers of neuronal trauma [26–37]. S100B is the glial-specific member of the S100 calcium-binding protein family and is responsible for producing neurotrophin mainly in astrocytes of the central nervous system (CNS). It can act as an extensive marker for glial cell integrity [38]. S100B is a useful neurobiochemical marker of brain damage such as circulatory arrest, stroke and traumatic brain injury [39]. Studies have shown that the levels of S100B in serum are increased in patients with TBI and correlate with Glasgow Coma Scale scores and neuroradiological findings at hospital admission [2]. It has also been found that S100B serum concentration a few hours post mTBI is a suitable predictor for post-concussion syndrome in later times [40].

Positron emission tomography (PET) conducted with a radiotracer specific to a biomarker of neuronal trauma, like S100B, could provide diagnostic and prognostic information in concussion patients if employed correctly. PET is one of the most powerful functional imaging tools used in nuclear medicine [41]. PET offers the ability to noninvasively image biological functions *in vivo* while providing both qualitative and quantitative information [42, 43]. This work looks to fill the void in concussion diagnostics with the development of a PET diagnostic tracer for neuronal trauma.

2 Results and Discussion

2.1 Design

AutoDock Vina [44] was employed to select structures most likely to bind to the biomarker of interest, S100B. AutoDock Vina is a program for molecular docking and virtual screening built in the same research lab as the popular tool AutoDock4 [45, 46]. AutoDock Vina employs a scoring function that combines advantages of knowledge-based potentials and empirical scoring functions [44].

An S100B structure (PDB: 3D0Y), obtained using X-ray diffraction at a resolution of 1.5 Å, was selected from the RCSB Protein Data Bank (www.rcsb.com) [47]. Validation of the virtual ligand screening (VLS) protocol was completed with a training set comprised of 7 known ligands of S100B with K_d values in the range of 1 μM to 120 μM [48] along with 765 decoy ligands generated using the "make decoys" function of A Database of Useful Decoys: Enhanced (DUDE) (http://dude.docking.org/) [49, 50]. AutoDock Vina performed very well in the validation yielding an area under the curve (AUC) of a receiver operating characteristic (ROC) curve of 0.82, which is above the generally accepted cut-off of an AUC of 0.7, to indicate the efficient concentration of active compounds at the top of the ligand ranking.

After validation, a library of 8573 ligands was screened against the S100B protein structure (PDB: 3DY0) and then clustered into structurally similar groups using MOE (www.chemcomp.com). Cluster 7930 appeared many times in the top 5% of the ligand ranking (Fig. 1).

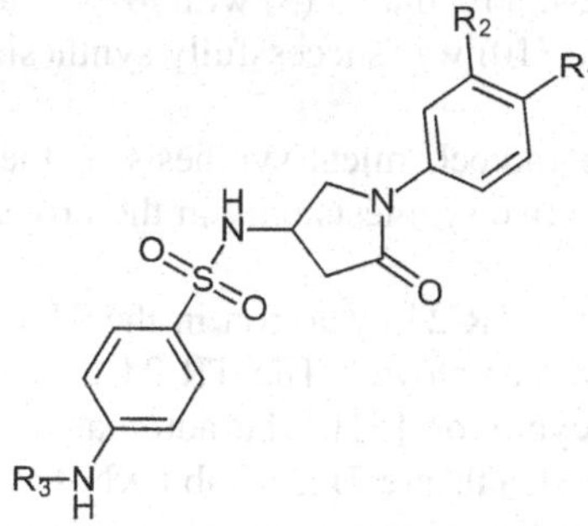

R_1 = F, H
R_2 = F, H
R_3 = CH_2CH_3, $COCH_3$

Fig. 1. General configuration of cluster 7930 ligands

2.2 Synthesis

Cluster 7930 (Fig. 1) is structurally like a known ligand of S100B (Fig. 2B), the scaffolds were combined to come up with a new suggested structure for the radiotracer (Fig. 2A). This structure was put through the AutoDock Vina VLS protocol and was found to bind with a free energy of binding similar to that of the cluster 7930 scaffold (–6.1 kcal/mol).

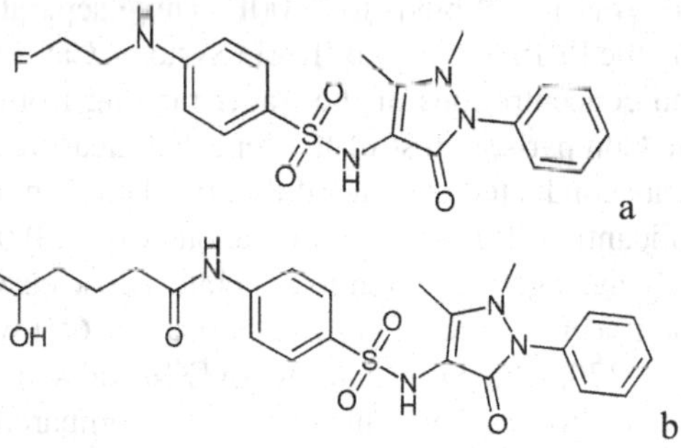

Fig. 2. The suggested structure resulting from VLS (A), the known ligand of S100B used as a reference for hit design (B).

Therefore, the proposed structure (Fig. 2A) was synthesized (Scheme 1). The scheme begins with the combination of 4-aminoantipyrine (1) (Fisher Chemical, 01123-100, CAS: 83-07-8) and 4-nirobenzeenesulfonyl chloride (2) (Alfa Aesar, A18512, CAS: 98-74-8). These reagents were combined in acetonitrile with potassium carbonate to yield 1-Methyl-5-methyl-4-(*p*-nitrophenylsulfonylamino)-2-phenyl-1, 2-dihydropyrazol-3-one (3), with an 83% yield. The hydrogenation of 3 resulted in the amine precursor 4-(*p*-Aminophenylsulfonylamino)-1-methyl-5-methyl-2-phenyl-1, 2-dihydropyrazol-3-one (4) in quantitative yields. The amine precursor (4) was then combined with the fluoroethyl tosylate prosthetic group (7) to yield our desired compound 4-[*p*-(2-Fluoroethylamino)phenylsulfonylamino]-1-methyl-5-methyl-2-phenyl-1,2-dihydropyrazol-3-one (10) in moderate yields of 62%. The fluoroethyl tosylate prosthetic group (7) was synthesized by reacting 2-fluoroethanol (5) with tosyl chloride (6) (72% yield). Therefore, the desired compound (10) was successfully synthesized with an overall yield of 37% as pale beige crystals.

This synthesis was followed up with the radiochemical synthesis of the desired compound, which differs from the non-radioactive synthesis only in the production of the prosthetic group (Scheme 2).

For the radiolabelling of the radiotracer, the TR-24 cyclotron in the Thunder Bay Cyclotron and Radiochemistry Laboratory was employed. The TR-24 cyclotron is a medium energy (18–24 meV), high current cyclotron [51]. The automated synthesis box used in this research is a General Electric Healthcare TracerLab FXN-Pro [52]. To determine the success of the radiosynthesis, a radiochromatogram was carried out using the LabLogic Scan-RAM Radio-TLC Detector (Fig. 3). The retention factor (Rf) in 9:1 dichloromethane:methanol of the radioactive product ($Rf = 0.53$) was similar to that of the non-radioactive product ($Rf = 0.54$), which had been conventionally characterized, indicating the successful synthesis of the desired compound with a radioactive-decay corrected radiochemical yield of 58%. Good chemical and radiochemical purity were also obtained.

2.3 Characterization

An enzyme-linked immunosorbent assay (ELISA) experiment was conducted to determine whether the radiotracer (10) binds to S100B. Three separate ELISA experiments were carried out using the ELISA assay kit (R&D Systems Cat. #DY1820-05), 3 ng/mL of S100B protein and concentrations of the tracer ranging from 0.0001 to 1000 μM. A Dunnett's Multiple Comparison Test of the repeated measures one-way ANOVA of the ELISA experiments conducted concluded that the data from each experiment were not statistically significantly different from one another ($p < 0.05$). The data from the three experiments were averaged and used to generate a dose curve (Fig. 4) to calculate the EC_{50} value of the tracer. The $\log(EC_{50})$ value was –1.659 with a 95% confidence interval of –1.992 to –1.326, which translates to an EC_{50} value of 21.93 nM with a 95% confidence interval of 10.2 to 47.2 nM. This EC_{50} value compared very well to the EC_{50} value of a known ligand of S100B, pentamidine isethionate (Millipore Sigma, P0547, CAS 140-64-7) determined using an identical ELISA protocol (15.5 nM with a 95% confidence interval of 9.5 to 27.5 nM).

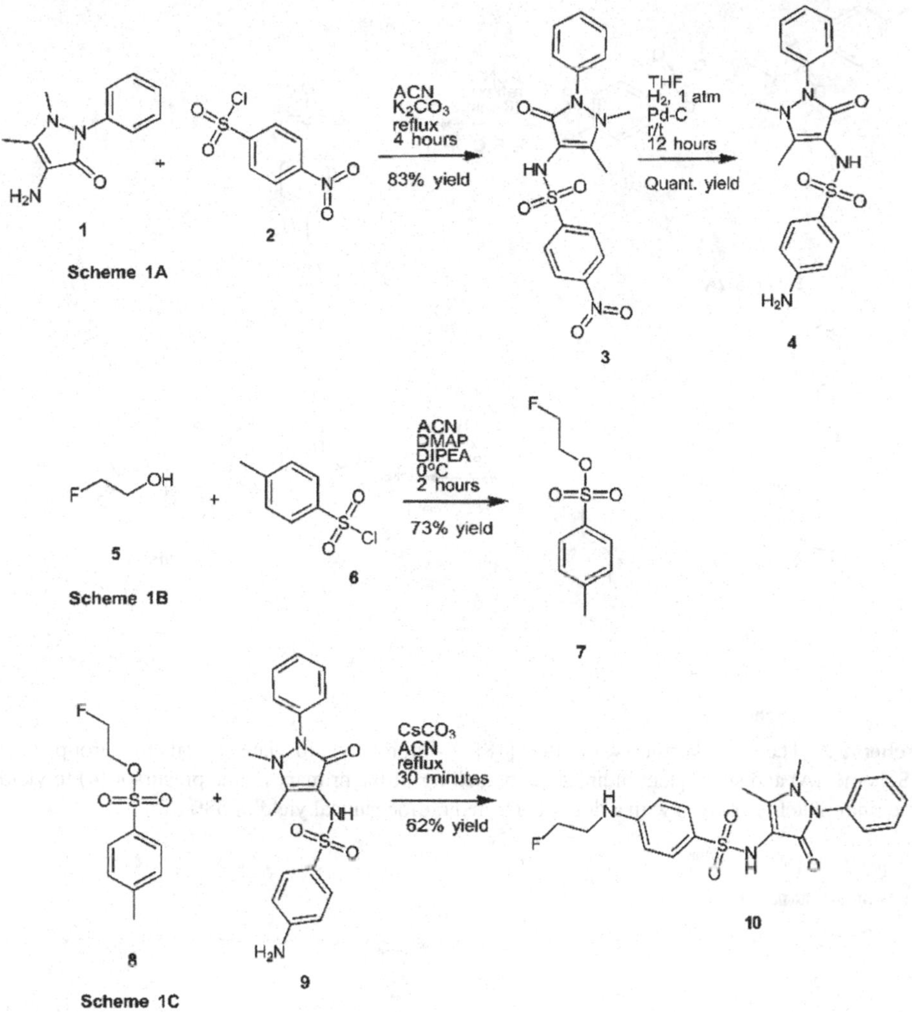

Scheme 1. The synthesis of a primary amine precursor (4) (Scheme 1A) and the fluoroethyl tosylate prosthetic group (7) (Scheme 1B), as well as their subsequent addition reaction (Scheme 1C) to produce our desired compound (10) (Fig. 1A) with an overall yield of 37%.

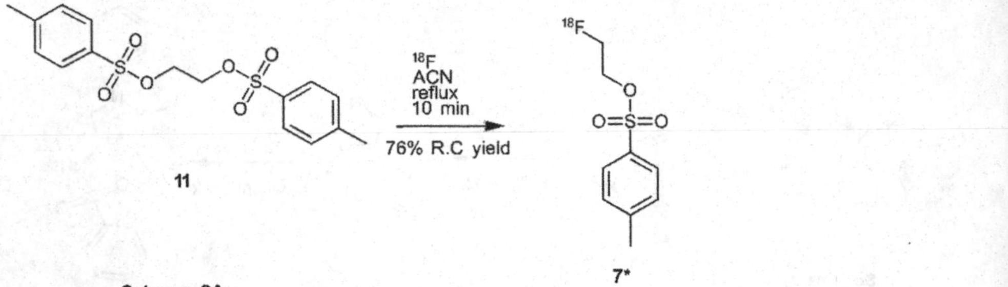

Scheme 2A

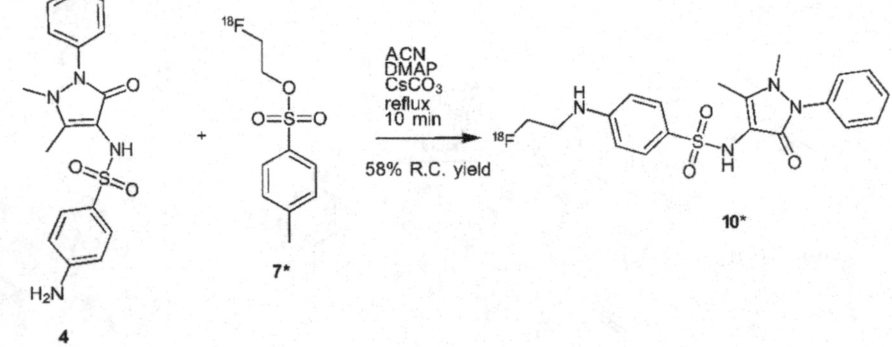

Scheme 2B

Scheme 2. The radiosynthesis of the [18] F-fluoroethyl tosylate prosthetic group (7*) (Scheme 2A) and subsequent indirect radiolabelling of the primary amine precursor (4) to yield the final radiotracer (10*) with a decay corrected radiochemical yield of 58%.

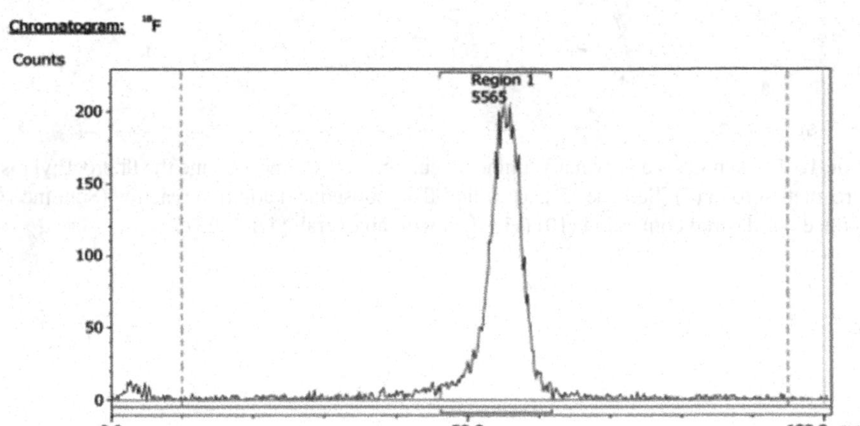

Fig. 3. The radiochromatogram of the desired radiotracer ran in 9:1 dichloromethane: methanol and read using the LabLogic Scan-RAM Radio-TLC Detector. The retention factor of the radioactive product was determined to be 0.53, which compares well to the retention factor of the characterized non-radioactive product (0.54).

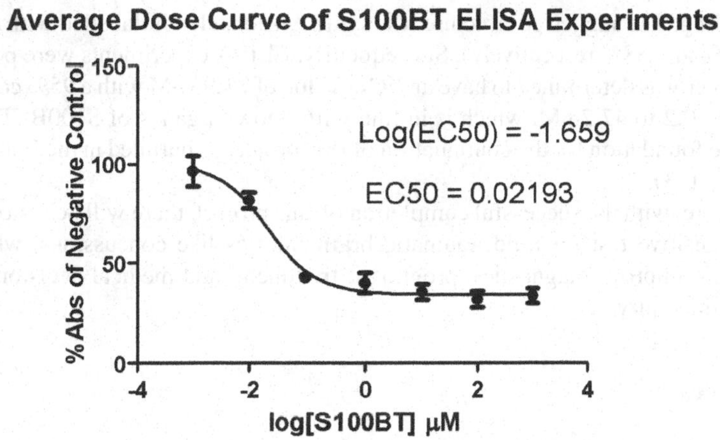

Fig. 4. The dose-response curve of the three ELISA experiments averaged together plotting the reference corrected absorbance of each concentration as a percentage of the negative control (just S100B) against the logarithm of the concentration of the tracer. Each concentration was run in triplicate and three experiments were conducted, therefore, nine measurements were utilized to calculate each average value, except for the average values at concentrations 0.033 and 0.066 μM, since these concentrations were only run in two of the three experiments ($n = 6$ for those concentrations). The log (EC_{50}) value was -1.659 with a 95% confidence interval of -1.992 to -1.326.

3 Future Work

To continue the evaluation of the radiotracer, a cell-based assay will be carried out using human astrocyte cells, which are known to produce S100B. To emulate a concussion and an increase in S100B concentration, the astrocyte cells will be treated with the anti-depressant fluoxetine hydrochloride (Millipore Sigma, F132, CAS: 56296-78-7). Fluoxetine has been found to increase the expression of S100B in rats [53, 54]. It has also been found that fluoxetine could increase adult neurogenesis by stimulating astrocytic synthesis and release of S100B [55]. The treated cells (concussed) and untreated cells (healthy) will both be subjected to varying concentrations of the tracer. The cells will then be lysed and ran through an ELISA experiment to determine whether binding occurred in a concentration-dependent manner.

Upon successful completion of the cell-based assay, the tracer will move forward into animal modelling using mice. High-intensity focused ultrasound (HIFU) will be employed to administer the concussions. Shortly after the injury is administered, the mice will be injected with the radiotracer and imaged using a micro-PET scanner to gain more insight into the pharmacokinetics of the tracer.

4 Conclusion

In this work, virtual ligand screening on a well-studied biomarker of neuronal trauma, S100B, yielded a very promising hit structure that was modified for ease of synthesis and radiolabelling. The suggested structure was synthesized and radiolabelled with adequate yields (37% and 58% respectively). Subsequently, ELISA experiments were performed and the tracer was determined to have an EC_{50} value of 21.93 nM with a 95% confidence interval of 10.2 to 47.2 nM, which is in line with known ligands of S100B. This work has laid the foundation for the continuation of this project as outlined in the Future Work section (Sect. 3).

Therefore, with the successful completion of this project, there will be a more objective and sensitive test for mild traumatic brain injuries like concussions, which will substantially improve diagnostics, prognosis, treatment, and medical decision-making regarding the injury.

References

1. Foundation, C.L.: Concussion Resources (2019). https://concussionfoundation.org/concussion-resources
2. Mondello, S., et al.: Blood-based diagnostics of traumatic brain injuries. Expert Rev. Mol. Diagn. **11**, 65–78 (2011). https://doi.org/10.1586/erm.10.104
3. Dikmen, S.S., Levin, H.S.: Methodological issues in the study of mild head injury. J. Head Trauma Rehabil. **8**, 30–37 (1993)
4. Kibby, M.Y., Long, C.J.: Minor head injury: attempts at clarifying the confusion. Brain Inj. **10**, 159–186 (1996). https://doi.org/10.1080/026990596124494
5. Lewis, L.M., et al.: Utility of serum biomarkers in the diagnosis and stratification of mild traumatic brain injury. Acad. Emerg. Med. **24**, 710–720 (2017). https://doi.org/10.1111/acem.13174
6. Benson, R.R., et al.: Detection of hemorrhagic and axonal pathology in mild traumatic brain injury using advanced MRI: implications for neurorehabilitation. NeuroRehabilitation **31**, 261–262 (2013)
7. Govind, V., et al.: Whole-brain proton MR spectroscopic imaging of mild-to-moderate traumatic brain injury and correlation with neuropsychological deficits. J. Neurotrauma **27**, 483–496 (2010). https://doi.org/10.1089/neu.2009.1159
8. Gajawelli, N., et al.: Neuroimaging changes in the brain in contact versus noncontact sport athletes using diffusion tensor imaging. World Neurosurg. **80**, 824–828 (2013). https://doi.org/10.1016/j.wneu.2013.10.020
9. Bazarian, J.J., Zhu, T., Blyth, B., Borrino, A., Zhong, J.: Subject-specific changes in brain white matter on diffusion tensor imaging after sports-related concussion. Magn. Reason. Imaging **30**, 171–180 (2012)
10. McAllister, T.W., Sparling, M.B., Flashman, L.A., Guerin, S.J., Mamourian, A.C., Saykin, A.J.: Differential working memory load effects after mild traumatic brain injury. Neuroimage **14**, 1004–1012 (2001)
11. Ptito, A., Chen, J.K., Johnston, K.M.: Contributions of functional magnetic resonance imaging (fMRI) to sport concussion evaluation. NeuroRehabilitation **22**, 217–227 (2007)
12. Lipton, M.L., et al.: Multifocal white matter ultrastructural abnormalities in mild traumatic brain injury with cognitive disability: a voxel-wise analysis of diffusion tensor imaging. J. Neurotrauma **25**, 1335–1342 (2008). https://doi.org/10.1089/neu.2008.0547
13. Gasparovic, C., et al.: Neurometabolite concentrations in gray and white matter in mild traumatic brain injury: an 1H-magnetic resonance spectroscopy study. J. Neurotrauma **26**, 1635–1643 (2009). https://doi.org/10.1089/neu.2009-0896

14. Slobounov, S.M., et al.: Alteration of brain sports concussion biomarkers 669 functional network at rest and in response to YMCA physical stress test in concussed athletes: RsFMRI study. Neuroimage **55**, 1716–1727 (2011)
15. Zhang, K., et al.: Default mode network in concussed individuals in response to the YMCA physical stress test. J. Neurotrauma **29**, 756–765 (2012). https://doi.org/10.1089/neu.2011.2125
16. Slobounov, S.M., et al.: Functional abnormalities in normally appearing athletes following mild traumatic brain injury: a functional MRI study. Exp. Brain Res. **202**, 341–354 (2010). https://doi.org/10.1007/s00221-009-2141-6
17. Bazarian, J.J., et al.: Diffusion tensor imaging detects clinically important axonal damage after mild traumatic brain injury: a pilot study. J. Neurotrauma **24**, 1447–1459 (2007). https://doi.org/10.1089/neu.2007.0241
18. Huang, M.X., et al.: Integrated imaging approach with MEG and DTI to detect mild traumatic brain injury in military and civilian patients. J. Neurotrauma **26**, 1213–1226 (2009). https://doi.org/10.1089/neu.2008.0672
19. Vakorin, V.A., et al.: Detecting mild traumatic brain injury using resting state magnetoencephalographic connectivity. PLoS Comput. Biol. **12**, e1004914 (2016). https://doi.org/10.1371/journal.pcbi.1004914
20. Dashnaw, M.L., Petraglia, A.L., Bailes, J.E.: An overview of the basic science of concussion and subconcussion: where we are and where we are going. Neurosurg. Focus **33**, 1–9 (2013)
21. Kochanek, P.M., et al.: Biomarkers of primary and evolving damage in traumatic and ischemic brain injury: diagnosis, prognosis, probing mechanisms, and therapeutic decision making. Curr. Opin. Crit. Care **14**, 135–141 (2008). https://doi.org/10.1097/MCC.0b013e3282f57564
22. Papa, L., et al.: Systematic review of clinical research on biomarkers for pediatric traumatic brain injury. J. Neurotrauma **30**, 324–338 (2013). https://doi.org/10.1089/neu.2012.2545
23. Papa, L.T.K.M., Flores, R.J.: Exploring the role of biomarkers for the diagnosis and management of traumatic brain injury patients. In: Poteomics—Human Diseases and Protein Functions. Tech Open Access Publisher (2012). https://doi.org/10.5772/31776
24. Papa, L., Randolph, J., Sebastianelli, W.: Biomarkers for Concussion, in: Concussions in Athletics: From Brain to Behavior. Springer, Heidelberg (2014)
25. Papa, L., Ramia, M.M., Edwards, D., Johnson, B.D., Slobounov, S.M.: Systematic review of clinical studies examining biomarkers of brain injury in athletes after sports-related concussion. J. Neurotrauma **32**, 661–673 (2015). https://doi.org/10.1089/neu.2014.3655
26. Otto, M., et al.: Boxing and running lead to a rise in serum levels of S-100B protein. Int. J. Sports Med. **21**, 551–555 (2000). https://doi.org/10.1055/s-2000-8480
27. Dietrich, M.O., et al.: Increase in serum S100B protein level after a swimming race. Can. J. Appl. Physiol. **28**, 710–716 (2003). https://doi.org/10.1139/h03-054
28. Mussack, T., Dvorak, J., Graf-Baumann, T., Jochum, M.: Serum S-100B protein levels in young amateur soccer players after controlled heading and normal exercise. Eur. J. Med. Res. **8**, 457–464 (2003)
29. Stalnacke, B.M., Tegner, Y., Sojka, P.: Playing ice hockey and basketball increases serum levels of S-100B in elite players: a pilot study. Clin. J. Sport Med. **13**, 292–302 (2003). https://doi.org/10.1097/00042752-200309000-00004
30. Stalnacke, B.M., Ohlsson, A., Tegner, Y., Sojka, P.: Serum concentrations of two biochemical markers of brain tissue damage S100B and neurone specific enolase are increased in elite female soccer players after a competitive game. Br. J. Sports Med. **40**, 313–316 (2006)
31. Stalnacke, B.M., Tegner, Y., Sojka, P.: Playing soccer increases serum concentrations of the biochemical markers of brain damage S-100B and neuron-specific enolase in elite players: a pilot study. Brain Inj. **18**, 899–909 (2004). https://doi.org/10.1080/02699050410001671865
32. Hasselblatt, M., et al.: Serum S100beta increases in marathon runners reflect extracranial release rather than glial damage. Neurology **62**, 1634–1636 (2004)

33. Zetterberg, H., et al.: No neurochemical evidence for brain injury caused by heading in soccer. Brit. J. Sport Med. **41**, 574–577 (2007). ARTN 574, https://doi.org/10.1136/bjsm.2007.037143
34. Zetterberg, H., et al.: Sustained release of neuron-specific enolase to serum in amateur boxers. Brain Inj. **23**, 723–726 (2009). https://doi.org/10.1080/02699050903120399
35. Graham, M.R., et al.: Direct hits to the head during amateur boxing is associated with a rise in serum biomarkers for brain injury. Int. J. Immunopathol. Pharmacol. **24**, 119–125 (2011).https://doi.org/10.1177/039463201102400114
36. Neselius, S., et al.: CSF-biomarkers in Olympic boxing: diagnosis and effects of repetitive head trauma. PLoS ONE **7**, e33606 (2012). https://doi.org/10.1371/journal.pone.0033606
37. Neselius, S., et al.: Olympic boxing is associated with elevated levels of the neuronal protein tau in plasma. Brain Inj. **27**, 425–433 (2013). https://doi.org/10.3109/02699052.2012.750752
38. (NCBI), N. C. f. B. I. S100B (1988). https://www.ncbi.nlm.nih.gov/
39. Yardan, T.J.: Usefullness of S100B protein in neurological disorders. Park Med. Assoc. **61**, 276–281 (2011)
40. Papa, L.: Time course and diagnostic accuracy of glial and neuronal blood biomarkers GFAP and UCH-L1 in a large cohort of trauma patients with and without mild traumatic brain injury. JAMA **73**, 551–560 (2016)
41. Paans, A.M.J., Van Waarde, A., Elsinga, P.H., Willemsen, A.T.M. Vaalburg, W.: Positron emission tomography: the conceptual idea using a multidisciplinary approach. Methods **27**, 195–207 (2002). Pii, https://doi.org/10.1016/S1046-2023(02)00075-0
42. Skotland, T.: Molecular imaging: challenges of bringing imaging of intracellular targets into common clinical use. Contrast Media Mol. **I**(7), 1–6 (2012). https://doi.org/10.1002/cmmi.458
43. Ametamey, S.M., Honer, M., Schubiger, P.A.: Molecular imaging with PET. Chem. Rev. **108**, 1501–1516 (2008). https://doi.org/10.1021/cr0782426
44. Trott, O., Olson, A.J.: Autodock vina: improving the speed and accuracy of docking with a new scoring function, efficient optimization and multithreading. J. Comput. Chem. **31**, 455–461 (2009)
45. Morris, G.M., et al.: Autodock4 and autodocktools4: automated docking with selective receptor flexibility. J. Comput. Chem. **30**, 2785–2791 (2009). https://doi.org/10.1002/jcc.21256
46. Goodsell, D.S., Morris, G.M., Olson, A.J.: Automated docking of flexible ligands: applications of autodock. J. Mol. Recognit. **9**, 1–5 (1996). https://doi.org/10.1002/(sici)1099-1352(199601)9:1%3c1::aid-jmr241%3e3.0.co;2-6
47. Ostendorp, T., Diez, J., Heizmann, C.W., Fritz, G.: The crystal structures of human S100B in the zinc- and calcium-loaded state at three pH values reveal zinc ligand swapping. Bba-Mol. Cell Res. **1813**, 1083–1091 (2011). https://doi.org/10.1016/j.bbamcr.2010.10.006
48. Makowitz, J.: Identification and characterization of small molecule inhibitors of the calcium-dependent S100B–p53 tumour supressor interactions. J. Med. Chem. **47**, 5085–5093 (2004)
49. Mysinger, M.M., Carchia, M., Irwin, J.J., Shoichet, B.K.: Directory of useful decoys, enhanced (DUD-E): better ligands and decoys for better benchmarking. J. Med. Chem. **55**, 6582–6594 (2012). https://doi.org/10.1021/jm300687e
50. Huang, N., Shoichet, B.K., Irwin, J.J.: Benchmarking sets for molecular docking. J. Med. Chem. **49**, 6789–6801 (2006). https://doi.org/10.1021/jm0608356
51. Advanced Cyclotron Systems: I. TR-24 Cyclotrons (2019). https://www.advancedcyclotron.com/cyclotron-solutions/tr24
52. Healthcare, G.E.: Vol. DOC0735494 Rev 3 (2001)
53. Bock, N., et al.: Chronic fluoxetine treatment changes S100B expression during postnatal rat brain development. J. Child Adolesc. Psychopharmacol. **23**, 481–489 (2013). https://doi.org/10.1089/cap.2011.0065

54. Tramontina, A.C., et al.: Secretion of S100B, an astrocyte-derived neurotrophic protein, is stimulated by fluoxetine via a mechanism independent of serotonin. Prog. Neuro-Psychopharmacol. Biol. Psychiatry **32**, 1580–1583 (2008)
55. Whitaker-Azmitia, P.M., Murphy, R., Azmitia, E.C.: Stimulation of astroglial 5-HT1 receptors releases the serotonergic growth factor, protein S-100, and alters astroglial morphology. Brain Res. **24**, 155–158 (1990)

AI-Enabled Proactive mHealth: A Review

Muhammad Sulaiman(✉), Anne Håkansson, and Randi Karlsen

Department of Computer Science, UiT The Arctic University of Norway, Tromsø, Norway
{muhammad.sulaiman,anne.hakansson,randi.karlsen}@uit.no

Abstract. Digital health incorporates mHealth to provide digital transformation in healthcare. AI in mHealth has a significant impact on promoting self-management. Our current healthcare system is reactive that is to react when symptoms emerge a crisis occurs and then take steps. Proactive health in contrast is to predict risks and prevent them with supportive actions promptly. This allows people to take control of their health and be aware of their surrounding and wellbeing. To achieve proactive mHealth with the capability of predictions and preventions. AI can contribute by applying reasoning and negotiation to the available health data and recognizing patterns to automate processes and augment healthier behaviors. In this paper, we systematically reviewed existing research with AI in mHealth to establish proactive mHealth. This paper also explores the level of proactiveness in existing systems. Our review identified that digital interventions and recommender system form the basis of proactive mHealth. We found nine targeted groups most of them are for chronic disease management. With this review, we also evaluated AI-techniques and data sources used in modelling these systems.

Keywords: Artificial intelligence · mHealth · Proactive healthcare · Machine learning · Digital health · eHealth · Digital interventions

1 Introduction

Healthcare sector comprises of several areas that work together to provide quality medical services to the public. Public health by definition is "The science and art of preventing disease, prolonging life, and promoting health through the organized efforts and informed choices of society, organizations, public and private communities, and individuals" [1]. Healthcare today is facing several challenges various circumstances contribute to these challenges, such as a public health crisis and emergencies. Another challenge is the ageing population, which is a renowned factor for the development of multiple chronic diseases like cardiovascular disease, diabetes, stroke, cancer, osteoarthritis, and dementia [2]. This ageing population corresponds to a group of people with regular healthcare need. Finally, some organizational challenges like the need for more healthcare professionals and the hospitals capacity to deal with the increase in hospital visits. For instance, in Sweden, there are only 2.22 hospital beds per 1000 people [3] and the availability of 4.19 doctors per 1000 people [4].

E. Pissaloux et al. (Eds.): IHAW 2021, CCIS 1538, pp. 94–108, 2021.
https://doi.org/10.1007/978-3-030-94209-0_9

Traditionally healthcare system is based on a reactive approach. Which is to react when symptoms appear, crisis occur then take actions. This reactive approach is damage control [5]. Supporting patients after they became symptomatic with the disease has an adverse effect on the healthcare system. Healthcare involves different processes e.g., screening, prevention, diagnosis, and treatment [6]. In this reactive design, the patient is assigned a passive role which is to wait for a decision throughout these healthcare processes this reduces patient empowerment and minimizes the possibilities of self-management.

A definition of health was introduced by Huber as "The ability to adapt and to self-manage, in the face of social, physical and emotional challenges" [7]. With the rapid increase in mobile technologies [8] and the transformation of healthcare practices, individuals are becoming more aware and concerned about their health [9]. A survey conducted in U.S showed that 62% of smartphone owners search the internet for health-related information [10]. The recent development and availability of smart devices pave the way for the era of digital health.

Digital health incorporates eHealth and mobile health (mHealth) [11] to provide digital transformation in healthcare. eHealth does not only mean electronic health but instead, it indicates many other terms [12]. eHealth provides health services and information delivered or enhanced through the internet and communication technologies, to improve healthcare locally, regionally, and worldwide by using information and communication technology [13]. mHealth provides healthcare services using mobile and wireless technology. mHealth combines wearable sensing technology and medical technology for providing healthcare services [14]. Within digital health, mHealth incorporates all available resources of telecommunication and wireless technology for the delivery of healthcare and health information. WHO global observatory for eHealth (GOe) defined mHealth as "medical and public health practice supported by mobile devices, such as mobile phones, patient monitoring devices, personal digital assistants, and other wireless devices" [15].

Healthcare is shifting from reactive to proactive [16] with the support of Artificial Intelligence (AI), mHealth and Internet of things (IoT). Proactive healthcare is to predict risks and react with supportive actions with the focus on the user-centric approach rather than the traditional hospital-centric approach [17]. Every health problem can be easier to manage in earlier stages. Proactive healthcare can allow supportive actions before a crisis [17]. Predicting and preventing a situation on time enables care which empowers and gives the user an active role.

mHealth provides pervasiveness which minimizes the dilemmas of healthcare delivery. It provides healthcare to anyone at any time anywhere. With the emergence of cutting-edge technologies [18] in healthcare and AI, self-management or self-care is becoming more relevant. It will contribute to shifting healthcare to a new norm with a focus on the user.

Artificial Intelligence with "problem-solving, reasoning and decision making [19] in mobile health can support healthcare by augmenting human capabilities to develop awareness, promote wellbeing and self-care of healthy behaviors [20]. As healthcare is evolving and with the introduction of healthcare 4.0 to be more proactive and user-centric

[17] AI can help by applying reasoning and negotiation to the available health data and recognize patterns to introduce automation and finally to make decisions.

With healthcare becoming more proactive and user-centric true potential lies with AI to contribute to that by introducing AI-enabled proactive mHealth. AI with automated decision-making and predictive analytics can provide timely preventive measures and transform future health applications [21]. Proactive mHealth applications can predict (early detect) and prevent a situation with adaptive supportive actions to improve personalization and contribute to a healthy lifestyle.

This review paper investigates existing studies with a focus on AI-enabled proactive mHealth. We also examine studies which establish proactive mHealth with properties of prediction, prevention, and personalization. To our knowledge, there is no prior study which presented a review with the focus on proactive mHealth. The methodology of a systematic literature review (SLR) [22] is used for this review. We opted for an SLR because it allows rigorous analysis of a topic with lower inclination.

2 Methodology

A systematic literature review (SLR) is conducted to investigate the current state-of-the-art in AI-enabled proactive mHealth. An SLR is "a systematic, explicit, [comprehensive,] and reproducible method for identifying, evaluating, and synthesizing the existing body of completed and recorded work produced by researchers, scholars, and practitioners" [22]. SLR process has different stages identification, screening, eligibility, and selection. The inclusion and exclusion criteria provide the basis of selection.

2.1 Search Strategy

The search strategy is to create a search string and look for all the available studies within the relevant databases. In this study, we used the sources found in Table 1. The outcome of the search provides studies for each stage of the SLR. A significant aspect of an SLR process is string formation. A more precise string can provide better comprehensive result.

Table 1. Databases for the search.

Databases
ACM Digital Library
ScienceDirect
IEEE Xplore
ISI Web of knowledge
Cite Seer
SpringerLink
Google Scholar
Wiley inter Science

2.2 Search String and Stages of SLR

Table 2 shows the search string used for this SLR. Each scope provided synonyms which are grouped to form the search string. The focus is to be more precise in finding studies and grasping more by using refined keywords.

Table 2. Search string table.

Scope	String
A = Artificial Intelligence	"Artificial Intelligence" OR "AI" OR" Machine learning" OR "Deep learning" OR "Artificial neural network" OR "ANN"
B = mHealth	"mHealth" OR "mobile health" OR "eHealth" OR "m-health" OR "e-health" OR "eHealthcare" OR "mHealthcare"
C = Proactive	"proactive"
$A \wedge B \wedge C$	$([A, A1] \vee [A, A2] \vee [A, A3] \vee [A, A4] \vee [A, A5]) \wedge ([B, B1] \vee [B, B2] \vee [B, B3] \vee [B, B4] \vee [B, B5] \vee [B, B6]) \wedge C$

After search string formation, a comprehensive search is conducted within the databases. The first stage of SLR is the identification stage to recognize the studies for the screening stage. Using the search string available studies are collected from different sources (Table 1).

In the second stage of screening, gathered studies from the identification stage are examined. Screening is based on the criteria for inclusion and exclusion (Table 3). Initial screening is performed by analysis of the title and abstract of each study. The outcome of the first stage of screening formulates a list of studies. This list is passed to another stage of screening by analysis of introduction and conclusion. This more specific list is selected for the third stage of eligibility where full-text analysis is performed. The studies are then finally chosen for investigation in the final stage of selection. From the final list, analysis is done and discussed by providing key finding and limitations.

3 Criteria Inclusion and Exclusion of Studies

Table 3 presents the criteria for inclusion and exclusion of studies. A study is selected if it includes any of the given inclusion criteria and excludes all the exclusion criteria (Fig. 1).

Table 3. Criteria table.

Type	Criteria
Inclusion*	**IC1** The paper is focused on mHealth or eHealth with Artificial Intelligence and proactive healthcare **IC2** The paper illustrates user-centred self-management or self-care for proactive healthcare with mHealth **IC3** The paper evaluates AI techniques for establishing proactive mHealth with the focus on machine learning, deep learning, and artificial neural networks? **IC4** The paper introduces principles of proactive healthcare with personalization, prediction, and prevention
Exclusion*	**EC1** The paper is not written in English **EC2** The paper was published before January 2008 **EC3** The paper is more focused on clinical decision-making

*IC = Inclusion criteria
*EC = Exclusion criteria

4 Outcome and Results

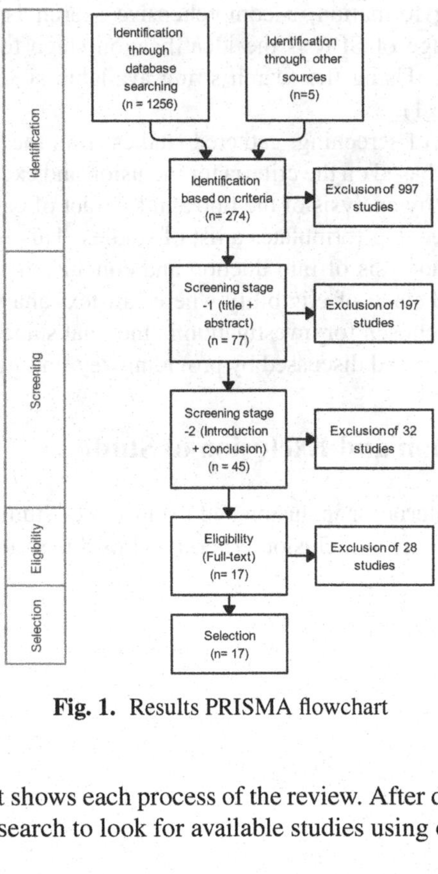

Fig. 1. Results PRISMA flowchart

PRISMA flowchart shows each process of the review. After defining the criteria, we started with extensive search to look for available studies using our search string.

- In the identification stage, we found 1256 studies and 15 more studies were included from references. These 15 studies were identified as relevant by keyword search performed on each of the references in the papers selected.
- By initial identification, we excluded 997 studies in stage 1 which were not based on our criteria of inclusion. 274 studies were selected to be screened. After reading the title and abstract we excluded 197 studies and only selected 77 studies for stage 2. In stage 2 of screening, studies were examined by reading the introduction and conclusion. At this stage, another 32 studies were excluded from the list.
- Finally, for the last stage before selection, only 45 studies were selected for full-text analysis.
- After final stage, only 17 studies were selected, and 28 studies are excluded.

Table 4. Selected studies with analysis.

Studies	Selection criteria	Outcome category	Predictive (P1), preventive (P2) & personalized (P3)	Patient-centered / User-centered	Self-management/Self-care	AI Techniques for predictive analytics	Data sources
Nitish Nag [23]	IC1, IC2 & IC4	Lifestyle	P1, P2, P3	✓	✓	Deep learning (overview only)	Sensors, activity data, expert systems, and dietary habits
Shubhi A [24]	IC1	Disease risk	P1	✗	✗	Machine learning classification model	EHR, personal history and disease history
Michael V [25]	IC1 & IC2	Cardiovascular disease (physical fitness)	✗	✓	✓	Not specified	Not specified
Mike B [26]	IC1& IC2	Nutrition (Dietary advice)	P1	✓	✓	Not specified	Physical activity (step counts), food consumption and medical history
Adrian A [27]	IC1	Physical activity (Diabetes)	P1	✓	✗	Reinforcement learning	Step counts
Yvonne J [28]	IC1 & IC2	COPD	P1	✓	✓	No implementation	Not specified
Talko B [29]	IC1 & IC3	Physical Activity	P3	✗	✗	8 machine learning classification models	Step counts over the intervention period
Robert S [30]	IC1, IC2 & IC4	Review	P1, P2, P3	✗	✓	Model (descriptive > predictive)	Not specified
Kashif N [31]	IC1 & IC3	Review analysis of predictive models with mHealth	P1	✗	✗	Review of machine learning techniques	Review of available data sources
Bertalan M [32]	IC1 & IC2	Discussion only	✗	✓	✓	Not specified	Not specified
J. Rojas [33]	IC1 & IC2	Sleep, Just-in-time adaptive	P1, P2, P3	✓	✓	Classifier model (MultiLayer Perceptron)	Sleep and activity
Mirza M [34]	IC1 & IC2	Diabetes	P1, P2, P3	✓	✓	AI model using adaptive-neuro fuzzy inference	Heart rate, breathing rate, activity. blood glucose, BMI
Usman I [35]	IC1	General public	✗	✗	✗	Not specified	Not specified
Marianne M [20]	IC1	Decision-making	P1, P2, P3	✗	✗	Focus on Reinforcement learning	Not specified
Michelle Nicole [36]	IC1	Depression	P1	✗	✗	Regression and decision trees	Phone sensors and GPS
Ramesh Manuvinakurike [37]	IC1	Weight management	P1	✓	✗	Adaptive boosting	Not specified
Morrison LG [38]	IC1 & IC2	Stress management	P1	✓	✗	Naïve Bayes classifier	User preferences

5 Analysis of Selected Studies

Table 4 presents the list of studies selected for this review paper. Each study is evaluated based on several criteria. The first column "studies" lists the identifier (author name) of the selected study. The second column "selection criteria" is based on Table 3 criteria of inclusion and exclusion. Column "outcome category" provides detail about the targeted outcome of the study. Next three columns assess the studies based on inclusion criteria IC2 and IC4 from Table 3. Last two columns provide details about the type of AI technique used and the data sources considered.

Most of the studies are focused on a particular group of people or chronic disease management [25, 27, 28, 34]. The studies targeted diabetes [27, 34], cardiovascular disease [25], chronic obstructive pulmonary disease (COPD) [28], nutrition [26], stress management [38], weight management [37], sleep [33], depression [36] and to promote physical activity [23, 29].

Only 4 studies are targeted towards individuals that do not possess any diagnosis of disease [23, 26, 29, 33]. Most of the studies illustrate the importance of personalization however studies [23, 29, 33] considered adaptive user preference into consideration.

Only two studies [29, 31] gave insight on details regarding the AI techniques used for prediction. Studies [29, 33, 34] considered wearables as a data source. A brief introduction of each of the selected papers is presented below in terms of purpose, outcome, methodologies, and results.

Nitish Nag et al. [23] described the importance of proactive health and significance of timely interventions by introducing a health navigation map which have a goal as desired state and the current state of the user as a starting point. They also described a P5 cybernetic multimedia health recommender system which has a personalized model connected with sensors to predict a new situation, and then provide a precise solution. Many different data sources are considered important. Some tools used for recognition are Clarifai and EventShop. The need for AI techniques and models for predicting events is depicted but no analysis on the available techniques to use. The primary focus of the study is on nutrition recommendation using multimedia sources.

Shubhi A et al. [24] explained the importance of proactive health monitoring using wearable sensors. The study focuses on health monitoring by first using a machine learning model with different datasets and person's electronic health record to identify the disease risk, and monitoring need. The paper only focuses on recommending the type of wearable device to the user based on the prediction of disease risk.

Michael V et al. [25] discusses the opportunities of providing proactive support for cardiovascular disease (CV) by early detection. The paper reviews the current state-of-the-art in mHealth to support CV. The main emphasis of the study is towards disease prevention with early detection. The study reviews available systems with mHealth to prevent CV disease no particular AI-techniques and are elaborated.

Mike B et al. [26] introduces eNutrition in the context of eHealth to provide designed nutrition to the users. It was argued that available systems are not personalized and cannot advise the user on what to eat, to keep track of the health information while giving recommendations. An example of an AI-engine is presented which takes the input of activity, preference, body data and consumption to give timely alerts to the user on what to eat and what to avoid including the portion size. The paper discusses available models and the gap but no information on modelling the AI-engine.

Adrian A et al. [27] is ongoing research targeting diabetic and mental health patients to improve physical activities using adaptive interventions. The applications hold a user-centered design (UCD) and provide interventions as an outcome of physical activity after

6 months. Step counts are gathered using Google fit and Apple HealthKit. Reinforcement learning is used as a technique for adaptive interventions.

Yvonne J et al. [28] discusses the importance of self-management in chronic patients for improving life and health outcomes. The main focus is on chronic obstructive pulmonary disease (COPD). The paper aims to describe in detail the whole process of developing UCD digital interventions.

Talko B et al. [29] uses a machine learning model to provide personalized coaching advice for an individual. They used step counts as a data source to train eight different machine learning models. Random forest algorithm performed best with the mean accuracy of 0.93, range 0.88–0.99 and the mean F1-score 0.90 with range 0.88–0.94. The proof-of-concept showed, machine learning can automate the process of physical coaching by predicting individual ability to reach their desired goal with timely interventions. Although the results of the study are promising but using step counts as a data source limits the system for interventions.

Robert S et al. [30] defines mHealth future trends with machine learning and deep learning in the current patient-centric model. A model of analytics is provided from descriptive analytics to predictive analytics. The paper provides insights to mHealth 2.0 with machine learning tools and patient-centric mHealth application design. The study lacks any implementation with these models.

Kashif N et al. [31] presented a review of available mHealth applications with prediction models using machine learning. A cloud-based secure architecture of a mHealth system is proposed which provides a platform for data acquisition and storage. They used CV as a use-case for training a model to provide outcome-based on the seriousness of the disease. The study gives great insight on available machine learning predictive models used in mHealth applications.

Bertalan M et al. [32] discusses wellbeing as a fundamental part of digital health. They introduced the definition of proactiveness as people are becoming more aware and have an active role in their health, they will be able to enter healthcare at an early stage. The paper emphasizes that digital health keeps people healthy instead of treating them when sick. The future depends on using AI systems, but the paper does not give any details on the type technologies to use for providing proactive health.

J. Rojas et al. [33] presented a personalized intervention system using mHealth and AI. They highlighted the importance of just-in-time interventions for continuous treatment and personalization based on lifestyle, environment, and genes. Two fundamental issues related to interventions are further discussed. They proposed a model aiming interventions for sleep. A Multilayer perceptron model was used instead of decision trees with the accuracy of the classifier as 88% and F1_score 0.54.

Mirza M et al. [34] used wearable devices for self-management of diabetes. The paper discusses the importance of early detection of diabetes. Data sources includes heart rate, breathing rate and volume, activity and manual data like blood glucose, BMI, and sex. AI model using adaptive-neuro fuzzy inference was proposed. The results showed good accuracy for the early detection of diabetes.

Usman I et al. [35] introduces earlier medicine and its importance. They discuss the contribution of AI in the initiative of "prevention is better than cure". In this study level of interventions is divided as actionable, accurate, timely and individualized.

Marianne M et al. [20] describes the importance of decision-making in mHealth using AI. They established that smartphones and wearables hold the key in providing health for anyone at any time with timely interventions. The paper focuses on decision-making with AI in terms of using Just-in-time adaptive interventions (JITAIs). Importance of decision rules which takes user current state as input and then decide when and what to deliver as an intervention. The study also provides the whole architecture of using AI with JITAIs. They proposed that AI-technique like reinforcement learning (RL) improves precision by learning optimal decision rules and RL also adapt and adjust to the user preferences.

Michelle N et al. [36] provided a machine learning intervention model to predict mood, emotions, motivational states, and activities for patients with depression. Phone data was used e.g., GPS and phone calls. The model with regression and decision trees proved to be accurate for predicting location but performed below par when it comes to predicting emotions. More parameters are needed for better accuracy.

Ramesh M et al. [37] developed an algorithm with adaptive boosting to focus on changes in weight loss through personal health behavior. The model used finds relevant stories based on demographics and emotional tone. The model provided an accuracy of 84%–98%. The outcome showed that there is an increase in efficacy for weight loss but the medium for the stories did not affect behavioral change.

Morrison LG et al. [38] provided a naive Bayes classifier for predicting when to send push notifications to the user and the best time for intervention. The study focused on push notifications for stress management. The results showed no major difference on outcomes of daily notifications and intelligent timely notifications.

6 Discussion

6.1 Principle Findings

This review systematically investigates existing studies with the focus on providing proactive health using mHealth and AI.

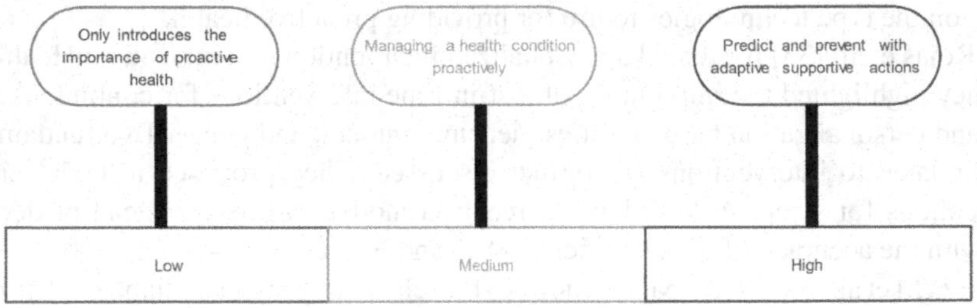

Fig. 2. Levels of proactive health

The Fig. 2 provides the parameter for identifying the level of proactiveness from each study. A "low" implies that the study only introduces the importance of proactive health. A "medium" level indicates that the study provides details about managing a situation or disease beforehand to avoid health risks. Finally, a "high" level presents the prediction and prevention capability to promote wellbeing.

Table 5. Key findings table.

Studies	Level of Proactiveness	Digital Interventions /Recommender systems	Automated decision-making /predictive analytics	P4/P5 principles	Just-in-time-adaptive Interventions (JITAI)	Real-time data from wearables
Nitish Nag [23]	Low	✓	×	✓	×	×
Shubhi A [24]	Low	✓	×	×	×	×
Michael V [25]	Medium	×	×	×	×	×
Mike B [26]	Low	✓	×	×	×	×
Adrian A [27]	Medium	✓	×	×	×	×
Yvonne J [28]	Low	✓	×	×	×	×
Talko B [29]	Low	✓	×	×	×	✓
Robert S [30]	Low	×	×	×	×	×
Kashif N [31]	Low	✓	×	×	×	×
Bertalan M [32]	Medium	×	×	×	×	×
J. Rojas [33]	Medium	✓	×	×	✓	✓
Mirza M [34]	Medium	✓	×	×	×	✓
Usman I [35]	Low	✓	×	×	×	×
Marianne M [20]	Low	✓	✓	×	✓	×
Michelle Nicole [36]	Low	✓	×	×	×	×
Ramesh Manuvinakurike [37]	Low	✓	×	×	×	×
Morrison LG [38]	Low	✓	×	×	×	×

✓ represents yes, × represents no

Table 5 presents key findings with different columns. Level of proactiveness is divided into three parameters as shown in the Fig. 2. Remaining columns provide details about different key findings that contribute to the discussion in this paper.

Our main finding is that digital interventions and recommender systems determine the basis of providing proactive mHealth. Most of the studies found were focused on disease management [25, 27, 28, 34]. With this review, we also found different implementations for proactive health. UCD is also given importance due to the reason that proactive health is user-centric, and it is away from the hospital settings.

Only one study [20] highlighted the importance of decision-making with AI and mHealth. No particular study focuses on automated decision-making with AI and implemented predictive analytics. Decision-making in mHealth has a significance. AI with automated decision-making can be an important factor when it comes to prediction and prevention of a situation. An AI-engine can provide automated decision-making to help users make healthier choices promptly.

With this review, we also found the importance of timely interventions for proactive health. Only two studies [20, 33] highlighted the importance of JITAI. Figure 3 provide details about JITAI challenges. Decision points show the time of intervention with "when". Intervention options give structure of intervention with "what" and tailoring variables shows the target assigned as "whom". So, moving forward challenge lies with when to intervene, with what information and to whom.

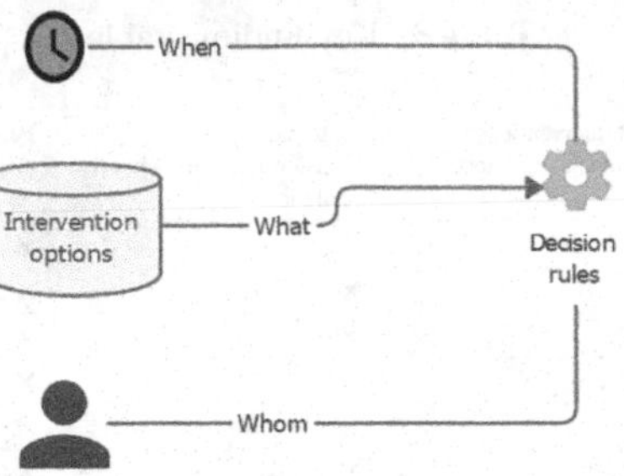

Fig. 3. JITAI points [39]

Only one study [23] highlighted the importance of P4 principles [40] for designing health systems which is personalization, prediction, prevention and participatory.

Our review found 9 different use-cases of interventions: diabetes, CV, COPD, nutrition, stress and weight management, sleep, depression, and physical activity.

We also found that existing studies used insufficient data sources. A few studies [29, 33, 34] used wearables but no study considered real-time data to represent the current state of the user. Wearables can play a vital role to provide more information on the current state of the user that can be very handy when it comes to interventions.

No existing system targeted the general population to improve wellbeing and promote health with proactiveness. A few examples targeted individuals [23, 26, 29, 33] but did not consider multiple factors e.g., user preferences and surroundings.

Nearby surroundings or environment factor was not considered by any study. Threats in the nearby environment can affect any individual. Timely intervention with a prediction and prevention mechanism can promote health and save lives. Accuracy of such a system depends on multiple data sources and sensors.

The selected studies also ascertained that mHealth implementation with sensors and mobile apps are used for providing digital interventions.

This review also provided insight into the type of AI-techniques used for mHealth applications to establish proactive health. A study [31] reviewed prediction models for mHealth applications. Depending on the use-case different studies included techniques for prediction. Only a few studies [23, 27, 29, 33, 36, 38] implemented a model and provided detailed results. A survey study was found [41] focusing on mHealth interventions using machine learning but without focusing on proactive aspect.

A recent study [42] presented a review of machine learning applications for big data analytics in healthcare. It explores the latest trends in using machine learning techniques for analytics in healthcare. Another contemporary survey study [43] surveys digital health role in nutrition support.

With this review, we conclude that there is no existing research conducted within proactive health with AI and mHealth to predict and prevent a situation beforehand. Which is targeted towards the general population to make them aware in a timely manner, so they do not become sick. Considering the context (surroundings/environment) of person. A system that is personalized and accounts for a person, not a patient. Automated decision-making (ADM) will be the core part of such a system.

6.2 Results and New Insights

The goal of proactive health is to make people proactive about their health, so they are aware of their surroundings and their well-being. To early detect a situation or anomaly and prevent it with actions in a timely manner for wellness promotion.

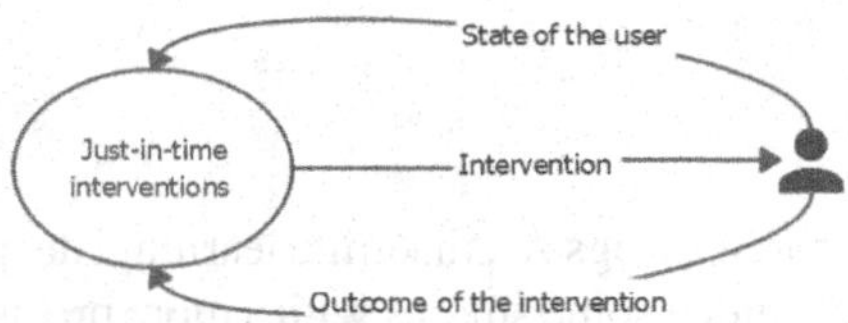

Fig. 4. JITAI [20]

Just-in-time adaptive interventions as shown in Fig. 4 can consider the current state of the user (from sensors) into account and provide timely interventions. Personalization of such interventions depends on user profiling and decision-making.

The world is currently experiencing a pandemic (COVID-19) which had an impact on our everyday life [44]. Proactive mHealth with AI can automate processes and support healthcare empowering people to take care of their health before becoming sick. An example is of several people working in a closed space. A proactive system can early detect a situation (e.g., fever alert) and proactively ask for symptoms and to provide a decision (go home) also give an alert flag for a possible outbreak.

An AI-engine can provide automated decision-making on a user-level to support self-care. An example is to identify someone in the risk of getting infected based on their profile and no. of cases in the city and reach out with timely advice (stay home). ADM can provide people with initial screening and advice on what steps to take.

AI systems are becoming intelligent and more automated in healthcare, in health decision-making it is vital to have transparency. System performance and transparency doesn't go well together. AI systems opacity and black-box decision-making approach directly influence trustworthiness. A novel concept of eXplainable AI (XAI) [45] is introduced which proposes AI-techniques that are more explainable and do not affect performance of the model. A system that is understandable by humans.

Environment factor along with health information gathered can lead to beneficial outcomes for people in danger e.g., an avalanche, to identify risks in nearby environment or an adverse effect on people's health. A proactive system can provide interventions based on individual or community level to save lives and promote wellness.

Real-time data from wearables like heart rate, activity, SpO2 etc. and user-profile can equip the system to be adaptive with current state for timely interventions.

Adopting the precise technique depends on the type of datasets and the desired outcome. Two studies [20, 27] opted for reinforcement learning for adaptive interventions, the reason is it improves precision by learning optimal decision rules, adapts and adjusts to user preferences.

Contribution for AI-Enabled Proactive mHealth. This review presented current state-of-the-art when it comes to AI-enabled proactive mHealth. The study identified

AI algorithms and techniques used in existing studies, along with the target group. The SLR presents which studies considered proactiveness with prediction and prevention capabilities. The analysis provides insights into data sources considered for modelling. This study also explores the level of proactiveness in selected studies. The detailed review of existing research prompted new insights for future work.

7 Limitations

For this review, broader search strings AI, machine learning, deep learning and ANN are used, which might have excluded some studies with a more precise title. While assessing the selected studies reliability in terms of data inputs (no. of people that participated) is not considered. Instead, the selection is based on multiple parameters.

8 Conclusion and Future Work

This paper presents a review of existing research with AI in mHealth to establish proactive mHealth. The review shows that proactive mHealth is complex and AI-enabled digital interventions and recommendation systems form the basis of proactive mHealth. The studies examined in this review show the effectiveness of being proactive but in the context of managing a certain health condition. We conclude that there is no existing research found for AI-enabled proactive mHealth that predicts and prevents a situation beforehand and targets the general population. A system that can consider multiple parameters of wellbeing e.g., environment or surroundings, and provide timely interventions before someone becomes sick. Furthermore, it is personalized and accounts for a person, not a patient. With this review, it is also concluded that the foundation of proactive mHealth lies with AI to provide automated decision-making with predictive analytics. P5 approach to mHealth and JITAI can contribute to the system design and implementation. These all pieces fit together to form the framework of AI-enabled proactive mHealth.

Future research must consider an iterative approach to establish AI-enabled proactive mHealth first step is to select multiple parameters (attributes) and a target group. Wearables and other sensors can be vital data sources. The next step is to identify these data sources based on the parameters and collect data. Finally, choosing a precise model which can not only provide timely intervention but can learn and adapt.

References

1. Winslow, C.: Introduction to Public Health CDC. https://www.cdc.gov/training
2. Atella, V., Piano Mortari, A., Kopinska, J., Belotti, F., Lapi, F., Cricelli, C.: Trends in age-related disease burden and healthcare utilization. Aging Cell. **18**, e12861 (2018)
3. Hospital beds (per 1,000 people) - Sweden | Data. https://data.worldbank.org/indicator
4. Physicians (per 1,000 people) - Sweden | Data. https://data.worldbank.org/indicator
5. M, A.: The Shift from Reactive to Proactive Healthcare. https://blackcreek.io/insights

6. Bergman, B., Neuhauser, D., Provost, L.: Five main processes in healthcare: a citizen perspective. BMJ Qual. Saf. **20**, i41–i42 (2011)
7. Huber, M., et al.: How should we define health? BMJ **343**, d4163 (2011)
8. Number of smartphone users in the U.S. 2025 | Statista. https://www.statista.com/statistics
9. Betts, D., Korenda, L., Giuliani, S.: Are consumers already living the future of health? Key trends in agency, virtual health, remote monitoring, and data-sharing (2020)
10. Smith, A.: U.S. Smartphone Use in (2015). https://www.pewresearch.org/internet
11. What is Digital Health? https://www.fda.gov/medical-devices
12. Eysenbach, G.: What is e-health? J. Med. Internet Res. **3**, e20 (2001)
13. Kluge, E.: Framework considerations. In: The Electronic Health Record, pp. 105–133 (2020)
14. Zhang, Y., Pickwell-Macpherson, E.: 5G-based mhealth bringing healthcare convergence to reality. IEEE Rev. Biomed. Eng. **12**, 2–3 (2019)
15. 71st World Health Assembly: Global Observatory for eHealth, Geneva (2018)
16. Waldman, S., Terzic, A.: Health care evolves from reactive to proactive. Clin. Pharmacol. Ther. **105**, 10–13 (2018)
17. Sharma, D., Singh Aujla, G., Bajaj, R.: Evolution from ancient medication to human-centered healthcare 4.0: a review on health care recommender systems. Int. J. Commun. Syst. e4058 (2019)
18. Chanchaichujit, J., Tan, A., Meng, F., Eaimkhong, S.: Healthcare 4.0 Next Generation Processes with the Latest Technologies. Palgrave Pivot, Singapore (2019)
19. Russell, S., Norvig, P., Chang, M.: Artificial Intelligence-A Modern Approach. Pearson Education Limited, London (2021)
20. Menictas, M., Rabbi, M., Klasnja, P., Murphy, S.: Artificial intelligence decision-making in mobile health. Biochemist **41**, 20–24 (2019)
21. EiT Health: Transforming healthcare with AI: The impact on the workforce and organizations. McKinsey & Company (2020)
22. Okoli, C.: A guide to conducting a standalone systematic literature review. Commun. Assoc. Inf. Syst. **37** (2015)
23. Nag, N., Pandey, V., Jain, R.: Health multimedia: lifestyle recommendations based on diverse observations. In: Proceedings of the 2017 ACM on International Conference on Multimedia Retrieval, pp. 99–106. Association for Computing Machinery (2017)
24. Asthana, S., Megahed, A., Strong, R.: A recommendation system for proactive health monitoring using iot and wearable technologies. In: Proceedings of the 2017 IEEE International Conference on AI & Mobile Services (AIMS), pp. 14–21. IEEE (2021)
25. McConnell, M., Turakhia, M., Harrington, R., King, A., Ashley, E.: Mobile health advances in physical activity, fitness, and atrial fibrillation. J. Am. Coll. Cardiol. **71**, 2691–2701 (2018)
26. Boland, M., Bronlund, J.: eNutrition–the next dimension for eHealth? Trends Food Sci. Technol. **91**, 634–639 (2019)
27. Aguilera, A., et al.: mHealth app using machine learning to increase physical activity in diabetes and depression: clinical trial protocol for the DIAMANTE study. BMJ Open **10**, e034723 (2020)
28. Korpershoek, Y., Hermsen, S., Schoonhoven, L., Schuurmans, M., Trappenburg, J.: User-centered design of a mobile health intervention to enhance self-management in patients with COPD (Copilot): mixed methods study. JMIR **22**, e15449 (2020)
29. Dijkhuis, T., Blaauw, F., van Ittersum, M., Velthuijsen, H., Aiello, M.: Personalized physical activity coaching: a machine learning approach. Sensors **18**, 623 (2018)
30. Istepanian, R., Al-Anzi, T.: m-Health 2.0: new perspectives on mobile health, machine learning and big data analytics. Methods **151**, 34–40 (2018)
31. Naseer Qureshi, K., Din, S., Jeon, G., Piccialli, F.: An accurate and dynamic predictive model for a smart m-Health system using machine learning. Inf. Sci. **538**, 486–502 (2020)

32. Mesko, B.: Digital health technologies and well-being in the future. IT Prof. **22**, 20–23 (2020)
33. Ramos Rojas, J., Dey, A.: The personalization of mobile health interventions (2019)
34. Baig, M.: Early detection and self-management of long-term conditions using wearable technologies (2017)
35. Iqbal, U., Celi, L., Li, Y.: How can artificial intelligence make medicine more preemptive? J. Med. Internet Res. **22**, e17211 (2020)
36. Burns, M., et al.: Harnessing context sensing to develop a mobile intervention for depression. J. Med. Internet Res. **13**, e55 (2011)
37. Manuvinakurike, R., Velicer, W., Bickmore, T.: Automated indexing of internet stories for health behavior change: weight loss attitude pilot study. JMIR **16**, e285 (2014)
38. Morrison, L., et al.: The effect of timing and frequency of push notifications on usage of a smartphone-based stress management intervention: an exploratory trial. PLOS ONE **12**, e0169162 (2017)
39. Trujillo, A., Senette, C., Buzzi, M.C.: Persona design for just-in-time adaptive and persuasive interfaces in menopause self-care. In: Marcus, A., Wang, W. (eds.) DUXU 2018. LNCS, vol. 10920, pp. 94–109. Springer, Cham (2018). https://doi.org/10.1007/978-3-319-91806-8_8
40. Sagner, M., et al.: The P4 health spectrum–a predictive, preventive, personalized and participatory continuum for promoting healthspan. Prog. Cardiovasc. Dis. **59**, 506–521 (2017)
41. Triantafyllidis, A., Tsanas, A.: Applications of machine learning in real-life digital health interventions: review of the literature. J. Med. Internet Res. **21**, e12286 (2019)
42. Li, W., et al.: A comprehensive survey on machine learning-based big data analytics for iot-enabled smart healthcare system. Mob. Netw. Appl. **26**, 234–252 (2021)
43. Limketkai, B.N., Mauldin, K., Manitius, N., Jalilian, L., Salonen, B.R.: The age of artificial intelligence: use of digital technology in clinical nutrition. Curr. Surg. Rep. **9**(7), 1–13 (2021). https://doi.org/10.1007/s40137-021-00297-3
44. WHO Director-General's opening remarks on COVID-19–11 March 2020 (2020)
45. Barredo Arrieta, A., et al.: Explainable artificial intelligence (XAI): concepts, taxonomies, opportunities and challenges toward responsible AI. Inf. Fusion **58**, 82–115 (2020)

eSticky–An Advanced Remote Reminder System for People with Early Dementia

Lisa Fixl[1], Stefan Parker[1(✉)], Joanna Starosta-Sztuczka[2], Christos Mettouris[3], Alexandros Yeratziotis[3], Stavroulla Koumou[3], Michalis Kaili[3], George A. Papadopoulos[3], and Valerie Clarke[4]

[1] Kompetenznetzwerk KI-I, Altenbergerstraße 69, 4040 Linz, Austria
{lisa.fixl,stefan.parker}@ki-i.at
[2] Harpo Sp. z o.o., 27 Grudnia 7, 61-737 Poznan, Poland
jstarosta@harpo.com.pl
[3] Department of Computer Science, University of Cyprus, 2109 Nicosia, Cyprus
{mettour,ayerat01,skoumo01,mkaili02,george}@cs.ucy.ac.cy
[4] Assistenz24 gemeinnützige GmbH, Boltzmanngasse 24-26/EG, 1090 Wien, Austria
v.clarke@vcinfos.com

Abstract. While the European population is aging, the number of people with dementia is dramatically rising. With this comes an increased need for products that help affected people to be more independent and able to live in their own home for as long as possible. ESticky addresses this need by providing a sophisticated reminder system that replaces the old-fashioned sticky-notes by electronic versions thereof, which can be programmed from near and far in a device-independent manner via the internet and using a standard web browser. For this purpose, a set of low-cost ePaper-displays are used, accompanied by a small and unobtrusive base station. The displays can be placed at several strategically useful places in a user's home, to enable users and/or care persons to place reminders that will, based on the user's daily routines, most probably be read. Active displays even enable the user to press a confirmation button to show that he or she has actually read the reminder. The system is developed using a user centred design approach, to take all stakeholders' wishes and needs into account, in order to come up with a system that is easy to use and provides good service to many people.

Keywords: Reminder system · Dementia · Older adults · Independence

1 Introduction

The number of people living with dementia worldwide in 2013 was estimated at 44 million. By 2030 this number is expected to reach 76 million and by 2050 rise up to 135 million [1]. It is also foreseen that by 2030 one in five people will be older than 65 years of age and almost half of the people that are older than 84 will have dementia [2, 3]. In Europe, data shows that the age-specific prevalence rates have been constant over time and this trend is expected to continue in the future [4].

E. Pissaloux et al. (Eds.): IHAW 2021, CCIS 1538, pp. 109–123, 2021.
https://doi.org/10.1007/978-3-030-94209-0_10

Alzheimer Europe's 2013: The prevalence of dementia in Europe report [5] estimated that the average EU population who were living with dementia at the time was 1.55%. The report further indicates the population for Italy being 1,272,317 (2.09% of the total population), for Austria 145,431 (1.73% of the total population), for Cyprus 11,250 (1.07% of the total population) and for Poland 501,092 (1.31% of the total population). The fact that this report shows that there are people living with dementia in the age band of 30–59 is worth noticing. Even though the number of affected population within this age band in comparison to older age bands is considerably less, it indicates that dementia can also be experienced by younger adults too.

Studies in many countries have attempted to quantify the financial cost of dementia. This has proven to be a challenging task but what is clearly agreed upon is that these costs are large and growing. In OECD member countries, which include Italy, Austria and Poland, a significant portion of health spending is linked with the direct costs of dementia (e.g. nursing home care). A cross-country variation does apply nonetheless [5]. In addition to the direct costs of dementia there are also significant indirect costs too; the outcome of the impact on families, carers and the wider community. As previously mentioned, it is difficult to quantify the full cost because measuring and estimating the indirect costs presents methodological challenges (e.g. quantifying with a monetary value the cost of informal care). Hence, different approaches are used in different studies leading to uncertainty on the resulting numbers. From a European perspective, it is noticeable that we account for about a third of the annual global costs [5].

Insufficient support from professionals and health care services to stimulate self-management abilities is often experienced in the early stages of the disease, while interventions for coping with dementia are rare. Moreover, medical treatment still remains as the main focus of such interventions. Rather, an approach that adopts a more holistic view of the person and their needs is required, as was also proposed in [6]. Most people with dementia would prefer to continue living in their own homes. This situation would have a positive impact on their quality of life while also keeping them closer to their families. Furthermore, it would benefit them financially too, since formal care at home can be expensive and in some cases not even possible [7]. Either way, the burden for both family and paid caregivers is heavy. As the elderly population increases and the number of younger adults' decreases it will become even more unviable to expect younger adults to assist older persons with their long-term care needs in general, including those due to dementia. Long-term care workforce shortage, caregiver burden and high costs of care have led to an increase of interest in the potential of Assistive Technology (AT) to substitute for, complement, or supplement paid and unpaid caregiving for people with dementia [8].

AT that supports people who are living with dementia varies greatly. Their goals are commonly cited as maintenance of independence and providing a sense of autonomy, relieving caregiver burden and contributing to better safety. From simple standalone devices to more complex integrated systems, by helping a person remain independent for as long as possible, it enables them to live longer in their own homes than would otherwise be possible. Everyday living, monitoring, safety, communication, as well as automated prompts and reminders are areas where AT can be especially helpful for persons with dementia.

Since the purpose of AT for memory impairment compensation is to offer reminders or prompts, dementia has thus been equated to memory impairment. It must be noted however that people living with dementia are not just forgetful, but their ability to recall information, recognise objects and create new memories are also affected. As a result, storing, retaining and recalling new knowledge is a problem. In turn, their ability in learning and remembering how to use AT devices is likewise impaired. Existing products that offer reminders seem to have neglected this aspect and hence their design does not consider the type and range of cognitive impairments found with persons in this population.

The eSticky project aims to design and develop small and novel eSticky displays that provide reminders and prompts to people living with dementia. The novelty of the product will lie in its design and its affordability, as well as in the combination of several reminders into an integrated, remotely configurable and extendable system. Resembling traditional sticky notes, the proposed eSticky displays will be affordable to the point that a person living with dementia can purchase multiple displays and stick them in different areas of his or her home. By having eSticky displays located in every room of the home, family members and/or caregivers can predetermine, based on the normal daily routine of the person living with dementia, in what area of the home it will be more effective to set a reminder on the respective eSticky display. Reminders and prompts can be set using the eSticky web portal. Let us assume that a person living with dementia has a doctor's appointment at 12:00. The evening before the day of the appointment a family member uses the web portal to (remotely) set a reminder for 08:00 (the next morning) on the eSticky display that is located in the kitchen and also sets a reminder for 11:00 on the eSticky display that is located in the TV room. These eSticky displays were purposefully chosen by the family member since he or she is aware of the daily routine of the person living with dementia. This routine usually entails that the person be in the kitchen between 07:15–08:15 for breakfast and watch favourite TV shows between 10:30–11:30.

The user-friendly and intuitive design of eSticky makes it accessible to people with disabilities and easy enough to use to enable people with beginning dementia to set their own reminders.

2 IoT Importance for Older Adults

The Internet of Things (IoT) can improve older adults' quality of life. Additional important benefits resulting from their use include decrease of strain on national health systems and decrease of system operational costs overall [9, 13]. As an aging society, the use of such technology should be pursued for improved lifestyle, independence and home health care and promotion [10, 11]. Coupled with the design and development of this technology solutions and services, one needs to consider the five basic programs proposed by the General Assembly of the United Nations in 1991 (UN, 1991) when care is offered to older adults: independence, participation, care, self-fulfilment, and dignity [12, 13].

The potential of the IoT paradigm in the context of assisted living for older and fragile adults is discussed in [22]. Considering the peculiar requirements of this user group, the authors [22] evaluate the paradigm from functional and technological perspectives. In their review of the state-of-the-art, the authors [22] mention that research on matching users' needs, values, habits and lifestyles are evident in the literature, especially in the design of new IoT-based AAL systems [14–16]. One IoT platform that was implemented to take care of older adults at their home is presented in Pires et al. [17]. In their study [17], a smart TV was used to convey health-related information to the individual, using an unobtrusive method (i.e., as additional commercials). Others [18, 19] have focused on adopting user-centred design approaches for the design and development of an ehealth platform to assist older adults in smart cities. An IoT architecture was modified to also include an additional layer in [20] that would help address specific needs of people with diverse disabilities. Efforts have likewise been directed towards standardisation, focusing on effective user-centric IoT based AAL solutions [14]. Moreover, it was reported that more promotion is needed in this regard, since lack of standards is seen as a major challenge to the actual spread of IoT-based AAL systems in healthcare specifically. In [21] it is reported that in addition to efficiency and security, system flexibility and learnability are likewise key features of the user-centric IoT design that could significantly increase the level of system usability.

The study in [23] investigates the effectiveness of an electric calendar, showing the date and schedule automatically for older people, and to prove the characteristics of appropriate users. The participants were 27 older adults with or without dementia (9 men, 18 women, 72–94 years old). The study design was a cross-over randomized controlled trial, with 15 participants (55.6%) allocated to the first group to use the electric calendar, and 12 participants (44.4%) to the second intervention group. The outcome measures are daily behaviors and cognitive function assessed by the Mini-Mental State Examination and Neurobehavioral Cognitive Status Examination. Participants showed significant increase in total Mini-Mental State Examination score after intervention period, whereas there was no significant difference after no intervention. Daily activities related healthcare were improved. The participants with positive outcomes showed higher motivations and around 18 points in Mini-Mental State Examination. Most healthy older adults mentioned that electric calendars were useful, but unnecessary. Using the electric calendar was effective in improving global cognitive function and daily activities.

3 End User Aspects

The main target group of eSticky (potential end users) are people with age-related obliviousness, people with beginning stages of dementia and people with beginning Alzheimer's disease (only in an early or medium state), so-called primary users, who can live independently in their homes or professional institutions for older people without any special help. The stakeholders also include informal carers (e.g. family members, so-called secondary users) and formal carers – care service providers offering 24/7 assistance, retirement homes, nursery homes and their formal staff (healthcare professionals, i.e. tertiary users). eSticky will be used directly by older people with memory problems and their caregivers, families, etc. who will use it for the good of the primary users.

The main objectives of user involvement in the project are to:

1. Define the process and procedures for the recruitment and involvement of older adults.
2. Analyse the demand for assisted-living solutions based on data for the services operated by experts (i.e., end-user oriented consortium partners) to drive implementation.
3. Provide input about customer behaviour and attitude, purchasing processes, regulatory and other decision-making for validating the customer appreciation and evaluation of the solution, willingness to use it and willingness to pay for it (price sensitivity).
4. Identify security, safety and privacy issues for data collection and monitor compliance with the regulations.

In the initial phase, the project activity picked-up from the older adults and carers/families to analyse the demands and needs and the platform specification, to guarantee that these demands and needs are respected in the hardware configuration of the device and the adaptation of the software platform and services. For the evaluations that are being conducted in the project, a total of 40 older adults will participate, in two countries, i.e. in Austria and Poland. In a full user-centred design approach (UCD), end-user oriented partners will constantly monitor, discuss, evaluate and provide feedback based on the system development activities, so as to guarantee the proper implementation, integration and optimization of the platform.

To achieve it, the development of eSticky notes is user driven right from the beginning of the project. First, the methodology has consisted of studying existing results from requirements analysis conducted in other projects, where relevant and freely available. For this purpose the other assistive technology (AT) tools, devices and past Active and Assisted Living (AAL) projects from 2014–2018 were analysed pointing out the differences between various solutions and to confirm that there are a lot of prototypes and products for older adults, including people with memory problems, but none of them are similar to the eSticky solution. The end-user partners shared their research and analysis of AAL and AT, and personal experience in the usage of AAL. Moreover, they analysed trends in business models of these systems. The important aspect of planning user requirements was to define the process of recruiting users, policy for user involvement, taking into account local cooperation organisations (national associations, centres and non-governmental organisations), own contacts and communication channels of end-user partners in Austria and Poland, as well as inclusion and exclusion criteria of users, exit strategy, data collection methods, privacy design and ethical issues.

The next task has focused on choice and usage of investigative methods for user-centred design to fulfil the goal of a product engineered for its users including: ethnographic study, contextual inquiry, prototype testing, usability testing and other methods. Generative methods may also be used in the project including: card sorting, affinity diagramming and participatory design sessions. The goal of the user-centred design is to make products which have very high usability. This includes how convenient the product is in terms of its usage, manageability, effectiveness and how well the product is mapped to the user requirements. The end-user partners provided the review of standards for eSticky design (ISO norms, Universal design, Privacy by Design, World Wide Web Consortium (W3C) standards, Web Content Accessibility Guidelines (WCAG), Mobile

Web Best Practices, Design for All), review of business tools (like SWOT, PESTLE analysis, Business Model Canvas, Stakeholder analysis, User stories) and proposed different materials and forms for work with users.

An analysis of usable products similar to the product being designed in eSticky was also prepared, including the review of other electronic displays, watches and wristbands, sound players, automatic and electronic pillboxes, providing the conclusions and suggestions for further design process in the project.

Then, an initial user research was conducted to test the user interface (UI) mock-ups and to help generate the requirements focus groups with primary and secondary users to assess the prototype and field trials with primary users in the second testing phase. The results from the focus groups have generated input for the development of the prototype and will be continued to continuously improve the system, serving as a constant source of feedback.

Finally, the integrated prototype will be installed in the user's homes and field trials will be conducted in order to define further requirements for the development of the final product. The purpose of end-user involvement in the project is to create a solution that will meet potential users' needs and expectations. Nobody knows the requirements of people with dementia better than affected people themselves do (and their families and caregivers). Involving end users right from the beginning will allow eliminating basic mistakes when designing, testing and implementing eSticky notes.

1. In the exploratory and creative phases of the innovation process, the wishes and needs of the end-users serve as input to the development of the new solution and design of the business plan.
2. In development phases, the end-users provide the feedback loops validating and verifying the progress of the development work.
3. In business plan development, end-users provide input about customer behaviour and attitude, purchasing processes, regulatory and other decision-making. End-users are also crucial for validating the customer appreciation and evaluation of the solution, willingness to use it and willingness to pay for it (price sensitivity).

Since this qualitative approach towards user-involvement takes a significant amount of supervision, only a specified group of users can participate in the project. These are spread across our 2 user sites in Austria and Poland and user partners make sure that as many different user-profiles as possible will be included.

Since depending on users' condition some of them will have reduced cognitive capabilities, there are certain additional ethical issues that need to be taken care of. Legal and ethical issues will be especially considered for the testing and evaluation phases of the application with the end users. In these phases, data is obtained by monitoring the behaviour of the elderly people while at home, and this data will be processed and analysed. This will require the authorization by the end user and/or his family. The end-user partners have produced a detailed "Informed Consent" process (signed by either the users themselves or their legally assigned representatives) that guarantees transparency and include information such as a description of the project and its aims, a specification of the role of different end-users in the project, self-determination of the end-users (to be able to turn off systems or services at their own discretion), contact person in the project (for ethical issues and related questions) and exit rights for individual end-users (withdrawal possible at any time, without a reason and costs).

Moreover, one very important issue is that the privacy of the elderly people must be respected. Therefore, user data will be (a) fairly and lawfully processed, (b) processed for limited purposes, (c) adequate, relevant and not excessive, (d) accurate, (e) not kept longer than necessary, (f) processed in accordance with the patient's rights, (g) secure and (h) not transferred without adequate protection.

It is worth underlining that the end-user partners have applied for ethical considerations by ethical committees in Poland and Austria to ensure compliance with national guidelines regarding Informed Consent and confidentiality. The consortium also acts in compliance with the EU's General Data Protection Regulation (GDPR) 2016/679 and respective national regulations in Austria and Poland, where these are more restrictive than the GDPR.

Another important goal of this project is that the system can be used by as many people of the target group as possible. Therefore the consortium follows the "Design for All" principle during all evaluation, design and implementation steps to fulfil this criterion.

The eSticky UI mock-ups were tested so far by older adults and their caregivers in two European countries, namely Austria and Poland. Due to the social distancing measures imposed amid the COVID-19 pandemic, each end-user site implemented the testing via small focus groups, one-to-one meetings or virtual meetings according to their resources and national restrictions in place at the time of the recruitment. In total, 27 persons (age range: 34–67, gender: 9 men and 18 women) of primary, secondary (some participants had both roles) and tertiary users (professional carers) evaluated the UI mock-ups. The majority of users were from urban areas, some of them from rural areas and had between little, medium and high IT literacy (but all users had at least a little experience with IT systems). The end-user partners received so far quite positive feedback and good opinions from the users in both countries, as well as the comments and suggestions for improvement of the system. Section 5 summarizes the UI mock-ups in detail and provides the conclusions from user feedback.

4 High-Level System Architecture

The high-level system architecture shows the relationships between the different sys-tem components (Fig. 1):

1. **Displays (passive)**: Passive displays simply show the reminder messages. The user has no possibility of interaction with a passive display. The base station sends messages to the displays (according to the database entries), which show these messages with the determined display parameters.
2. **Displays (active)**: Same as passive displays, only that the user can make simple interactions here, i.e. he or she can press a button to confirm. The user's answer will then be sent to the registration server and stored in the database. Relatives or carers can view this answer on demand via the web application. After confirmation by the user, the message is deleted on all displays.

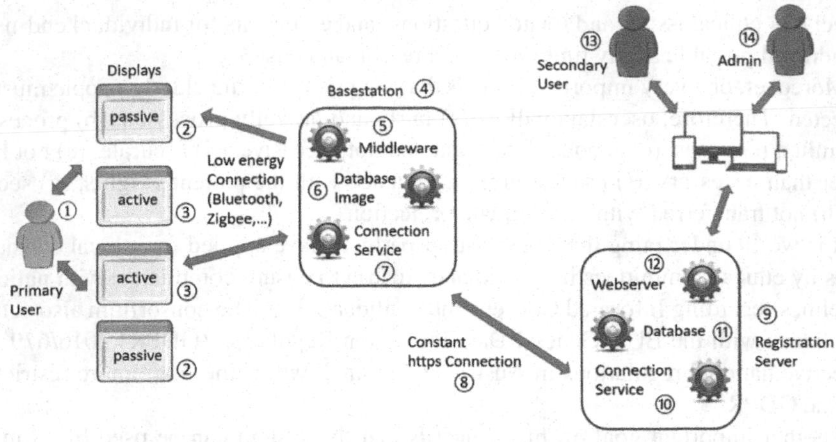

Fig. 1. High-level system architecture

3. **Base station**: The base station includes the middleware, an image of the database and a connection-service to interact with the registration-server. The base station has a pre-configured admin-user-account for service purposes.
4. **Middleware**: The middleware controls the displays. It uses an image of the database (located on the registration server). It registers new displays with a unique ID due an automatic pairing process.
5. **Database Image**: Image of the Database, which is located on the registration server.
6. **Connection Service**: Sets up and keeps alive an https-connection to the registration server.
7. **Constant https-Connection**: Connection between base station and registration server, used to get image of the database, get notifications, when the database has been updated and send users' confirmation messages to be stored in the database.
8. **Registration Server**: Contains a connection service, the database and a webserver.
9. **Connection Service**: Maintains the communication with the base stations.
10. **Database**: Stores all the messages and their schedule as well as the assignment to which displays every message will be sent. The users' confirmations will also be stored here.
11. **Webserver**: Delivers the web app that lets the secondary users configure the system (set user-friendly name for registered displays, user management, etc.), maintain the message schedule (incl. setting the message and its parameters) and view the primary users' confirmations. Special attention is paid to responsiveness, usability and accessibility (WCAG 2.1 AA) when implementing the GUI. When a secondary user changes something, it is stored in the database and the respective base station is notified via the connection service.
12. **Secondary User**: Relatives and carers (and also primary users, if their dementia still allows it) can communicate with the web application via different end devices (e.g. PC, tablet, smartphone). They can create new messages, parametrize messages (view), create schedules for the messages, select the displays on which the messages should appear and view the primary users' confirmations.

13. **Admin**: The admin configures all system relevant settings:

- A user-friendly name for the registered display-IDs
- User administration (user name, password, rights and roles).

5 UI Mock-Ups and Conclusions from User Feedback

With primary end user's needs in mind, a first set of UI mock-ups was designed by the technical and the design team. The goal was to design a UI, which is intuitive and guides an end user through the system configuration and message creation in an easy way. Although it was clear at the time of mock-up creation that further design steps were going to be needed, the mock-ups were created in a way that allowed the users to experience the planned basic structure and user guidance of the eSticky system, thus enabling them to give valuable feedback for further enhancement of the UI.

5.1 Description of UI Mock-Ups

When the system is started for the first time, the user chooses a language on a welcome page, before setting up the components. Once the user has given the base station a user-friendly name, he or she can login or register to the system depending if they already have an account or not. In the case of registration, users have to enter their first name, last name, email address and a chosen password. Afterwards the user, who is now the administrator of the base station, has to pair the displays with the system. Further, it is possible to add other supervisors to this base station by inviting them via their email address. Once this walkthrough has been completed, the login page appears. The users that have been invited via their email address get an email with a confirmation link, leading to the eSticky system to join the base station via login or registration.

After successful login, the message list is shown. The user can add a new message to the system via a "create"-button, which leads to a configuration page for a message. Here the user can enter the text for the message, the text colour, background colour, enter a start date as well as the repetition settings and decide if the message should be active or passive. If the message is active, only the active displays will be shown at the bottom of the page, where the user can choose on which displays the message is supposed to be shown later. If the message is passive, however, all displays will be shown, since active displays can serve both purposes. After submitting the message, the user will be linked to the message list again, where the message will be shown now and can be edited or deleted. When the user chooses to edit a message, the user will be linked to the same configuration page again, with the only difference that the fields are now prefilled. Furthermore, a preview of the message will be shown in this view, to give the user an idea of how the message will look like on the display.

As an alternative to the message list, the user can choose a calendar view in the main menu on the top of the page. In this view, the user can select a display and a week and then gets an overview of all the messages scheduled for that week, sorted by day and hour (see Fig. 2).

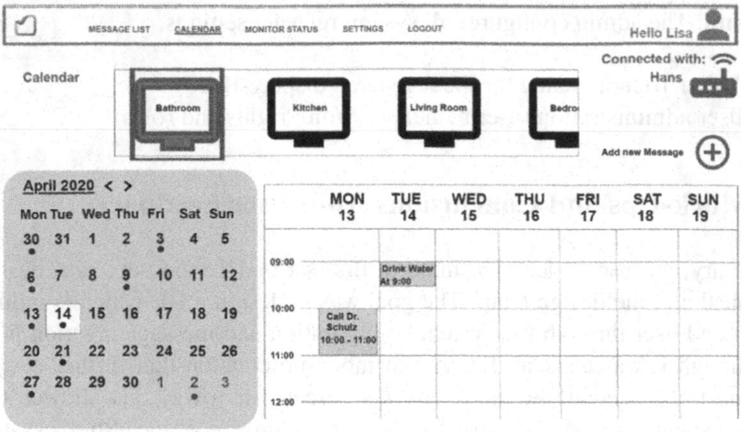

Fig. 2. Calendar view

Just like in the message list, messages can be added, edited and deleted here. The blue dots on the monthly calendar (left hand side) point out the days with at least one message already set for the display selected at the top.

The main menu item "monitor status" links to a page that shows all displays that are currently connected to the user's base station. This view includes the battery life, connection status and current message status of each display to give a quick overview of the connected components. This view also includes the possibility to edit or add a display. When a user decides to edit a display, he or she gets the same view as in the beginning when the initial display pairing took place.

A settings-view can also be shown if selected in the navigation. This page shows the whole information about the accounts that are registered for this base station. Editing an account is also possible here. The displays are also shown again on this page, split into active and passive and with a warning to check the display status in case this is necessary (i.e. low battery).

When a user logs out, the login page is shown again. When a user, who is already registered on the eSticky system for more than one base station, logs in, a page is shown after login where the user can choose to which base station he or she wants to connect. This is mainly relevant for professional careers, who might want to administer eSticky messages for several primary users.

5.2 Evaluation of User Feedback on Mock-Ups

The UI mock-ups were shown and explained to 27 users in Poland and Austria and quantitative as well as qualitative feedback was gathered and evaluated. Then conclusions were drawn on what changes have to be applied to the UI in order to meet user's needs and wishes. Some suggestions were outside the scope or possibilities of the project, like e.g. the wish to be able to use own photos on the displays, instead of icons (the envisaged low-power and low-cost e-paper displays do not provide enough colours and good enough quality for displaying photos). However, many of the user's suggestions will be taken up and implemented in the actual system prototype. In addition, a detailed manual will come with the system to clarify things that cannot be made implicitly clear in the UI. The following list gives an outline of the most important changes planned:

- The pairing process has been considered too complicated by many users. Therefore, either the displays will be shipped readily paired, or, in the ideal case, a possibility will be found how to do without pairing.
- Buttons need to have a consistent look and feel throughout the system and must always provide textual descriptions along with icons. Also the positioning of buttons needs to be adapted in some views.
- An explanation of what the "active" and "passive" message types (and display types) mean will be given directly in the interface.
- An icon-overview will be added instead of the search field.
- Most users had troubles understanding the many options for message repetition and activating and deactivating those options. Since providing so many possibilities is not possible without a certain extent of complexity, a decision has been taken, in the light of usability, to reduce the amount of options for message repetition, only allowing daily, weekly, monthly and yearly repetitions, as well as a choice of specific weekdays.
- In the calendar view the distinction between active and passive messages will be made clearer by adding an "A" in the corner of every active message. A confirmed message will be marked by green colour and a check mark, while a "!" and red colour signal that the message has expired without being confirmed.
- Horizontal scrolling will be avoided at all times.
- Generally, text size (compared to icon size) was an issue for some users. Text will be larger in the next version of the UI.
- Users asked for light signals and sounds to attract the user's attention. There is an ongoing discussion about adding sound and LEDs to the displays. The main issue here is the power consumption, which must not interfere too much with long battery lifetime. Therefore, the final decision on this issue is still pending. It depends on the outcome of further tests.
- To allow messages of a certain length, but also to allow large messages for people with vision impairments, different font sizes for the message text will be possible in future.

6 Middleware and Connectivity

The aim of the middleware is to forward the appropriate messages to the corresponding displays, according to a predefined schedule. The middleware runs on the base station that is situated at the home of the primary user. It connects to the webserver to acquire message updates for the particular primary user, as well as the messages' schedule. The middleware consists of 3 modules: the reasoner, the scheduler and the sender. In addition, it also interacts with a local MySQL database (DB) where it stores the messages as they arrive from the webserver in order to send them to the displays at the appropriate time for each message. In addition, the local DB also serves as a means to support the system for several hours in case of internet connection failure, as the messages will be retrieved from there and sent to the displays according to their initial (prior to internet connection failure) schedule.

6.1 Components

In the following paragraphs we describe the components that compose the middleware. Figure 3 shows the system workflow.

Reasoner

The Reasoner Component retrieves the user-scheduled messages from the webserver and stores them in the middleware's local DB. A set of appropriate REST calls are issued to receive new messages, as well as updates for existing messages. Other information retrieved include details about how the messages should appear on the display of choice (i.e., the "designs" of the messages, see Fig. 3). All retrieved data are stored into the middleware's local DB on the base station. The messages will be sent to the displays at the appropriate point in time, decided by the Scheduler Component based on the messages schedule. There is a distinction between "complex" and "simple" messages, where complex messages are "iterative", meaning that they appear more than once on a display. Simple messages define a single appearance on the display.

Scheduler

One of the major roles of the base station is to decide when and where messages need to be sent. This task is being handled by the scheduler which is responsible for figuring out what messages are in line to be displayed, which monitors will display them and when these messages should be sent. The scheduler accomplishes this task by regularly checking the DB table containing the messages as inserted by the reasoner beforehand. If any messages are to be displayed in a specific time span, then the scheduler will retrieve them and place them in a queue. The messages in the queue will be sent to the appropriate displays and will be handled by a different module, namely the sender. Once a message is placed in the queue, the scheduler marks the message as "in queue" and moves on to the next messages.

The sender is the module responsible for sending the messages in the queue. It is a simple and fast module that is able to read the messages, connect to the corresponding display and send the messages, logging at the same time any errors.

Having two separate modules for the scheduler and sender is considered a preferred approach, as opposed to having a single module doing all, as this process is very sensitive when it comes to punctuality through long time periods and needs to be able to recover from any unexpected issues/failures that may occur. Having two different modules ensures that, in case the sender fails to send a message to a display for any reason and stalls (e.g. network or connectivity problems), the scheduler will continue functioning as normal, ensuring that no other messages are lost due to issues. Additionally, if these modules were to be combined in one, a possible delay would become a possibility as well. As the sending procedure may be time consuming compared to other functionalities of the system after the continuous use of the system through time, a delay could accumulate which may result in missed messages. This possibility is eliminated by the separation of the two modules.

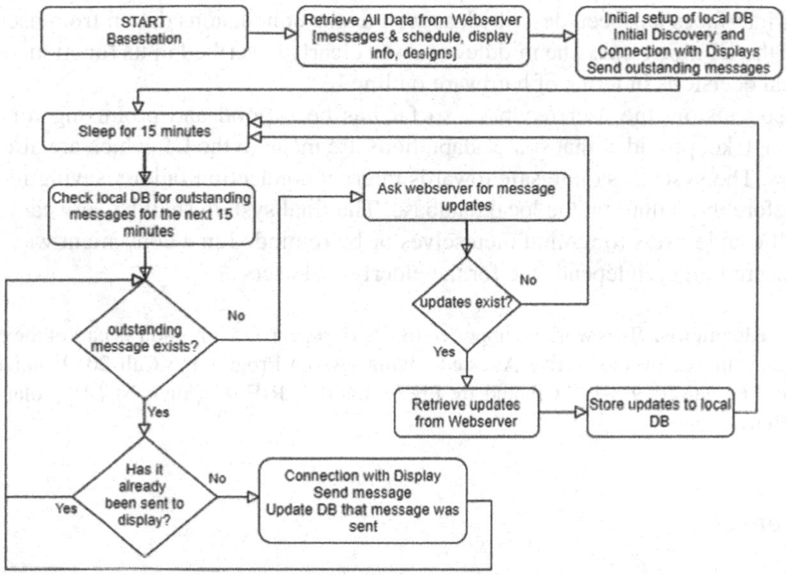

Fig. 3. The Middleware's workflow

7 Alternative Displays Solutions

An important requirement of the project in terms of the hardware components was to find an appropriate solution to facilitate the displays that will be placed in the local environment, i.e. the end user's house. Prior to defining the final design, that is based on the ESP32 microcontroller, the consortium was also considering two alternative solutions from the market. Both solutions satisfied the specifications of the project and provided pre-programmed displays that can be easily set up in the end user's house. The specifications for the displays included among other, long battery life to avoid recharging in time intervals that are less than 6 months. That would allow for a technician or a family member/healthcare professional to undertake this task. The first solution was rejected due to the fact that it required an extra device, a hub that was responsible for connecting with the displays and sending them the messages to be displayed. This process is facilitated by the base station. In addition, some displays did not support the decided communication protocol, while those that did, were extremely energy consuming. About the second solution, while it did not require any extra devices and all of the displays supported the communication protocol, it did not provide enough support in terms of maintenance, configuration and programming of the displays.

8 Conclusions

The development of the eSticky system as it is going on at the moment has been described in this paper. The background has been given and the user involvement thoroughly discussed. After an outline of the high-level system architecture, the work that has happened on user interfaces has been described, as well as the conclusions drawn from user feedback to the UI mock-ups. The middleware was clearly described in its functionality and technical decisions in terms of hardware outlined.

In conclusion, the user feedback so far has been good and promising for future system uptake, provided that some adaptations are made to the UI, which are already in progress. The system is quite safe towards internet connection failure, saving its status from before the failure on the local database. The final system shall be very easy to use and will enable users to remind themselves or be reminded in a convenient way that is fit to ensure longer independence for the elderly end users.

Acknowledgements. This work is supported by the European Commission as part of the eSticky EU project funded by the Active Assisted Living (AAL) Programme Call 2019–under grant agreement no aal-2019-6-179-CP, and by FFG (Austria), RIF (Cyprus), NCBR (Poland) and MIUR (Italy).

References

1. Alzheimer's Disease International. Policy brief for heads of Government: the global impact of dementia 2013–2050. mLondon: Author (2013)
2. Wild, S., Roglic, G., Green, A., Sicree, R., King, H.: Global prevalence of diabetes estimates for the year 2000 and projections for 2030. Diabetes Care **27**(5), 1047–1053 (2004)
3. Umphred, D.A., Lazaro, R.T., Roller, M., Burton, G.: Neurological Rehabilitation. Elsevier Health Sciences, Amsterdam (2013)
4. OECD (2015): Addressing Dementia: The OECD Response, OECD Health Policy Studies, OECD Publishing, Paris (2015).https://doi.org/10.1787/9789264231726-en
5. Alzheimer Europe: 2013 Dementia in Europe Yearbook (2013). http://www.alzheimer-europe.org/Publications/Dementia-in-Europe-Yearbooks
6. Kerkhof, Y.J.F., Bergsma, A., Graff, M.J.L., Dröes, R.M.: Selecting apps for people with mild dementia: Identifying user requirements for apps enabling meaningful activities and self-management. J. Rehabil. Assist. Technol. Eng. **4**, 2055668317710593 (2017)
7. Wimo, A., Winblad, B., Jönsson, L.: The worldwide societal costs of dementia: estimates for 2009. Alzheimer's Dementia **6**(2), 98–103 (2010)
8. O'Keeffe, J., Maier, J., Freiman, M.P.: Assistive technology for people with dementia and their caregivers at home: what might help. Administration on Aging, Washington (2010)
9. Tun, S.Y.Y., Madanian, S., Mirza, F.: Internet of things (IoT) applications for elderly care: a reflective review. Aging Clin. Exp. Res. **10**, 1–3 (2020). [CrossRef] [PubMed]
10. Akyildiz, F., Su, W., Sank, Y., Cyirci, E.: A survey on sensor networks. IEEE Commun. Mag. **40**, 102–114 (2002)
11. TTablado, A., Illarramendi, A., Bagüés, M.I., Bermúdez, J., Goni, A.: Aingeru: an innovating system for tele-assistance of elderly people. In: Telecare, pp. 27–36. Porto, Portugal (2004)
12. General Assembly Resolution 46/91 of 16 December 1991. https://www.ohchr.org/Documents/ProfessionalInterest/olderpersons.pdf. Accessed 02 July 2021
13. Liu, C.H., Tu, J.F.: Development of an IoT-based health promotion system for seniors. Sustainability **12**(21), 8946 (2020)
14. Domingo, M.C.: An overview of the internet of things for people with disabilities. J. Netw. Comput. Appl. **35**(2), 584–596 (2012)
15. Miranda, J., et al.: From the internet of things to the internet of people. IEEE Internet Comput. **19**(2), 40–47 (2015)

16. Soro, A., Ambe, A.H., Brereton, M.: Minding the gap: reconciling human and technical perspectives on the iot for healthy ageing. Wirel. Commun. Mob. Comput. **2017** (2017)
17. Pires, G., et al.: Vitasenior-mt: a telehealth solution for the elderly focused on the interaction with tv. In: 2018 IEEE 20th International Conference on e-Health Networking, Applications and Services (Healthcom), pp. 1–6. IEEE (2018)
18. Mangano, S., Saidinejad, H., Veronese, F., Comai, S., Matteucci, M., Salice, F.: Bridge: mutual reassurance for autonomous and independent living. IEEE Intell. Syst. **30**(4), 31–38 (2015)
19. Hussain, A., Wenbi, R., da Silva, A.L., Nadher, M., Mudhish, M.: Health and emergency-care platform for the elderly and disabled people in the smart city. J. Syst. Softw. **110**, 253–263 (2015)
20. Lopes, N.V., Pinto, F., Furtado, P., Silva, J.: Iot architecture proposal for disabled people. In: 2014 IEEE 10th International Conference on Wireless and Mobile Computing, Networking and Communications (WiMob), pp. 152–158. IEEE (2014)
21. Thomas, M.O., Onyimbo, B.A., Logeswaran, R.: Usability evaluation criteria for internet of things. Int. J. Inf. Technol. Comput. Sci. **8**, 10–18 (2016)
22. Zanella, A., Mason, F., Pluchino, P., Cisotto, G., Orso, V., Gamberini, L.: Internet of things for elderly and fragile people (2020). arXiv preprint arXiv:2006.05709
23. Nishiura, Y., Nihei, M., Nakamura-Thomas, H., Inoue, T.: Effectiveness of using assistive technology for time orientation and memory, in older adults with or without dementia. Disabil. Rehabil. Assist. Technol. **16**(5), 472–478 (2021). https://doi.org/10.1080/17483107.2019.1650299

Brain Functions Support and Oncology

Bibo the Dancing Cup: Reminding People with Dementia to Drink

Avgi Kollakidou[1(✉)], Kevin Lefeuvre[2], Christian Sønderskov Zarp[1], Oskar Palinko[1], Norbert Krüger[1], and Eva Hornecker[2]

[1] University of Southern Denmark, 5230 Odense M, Denmark
{avko,csz,ospa,norbert}@mmmi.sdu.dk
[2] Bauhaus-Universität Weimar, Bauhausstr. 11, 99423 Weimar, Germany
{kevin.lefeuvre,eva.hornecker}@uni-weimar.de

Abstract. We present the concept and technical realisation for a cup that moves and lights up so as to bring itself to the attention of a person with dementia, to trigger taking a sip as a response. The concept is aimed at people with dementia in home or resident care who still have the ability to act, but tend to mentally drift away and thus require external impulses and triggers. The cup moves and lights up in regular intervals if it has not been picked up recently. Once it is emptied, it alerts a caregiver to refill. Moreover, the degree or level of movement and light can be configured, depending on the person's needs and reactions. This paper describes the core idea and focuses on the technical aspects of building a prototype on Technology Readiness Level (TRL) 3.

Keywords: Dementia · Dehydration · Elderly care

1 Introduction

In elderly care, a general concern is to prevent dehydration of elderly residents [7,21]. The elderly often do not perceive being thirsty and therefore do not drink enough. For people with dementia at severe stages, this becomes even more problematic. In the authors' previous fieldwork in an elderly care home, where staff was shadowed and assisted in their daily work by project members, it was observed that a resident would take a sip, put down the cup, and then stare into space again, until a staff member would move the cup towards their hand. The resident then smiled, looked at and took the cup up again to drink. This procedure was repeated until the cup was emptied, posing a significant workload to staff. The resident appeared to need an external trigger that brought the cup to their awareness again, while still being able to associate the act of drinking with the cup and to drink without assistance.

This observation motivated the concept of the 'dancing cup' which brings itself to attention (as illustrated in Fig. 1). The concept goes beyond existing products that integrate blinking lights as a reminder to drink [1,3,4,6]. It is based on the hypothesis that the movement of the cup itself (Fig. 1b), along

E. Pissaloux et al. (Eds.): IHAW 2021, CCIS 1538, pp. 127–140, 2021.
https://doi.org/10.1007/978-3-030-94209-0_11

(a) The caregiver activates the cup

(b) The cup moves and blinks to attract the individual's attention

(c) The cup prototype rendering

(d) First prototype

Fig. 1. Envisioned use of cup, prototype design and current working prototype

with slight sound produced by the cup's vibration, provides a stronger trigger than simply integrated lights. Moreover, it does not interfere with the habituated appearance of a cup or glass, and thus may be more appropriate for people with dementia, where it is important that objects look familiar and can be recognised [10,14].

The use of familiar objects can support daily practice, since patients will still be able to spontaneously relate to and use familiar-looking objects, even if dementia prevents them from understanding the function of new unfamiliar objects [10,11]. The cup aims to support the person's remaining ability for action, a principle in elderly care where it is aimed to keep residents active and involved as this can delay the (inevitable) decline [12,22] (see [9,14]). Staff at the facility where the research team did observations and interviews had described this as an important strategy, e.g. preferring to accompany slow walking residents to the dining area instead of pushing them in a wheelchair, even if the latter would be faster.

Feedback from care staff as well as from geriatrics experts confirmed that they find the concept promising, and would like to see it tested. Therefore it was decided to create a working prototype that would both serve to better illustrate the concept and to enable user tests. In the current paper, the focus is on the technical realisation, including initial expert feedback that influenced the design. Figure 3 shows our current prototype in action.

In the following sections, the effect of dehydration on elderly people is discussed as well as investigated solutions for the issue (Sect. 2); the prototype and its intended use is described in Sect. 3; the cup functionalities, their implementations and reasoning behind them are specified in Sect. 4; the achieved results are discussed in Sect. 5 and finally conclusions and future work are considered.

2 State of the Art

Dehydration affects 20–30% of older adults and increases reported health issues [23]. Dehydration is even more perilous for people with dementia, as it poses one of the main, often less thought of, causes of death. More people with dementia, once they reach a late stage in the disease, die from cachexia or dehydration rather than of any other cause of death [19]. Dehydration has been found to be more severe in people with advanced cognitive impairments [20]. According to [24], on average 5.5 billion dollars are spent in the USA annually to treat hospitalisations caused by dehydration.

Dehydration in the elderly happens for multiple reasons. Fluid reserve is decreased compared to their younger selves, liquid loss is more frequent and the sense of thirst is not as intensive [18]. A combination of these reasons, among others, can co-exist in a person causing severe dehydration.

Most of the solutions that encourage people to drink have taken the form of augmented bottles or cups (e.g. [2–5,8,15,16]), while others take the form of add-ons to be combined with existing objects (e.g. [1,6,25]). The most common method seems to consist of grabbing the attention with a visual trigger through light effects (e.g. [1,3,4,6]), via an audio signal (e.g. [8]), or through a combination of both (e.g. [2,15,16]).

The option of using vibrations to attract attention has been utilised in Ozmo [5], a bottle that reminds you to drink by vibrating (which might constitute rather an audio or haptic signal). Visible movement as an attention trigger has been explored more explicitly with the Bionic water drinking reminder [25], an additional attachment to a cup, shaped as a butterfly, which uses a vibration motor to flap its wings when triggered, to attract attention. However, the cup itself does not move.

Several of these products offer additional functions, such as monitoring water consumption (e.g. [3–5,15,16]), the frequency of drinking (e.g. [2]), or keeping the temperature (e.g. [3,4]). Some products are paired with applications that allow to monitor daily fluid consumption, record hydration history and calculate personal hydration goals (e.g. [3–5]). Most existing products are general consumer products, and very few are aimed for elderly and persons affected by illnesses and offer specific functions for care, such as Drink Smart [15,16], a cup connected to a digital care documentation, or Droplet [2], a dementia-friendly mug that alerts caregivers with flashes.

3 Product Description and Envisioned Use

Through a few iterations and feedback from experts in geriatrics and elderly care, a prototype was designed (Figs. 1b and 1c) as a proof of concept as well as demonstrator for planned user tests (Fig. 1d). As a general design constraint, the shape and look needed to be recognisable as a cup and look familiar, so that it can evoke spontaneous use as response from elderly residents with dementia. The cup is small enough in diameter and light enough to be handled easily. The possibility of adding a supplementary handle for residents with limited hand functionality was added as an option (Fig. 1c), based on recommendations from elderly care experts.

The cup consists of two parts. The lower part will be made of coloured polyamid and houses all electronic components and sensors. A coloured cup is considered easier to perceive, as intense colours aid visual perception in people with dementia. At the moment, the cup is made from a photopolymer (VeroWhite) for a Stratasys Objet30 Prime 3D printer to enable iterations within tests and development. Detailed consideration was given to the upper part, which holds the beverage. A food-safe and transparent material is used to facilitate diffusing of the coloured light (Figs. 4b and 7) as well as to keep the appearance of a regular cup or glass.

The envisioned scenario of use is that care staff places the cup in the field of view of its user (usually on a table) and activates it via a switch. If the cup is not picked up for a (predetermined) time, it will start to move and blink, thereby alerting to its presence. This would then attract the attention of the resident, who perceives and recognises the cup, thereby prompting them to drink. The activation (movement and light) is executed in spaced-out intervals, to enable the intermittent drinking and avoid overly disturbing the resident. If the cup is not picked up, the activation will be repeated after a predetermined time has passed. If a pickup is detected, the cup stops moving and will restart the countdown for a subsequent activation at a later time.

The device can be configured and personalised according to the individual's needs via physical sliders (Fig. 2). Geriatric experts recommended providing the ability for configuration, because of the differences in each stage and form of the disease, where each individual might react differently, impacting on how strong the visual and/or movement signal needs to be (or what would be too much). They also stressed that such controls need to be simple and physical-tangible (not via a mobile app), since any caregiver (or temporary help) should be able to do this, and care staff often have little affinity with technology. The configurable parameters are the intensity of movement, intensity of blinking and light colour.

If the resident picks up the cup, this is detected by an accelerometer. The cup then ceases to move, so that they can drink. When the cup is empty, the cup will repeatedly flash on and off in a predetermined colour to alert the stuff for refill as well as aid in liquid intake monitoring.

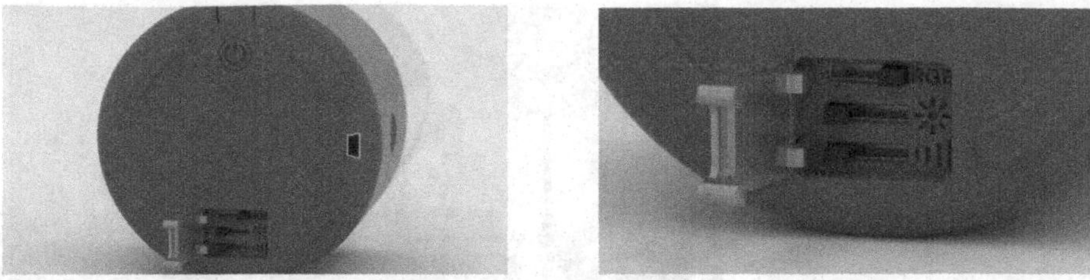

(a) Configuration and power on/off switches on the bottom

(b) Zoom in on configuration switches

Fig. 2. Activation and configuration switches

4 Detailed Overview of Functionalities

We now describe the cup functionalities and details of the mechanical and electronic realisation. This is structured along the core functionalities of our prototype: Grabbing attention (Sect. 4.1); Water Level Detection (Sect. 4.2); Activation, De-Activation (Sect. 4.3); Pick up Detection (Sect. 4.4); Configurability (Sect. 4.5).

4.1 Grabbing attention

Two actions are implemented to attract the attention of the residents; movement (and the implicit sound from its production), and coloured light impulses that create visual stimulation. These occur in bursts, to enable drinking in between those phases and to avoid over-stimulation. Ideas for sound output as an explicit signal were discarded and we aim for fairly subtle motor sounds. This is because care experts advised that if the cup is used e.g. in the social setting of a care home's dining area or sitting/common room, this could overstimulate and annoy people (including the staff), in particular if several such cups are in use.

The movement (dancing) of the cup is generated using a small 3V DC motor mounted in the bottom of the cup (Fig. 4a). A plastic lever is attached to the motor shaft. The end of the shaft holds a small steel puck which acts as an unbalanced Eccentric Rotating Mass (ERM) which generates instability resulting in a centripetal force, forcing the cup to rotate, and a centrifugal force away from the centre of the motor shaft. The motor rotates the lever arm at a variable speed, depending on the measured water contents of the cup (see Sect. 4.2), generating the needed forces/vibrations to correctly rotate the cup, without spillage. With the eccentric rotation of the motor and of the cup itself, the cup moves on the table, changing its position and thus visually stimulating the resident. To avoid moving too far from the resident and prevent the cup falling off the table, the motor changes direction of rotation between activations, thus moving in opposite directions in consecutive bursts. The specific speed of the motor at the respective water levels was determined based on lab-tests (see Sect. 4.2).

(a) Placement of PCB 1 in cup

(b) PCB 1, side A. Battery, interface with switches, USB port

(c) PCB 1, side B. Microcontroller, motor driver, battery driver

(d) Placement of PCB 2 in cup

(e) PCB 2, side A. Accelerometer, touch sensor interface

(f) PCB 2, side B. LED ring, capacitive sensor

Fig. 3. Prototype components

As a complementary way of attracting attention, the cup subtly blinks (Fig. 4b when activated, using an Adafruit Neopixel ring (Fig. 3f). The colour and intensity of the light can be configured according to individual's needs as explained in Sect. 4.5, see (Fig. 2a). As a default, the colour red was chosen, as studies show that red or similarly intense hues increase liquid intake in people with dementia by ca. 80% [13].

4.2 Water Level Detection

Two approaches for water detection methods were explored, a capacitive sensor, that roughly detects the presence (not quantity) of water and a strain gauge bridge, which is also able to measure quantities. As it works contact-less, a capacitive sensor can be embedded in the plastic shell, (Fig. 5a), and thus does not require waterproofing. The current version of the prototype works with a capacitive sensor.

An additional method for detection is currently in the final stages of development. The strain gauge method measures the weight of the water content in the

(a) The bottom of the cup containing the ERM mechanism for the cup movement

(b) Cup blinking with a green light, diffused in water and visible through the material

Fig. 4. Cup attention grabbing functions (dancing and blinking) (Color figure online)

cup. This information can be used to adjust the RPM of the motor making the cup dance/rotate. The more water the cup contains, the faster the motor will spin (the more RPM the motor has), enabling movement even with the added weight.

The cup is comprised of a top and a bottom half, where the bottom contains the electronics. The top half, which contains the water, is fitted with a flexible bottom made of food-approved plastic, and has four strain gauges glued to it (Fig. 5b). The strain gauges circuit is set up as a full Wheatstone bridge. [17], Physically this appears as strain gauges in pairs in two circles (see Fig. 5b). A pair of strain gauges in this case, is two strain gauges placed with an equal distance from the center of the flexible bottom mirroring each other, which makes up the full Wheatstone bridge. A full Wheatstone bridge is needed to neutralise the effects of temperature changes which the strain gauges are sensitive to. The strain gauges deform due to the increased weight of water in the cup, thus changing resistance, making it possible to algorithmically correlate changes in strain gauge resistance to change in weight. To determine the weight of the cup content, the voltage output from the strain gauge Wheatstone bridge is correlated to a unit of weight. To do this, a steel cylinder (Fig. 5c) is fitted with a 1 mm thick PETG plastic bottom (Fig. 5b), with the four strain gauges mounted on it. The Wheatstone bridge is connected to a micro controller which collects the data.

4.3 Activation and De-activation, Charging

The activation of the cup is done in two steps. First, a button is pushed on the cup's bottom (Fig. 2a). Once switched on, the LED ring blinks briefly, its colour indicating the battery status. After the cup flashes with a green light, indicating

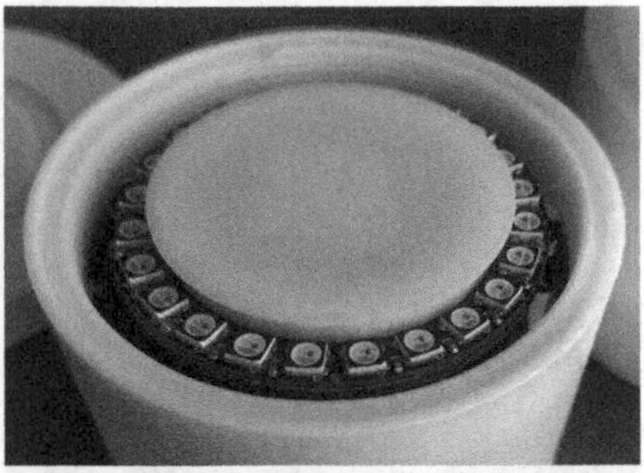

(a) Square capacitive sensor embedded in plastic shell (in center)

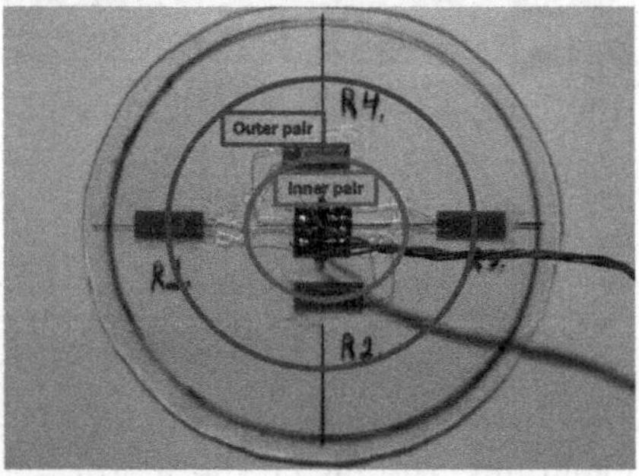

(b) Flexible bottom with physical wheat-stone bridge, outer strain gauge pair (green) inner strain gauge pair (yellow)

(c) Strain gauge water content measuring test setup

Fig. 5. Water level detection methods

sufficient battery power, the cup can be placed in front of the user, and is then activated by touching the two opposite finger recesses simultaneously (Fig. 6a), thus preventing unintentional activation.

The main process then starts and will continue only if the cup contains fluid and is not grabbed. Once the battery is low, this stops and the LED ring starts to blink red. The cup must then be switched off by pressing the ON/OFF button at the bottom of the cup and placed on its induction charging base (Fig. 6b). Although less effective than USB-charging, induction was chosen for its practicality and ease of use.

4.4 Pick up Detection

The "dancing" of the cup should not continue when taken in hand. The accelerometer (Fig. 3e) enables monitoring any movement in elevation and change in inclination; two parameters innate to handling a drinking cup, first lifting the cup from the table and then inclining it to drink. Together, these

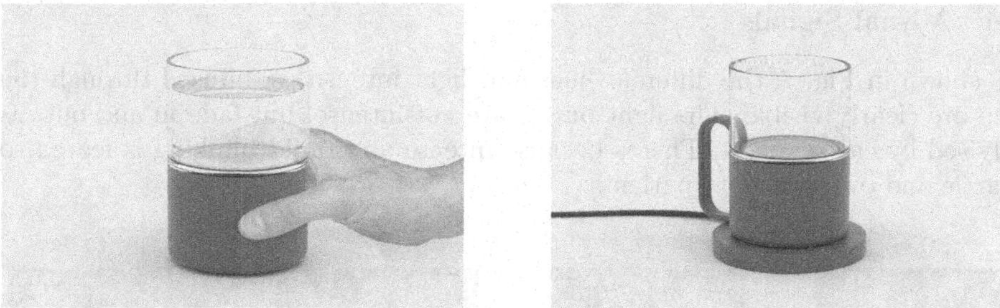

(a) Cup touch activation (b) Charging Platform

Fig. 6. Cup secondary activation method and inductive charging platform

parameters make it possible to detect if the cup is picked up, and then to stop the motor and the LED signal. If the cup is taken up before the movement even starts, the whole cycle is reset once the accelerometer does no longer detect any movement.

4.5 Configurability

Geriatric experts and care staff, who provided feedback on our concept, recommended that it should be quick and easy for the care staff to reconfigure the three key parameters - LED colour, LED brightness and motor speed - according to the resident's needs. As care staff may not be familiar with technological applications and since there are usually different staff members involved, including temporary helpers, we discarded the idea for a mobile app, prioritising work-efficiency and user-friendliness, and opted for on-product analogue/physical configuration modalities. To save space, we chose three slide switches (Fig. 2a), with four positions for configuring LED colour (Red, Yellow, Green, Blue), LED brightness and motor speed. After each colour change, the LED ring blinks in the selected colour as feedback (Figs. 7a and 7b); after an LED brightness change, the LED will blink with the currently selected colour in the chosen intensity (Figs. 7c and 7d); and a change in motor speed is shown with a blink in white colour with different intensities, to indicate the intensity of the movement (a decision to refrain from movement in the configuration process was taken). Following recommendations by care staff, we plan to conceal these switches with a safety strip (Fig. 2b) to avoid inadvertent changes of the configuration by the elderly residents.

5 Results

At its current state, the prototype was tested for functionality in the lab. The previously described capabilities have been implemented. The achieved results for the three main functionalities (visual signals, movement and water level detection are discussed in the following sections.

5.1 Visual Signals

As shown in Fig. 7, the different hues and light intensities diffused through the cup are clearly visible. The light bursts are not intense, but fade in and out, as advised by care experts. This is because intense and rapid blinking is feared to startle and overstimulate patients.

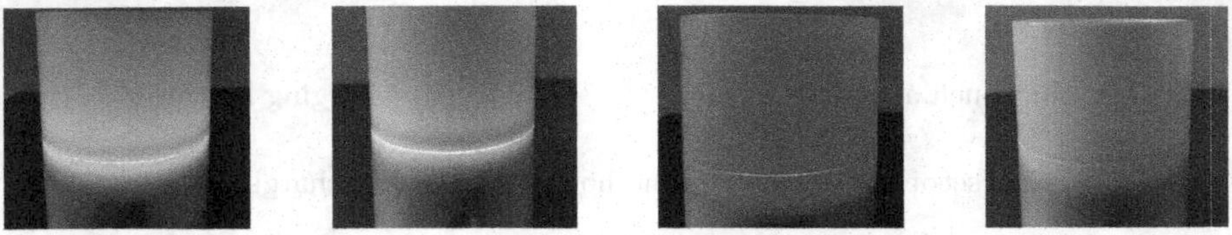

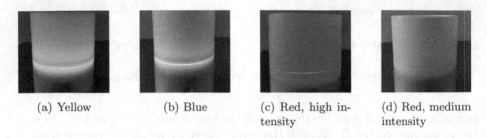

(a) Yellow (b) Blue (c) Red, high intensity (d) Red, medium intensity

Fig. 7. Light colours and intensities (Color figure online)

5.2 Movement

The cup rotates in opposite directions in subsequent turns. This leads to displacement in a constrained area and ensures that the cup does not fall off the table, given that it is placed within a minimum predefined distance from the edge before activation.

To quantify the movement, structured experiments were executed. The cup containing 150 ml of water, fitted with an ArUco marker, was activated and left to translate freely, as it would in a normal activation. A stationary camera placed above the area was used to record the movement (Figs. 8a and 8b). The Aruco marker was detected and used to extract the exact position of the cup relative to the camera. This process was repeated 10 times to acquire sufficient measurements. The translation of the cup depends, as expected, on the intensity of the motor rotation set by the configuration switches (Sect. 4.5). The movement was tested in two different surfaces, a wooden coffee table and linoleum flooring (Figs. 8c and 8d). The heatmap illustrates the positions of the cup on the surface and the frequency of the occupation of the specific position. The translation was found to be confined to an area of $0.08\,m^2$ for the highest intensity of movement on the coffee table and much lower on linoleum flooring ($0.01\,m^2$).

Considerations on controlling or restricting the movement of the cup have been made for later development. Firstly, a beacon to detect whether the cup has moved over a "movement safe area" threshold is considered. In case where the cup covers a larger distance than initially allowed, the cup should seize activation and alert the staff for repositioning. Additionally, the investigation of a controlled movement generation through additional motors is intended.

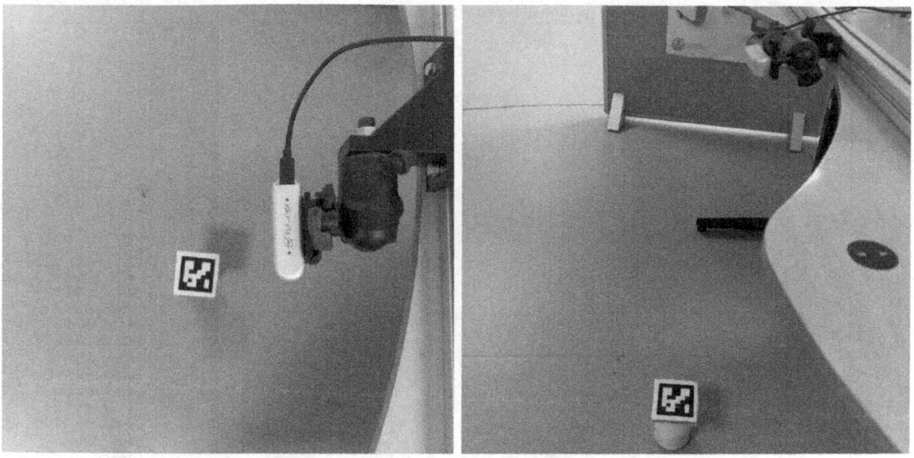

(a) Experimental Setup - top (b) Experimental Setup - side

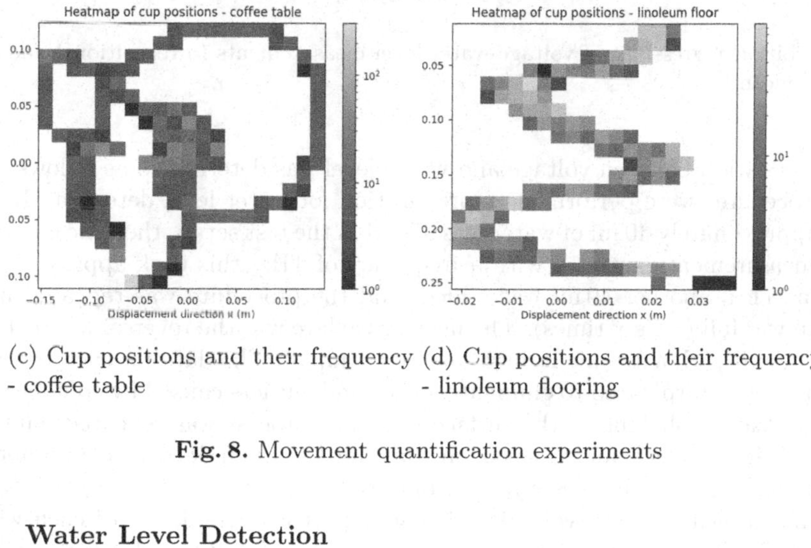

(c) Cup positions and their frequency - coffee table (d) Cup positions and their frequency - linoleum flooring

Fig. 8. Movement quantification experiments

5.3 Water Level Detection

The current prototype includes a capacitive sensor for water detection. The strain gauge method is however developed and planned to be included in a future second prototype, to test both possibilities. In laboratory tests, the strain gauges have proven to enable inferring the volume of water in the cup, with relative accuracy. Some instability is observed when less than ca. 50 ml is in the cup. To obtain a reliable reading of the cup contents, 1000 readings from the gauges are taken (which lasts ca. 2.5 min). This poses no issue as it is performed before and during the intermittent break from 'dancing'. Spikes and noise are removed using interpolation, as mentioned in Sect. 4.2, and a mean value is calculated. The linear regression coefficients are then used to infer the cup content and the appropriate motor speed. Less samples could also suffice if needed; as a minimum, 700 samples have proven adequate.

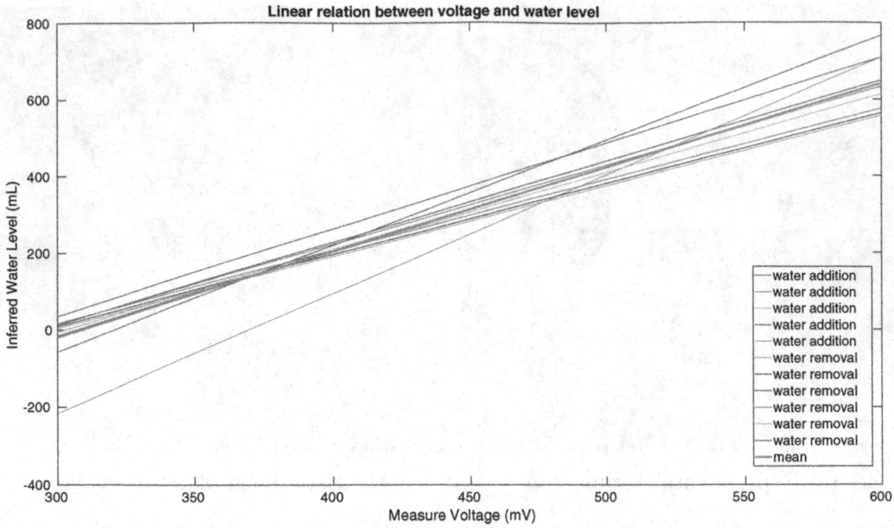

Fig. 9. Linear regressions of voltage-water level measurements (5 repetitions) and calculated mean

The relation between voltage and water level was determined as follows: two test procedures were performed as preparation for water level detection. In the first, approximately 40 ml of water was added in the test setup, then the cup took 1000 measurements/samples with a frequency of 4 Hz, this took approximately 2.5 min. Then another 40 ml was added, and the procedure was repeated until the cup was full (i.e. six times). The next procedure was the reverse, where 40 ml was removed with a sample interval of 1000 samples. The data for each test was then linearly interpolated to eliminate spikes and outliers caused by contact with the cup, sudden shaking of the surface, etc. The process was repeated multiple times in different days and times of the day, for thorough data collection and to ensure that climatic changes were not of effect.

A mean measurement value is calculated for each sample set of each water level, and a linear regression model is fitted to the readings. Each procedure is fitted separately to obtain linear model coefficients. The mean coefficients are then calculated. It was observed that a stable linear function can describe the relation between voltage and water level, with a small instability when the water is below 50 ml. The coefficients are plotted, along with the calculated mean coefficients (Fig. 9). The mean coefficients can then be used real-time in the cup to output the water level depending on the measured voltage. This calculation is used to adjust the rpm of the motor (Sect. 4.1).

6 Conclusion and Outlook

So far, our work has focused on creating a working prototype. The movement as well as the light stimulation have been implemented and initial tests in lab conditions for the movement and the water level detection have been carried out.

We are now at the stage were it is possible to test our idea, that such a "dancing" movement of a cup can trigger the attention of people with dementia and activate them to drink. Initial discussions with domain experts indicate this to be a promising idea. In such tests, we will need to determine the range of motion and visual stimuli that are acceptable for people with dementia (which stirs them out of their stupor but does not frighten them) and the need for personalisation or adaptivity.

In the future, investigations of different rotational bursts leading to different movement patterns as well as a variety of materials for the bottom of the cup (used for noise dampening and movement control), will be carried out. The water level detection functionality will be included and finally the behaviour of the cup will be tested on different surfaces to determine the adadptability of the cup on different tabletops.

Acknowledgment. This work was funded by Volkswagen Foundation, on the ReThiCare project. We thank the staff of Diakonie Sozialdienst Thüringen at Seniorenpflegeheim Sophienhaus for their collaboration and time during our initial ethnographic phase during which we encountered the use case for the cup. We also thank members of the project's advisory board for their feedback on our concepts.

References

1. Drink on. https://msd-projekte.de/schulz/drink-on/. Accessed 24 Feb 2021
2. Droplet. https://www.droplet-hydration.com/products/. Accessed 24 Feb 2021
3. Equa smart. https://myglassbottle.de/. Accessed 24 Feb 2021
4. Hidrate spark steel. https://hidratespark.com/. Accessed 24 Feb 2021
5. Ozmo. https://www.ozmo.io/. Accessed 24 Feb 2021
6. Ulla. https://www.ulla.io/. Accessed 24 Feb 2021
7. Begum, M.N., Johnson, C.S.: A review of the literature on dehydration in the institutionalized elderly. e-SPEN Eur. e-Journal Clin. Nutr. Metab. **5**(1), e47–e53 (2010)
8. Boyuan, C.: Healthful drinking reminder cup. China Patent CN000201822482U, 20 February 2010. https://depatisnet.dpma.de/DepatisNet/depatisnet?action=bibdat&docid=CN000201822482U
9. Bozeat, S., Patterson, K., Hodges, J.: Relearning object use in semantic dementia. Neuropsychol. Rehabil. **14**(3), 351–363 (2004). https://doi.org/10.1080/09602010343000264
10. Bozeat, S., Ralph, M.A., Patterson, K., Hodges, J.R.: The influence of personal familiarity and context on object use in semantic dementia. Neurocase **8**(1-2), 127–134 (2002). https://doi.org/10.1093/neucas/8.1.127, pMID: 11997491
11. Cox, C., Vassallo, M.: Fear of falling assessments in older people with dementia. Rev. Clin. Gerontol. **25**(2), 98 (2015)

12. Crawford, H., Anderson, S., TeKamp, R., Chatzikiriakos, V., Osborne, D.: A review of the literature on dehydration in the institutionalized elderly. Healthc. Manag. Forum **25**(1), 4–15 (2012). https://doi.org/10.1016/j.hcmf.2011.12.002
13. Dunne, T.E., Neargarder, S.A., Cipolloni, P.B., Cronin-Golomb, A.: Visual contrast enhances food and liquid intake in advanced Alzheimer's disease. Clin. Nutr. **23**(4), 533–538 (2004). https://doi.org/10.1016/j.clnu.2003.09.015
14. Harrison, B.E., Son, G.R., Kim, J., Whall, A.L.: Preserved implicit memory in dementia: a potential model for care. Am. J. Alzheimer's Dis. Other Dementias 286–93 (2007). https://doi.org/10.1177/1533317507303761
15. Haslinger-Baumann, E., Werner, F., Korak, G.: Drink Smart: Dehydratation wirksam vorbeugen. Pflegezeitschrift **73**(9), 52–55 (2020). https://doi.org/10.1007/s41906-020-0740-9
16. Haslinger-Baumann, E., et al.: Development of an intelligent drinking system for the prevention of dehydration in old age, pp. 31–34 (2017)
17. Hoffmann, K.: Applying the Wheatstone Bridge Circuit. HBM Germany (1974)
18. Hooper, L., Bunn, D., Jimoh, F.O., Fairweather-Tait, S.J.: Water-loss dehydration and aging. Mech. Ageing Dev. **136**, 50–58 (2014)
19. Koopmans, R.T., van der Sterren, K.J., Van der Steen, J.T.: The 'natural' endpoint of dementia: death from cachexia or dehydration following palliative care? Int. J. Geriatr. Psychiatry: A J. Psychiatry Late Life Allied Sci. **22**(4), 350–355 (2007)
20. Lauriola, M., et al.: Neurocognitive disorders and dehydration in older patients: clinical experience supports the hydromolecular hypothesis of dementia. Nutrients **10**(5), 562 (2018)
21. Lavizzo-Mourey, R., Johnson, J., Stolley, P.: Risk factors for dehydration among elderly nursing home residents. J. Am. Geriatr. Soc. **36**(3), 213–218 (1988)
22. Menner, H.: Aktivierende und Reaktivierende Pflege, pp. 23–34. Springer, Vienna (2004)
23. Miller, H.J.: Dehydration in the older adult. J. Gerontol. Nurs. **41**(9), 8–13 (2015)
24. Xiao, H., Barber, J., Campbell, E.S.: Economic burden of dehydration among hospitalized elderly patients. Am. J. Health Syst. Pharm. **61**(23), 2534–2540 (2004)
25. Xioadong, L.: Bionic water drinking reminder. China Patent CN000209993092U, 12 June 2019. https://depatisnet.dpma.de/DepatisNet/depatisnet?action=bibdat&docid=CN000209993092U

Don't Be Afraid! Design of a Playful Cleaning Robot for People with Dementia

Sophie Alice Grimme[2], Avgi Kollakidou[1], Christian Sønderskov Zarp[1], Eva Hornecker[2], Norbert Kruger[1], and Emanuela Marchetti[1](✉)

[1] University of Southern Denmark, 5230 Odense M, Denmark
{avko,csz,norbert}@mmmi.sdu.dk, emanuela@sdu.dk
[2] Bauhaus-Universität Weimar, Bauhausstr. 11, 99423 Weimar, Germany
{sophie.alice.grimme,eva.hornecker}@uni-weimar.de

Abstract. Robot technologies for care homes and people affected by dementia has become a popular research field. However, such technologies have not become mainstream in care homes yet, due to specific issues related to the well being of their residents. For instance, although existing robot vacuum cleaners can provide meaningful support to hygiene practices in care homes, their appearance and loud noise can negatively affect residents. Building on these insights, we developed a playful alternative design. By testing our design in a care home, we have found that a robotic vacuum cleaner can be accepted by residents affected by dementia, when it has a playful appearance and movement pattern, to elicit positive feelings and provide predictability of its actions.

Keywords: Elderly care · Mobile cleaning unit · Robotic pet

1 Introduction

In 2018, around 9.1 million people over 60 were diagnosed with dementia in EU states [12]. Dementia describes a variety of brain disorders which progressively lead to brain damage, causing deterioration in memory, thinking, behaviour and the ability to perform everyday activities [12]. Many of these individuals can still live at home, but when reaching a later stage of the disease, most will eventually move to a residential care facility.

Dementia affects not only its victims, but also caregivers and families, causing physical, psychological, social, and economic challenges [22]. Moreover, the number of people working in elderly care is decreasing. The job requires long working days and shifts, physically hard labour, often at relatively low wages and with too little time for caring for residents [4,11,18]. According to Riek [17], there is a substantial health-care shortage, because far more people need care than healthcare workers are available to provide. Therefore, researchers in healthcare robotics have proposed multiple robotic solutions for providing health support. Amongst other things, robots may help people with cognitive impairments, support caregivers, and aid the clinical workforce [17].

E. Pissaloux et al. (Eds.): IHAW 2021, CCIS 1538, pp. 141–155, 2021.
https://doi.org/10.1007/978-3-030-94209-0_12

Fig. 1. Our Sanne prototype moving across the shared room during tests. Left in the door: one researcher steers Sanne through the room. On the opposing side of the room, another researcher takes field notes.

A common and time-consuming task in care homes and hospitals is cleaning the floors. In the care home where we conducted our study, a robotic vacuum cleaner had been trialled. The caregivers reported that the residents, most of whom are at later stages of dementia, were overwhelmed by the robot, because they could not perceive it easily due to its dark colour, and felt unsettled by its unpredictable movement pattern and noise level. Therefore, the cleaning robot could not be used any further.

The project reported here focuses on developing a mobile cleaning unit with a playful design, to be used at care homes for people with dementia. We investigated the design of a robotic appliance, which has the functional purpose of cleaning the floors autonomously, but also a social purpose for residents. We aimed at a vacuum cleaner that does not elicit the feeling of being overwhelmed and may even lead to amusement. We designed our robot in the form a toy cat, so that it could serve as a pet-like companion (Fig. 1). Residents' reactions to the robot were investigated through in-situ observations in two Danish care homes. The focus of our analysis was: *whether a playful, zoomorphic design for such a robot, with a playful moving pattern, will be accepted by people with dementia, without them getting scared or overwhelmed.* In our study, we define residents' acceptance as a positive user experience, characterised by an open, possibly playful attitude towards our prototype [15]. In the following section (2), the background of our study and related work are discussed, while the design process is presented in Sect. 3. The user study and findings regarding the reaction of residents are described in Sects. 4 and 5. Hence Sect. 6 proposes a critical discussion of our results and future work, and Sect. 7 the conclusion.

2 Background and Related Work

The estimated number of cases of dementia will almost double by 2050, growing from 1.57 to 3.00% of the European population [8]. Studies show a positive effect on cognition through preventive interventions, a healthy diet, physical exercise, and cognitive training [22]. Nevertheless, there is no cure or disease-modifying treatment for dementia yet.

Although dementia mainly affects older people, it is not a normal part of ageing [22] and comes with different challenges for each patient. Dementia has different stages, characterised by different signs and symptoms. The late stage of the disease comes with behaviour changes and difficulties in recognition of humans and objects, causing an increased need for assisted self-care [22]. The participants of our study were almost all in this later stage, therefore their needs have to be considered when designing technology for care homes.

According to current literature [3], ageing adults affected by dementia experience changes in their perception of the environment and corresponding behaviour. This occurs in different ways, in some cases people may lose control of their emotional responses to environmental stimuli, leading to erratic behaviour and emotion, or show indifference to their surroundings [21].

In the study of dementia, it was found that laughter and humour can bring significant benefits to people affected [21]. Laughter has been acknowledged as a supportive method to complement clinical treatment, improving quality of life. Another important aspect for well-being is the use of familiar objects to sustain daily practices [3,6]. Dementia causes cognitive impairments, which hinder people from understanding the function of new unfamiliar objects. Nevertheless, when interacting with own objects and perceptually similar ones, people are able to spontaneously relate to and use those objects in their daily practices [3], whereas perceptually unfamiliar objects were not easily understood by the same study participants [3]. It seems that by using certain objects for many years, people internalise their physical use and context [3,5], so that despite of dementia they can still actively relate to these. This can be explained as an effect of implicit memory, an unconscious memory generated by previous experience of repeated task performances, not linked to specific episodes [10]. Repeated exposure to objects results in perceptual priming that is resilient to cognitive impairment and can support people affected by dementia in performing their daily practices [10]. Thus, the design of novel technologies and artefacts for residents in care homes should take into account perceptual familiarity, so that novel artefacts fit with residents' previous experiences and sociocultural context.

When designing a mobile robotic unit, we have to be careful to not trigger fear of falling [2]. Falling is acknowledged as "the second leading cause of death from unintentional injury" [2]. Dementia is known for leading to unconscious wandering, agitation, and perceptual difficulties, which in combination with the physical fragility associated with ageing might cause people to experience serious injuries [6]. As a consequence, ageing people affected by dementia, manifest a strong fear of falling [2,6].

The design of assistive robots for care homes typically includes automated mobile units, which are in charge of carrying things around, monitoring safety, engaging people in physical exercise, even including exoskeletons and wearable devices aimed at improving physical mobility [17]. Thus, no matter whether care home residents will actively use such robots, or just encounter them in their daily environment, fear of injuries should be considered as a key factor in such designs for the residents' safety.

Building on these insights, we aimed at designing a mobile floor cleaning unit, which could be perceived as nonthreatening, in relation to three main aspects: humour, familiarity of objects, fears of falling and injuries.

3 Designing Nonthreatening Robotic Cleaners

The work presented here is part of a larger research project on care home technologies. In this context, interviews and (participant as well as non-participant) observations at care homes were conducted. The researchers also visited the cooperating two care homes of OK-Fonden in Odense, Denmark[1]. Here, the inspiration and motivation for the reported work was gathered. This was complemented via a number of (online) interviews and meetings. When the design was finished, the pandemic situation allowed to test the prototype at the care homes of OK-Fonden.

3.1 Development Process

This research followed the Human-Centred Design approach (closely related to User-Centered Design), which aims to create usable and useful systems and products by focusing on users, their needs, and requirements [13,14,19]. During the initial stage of the project, the setting, the care staff and a clinical clown, whose role is to activate and engage the residents, were observed. The goal was to gain a first-hand understanding of the user group and context of use, identifying relevant users and stakeholders [9]. This yielded insights into the daily life in the care home, the activities, behaviour and challenges for residents and staff. It revealed the omnipresent problem of keeping the floors clean and the mentioned problems when using a vacuum cleaning robot. This robotic vacuum cleaner was hard to perceive for residents due to its dark colour and minimalist round shape, which, according to the staff, made it look like a black hole moving across the floor. Moreover, its movement pattern was unpredictable for the residents, making them restless. Therefore, the acquired robotic vacuum cleaner was discarded after only a few months, because of its negative impact on the residents.

The clinical clown was a source of inspiration for investigating patterns of movement and appearance of our robotic vacuum cleaner. She dresses as a cow and uses a slow and predictable as well as playful movement pattern to approach people. This was reported as being especially important for residents with dementia, who are not frightened by such a slow and playful approach pattern.

[1] https://ok-fonden.dk/.

After discussing requirements among the researchers, it was decided to design a playful interactive mobile cleaning unit. Given the positive effects documented of laughter and humour on people with dementia [21], we experimented with a playful, zoomorphic look for our prototype, to elicit positive emotion and laughter. The concept prototype is nicknamed "Sanne", short for'sanitizing unit. As according to [9] interviews with management and staff members of the care home, the board of OK-Fonden and a hygiene expert of a hospital, provided feedback to this idea as well as additional insight into residents' and stakeholders' needs. Staff argue that residents are cognitively and emotionally affected by colours; red and orange are stimulating due to its vibrant chroma [1,7], while white and black can be hard to perceive. On the other hand, blue and green were described as pleasant and relaxing, but easily ignored by residents. Therefore, it was suggested to colour our prototype red and orange to make it easily visible for residents. Potential shapes of the cleaning unit were also discussed. A staff member reported that the residents of this care home felt uncomfortable and'unnatural' while interacting with a toy resembling a seal, which sparked the idea to use the form of a domestic animal, which should be familiar to residents and can be expected of moving around (cp. [3,6]). The size of the cleaning robot was also decided in collaboration with the staff. According to a hygiene expert, the floor itself is considered potentially infectious and unhygienic, and thus the body of the robot (especially the head that might be touched by residents) needs to be at least at 20–30 cm height, to avoid contamination. On the other hand, the robot should still be able to drive under furniture (Fig. 1).

During the design process, the stakeholders continued to contribute feedback and ideas. After the first digital sketches, use cases and user scenarios were created, also considering potential challenges. Hence, a short video of animated sketches was created and distributed, to gain additional feedback. Finally, the first prototype was created based on our understanding of the users, tasks, and environment [13].

As mentioned, the shape of a cat was chosen as a familiar pet. The robot cat was intentionally designed to look toy-like, to avoid deceiving the residents about its nature as an inanimate object. Orange was picked because of its activating nature, and being easy to perceive to reduce the risk of tripping.

3.2 Proof of Concept Prototype

Our Sanne prototype was developed with the TurtleBot[2], a modular robotic unit widely used in teaching and research environments, due to its small size and flexible design. We selected the TurtleBot, mainly because it was within the desired size limits, price tag, and it can support a fast, modular prototyping process. The TurtleBot is equipped with a raspberry Pi, raspberry pi Camera, and 360° 2D LiDar among other sensors. These will be vital for further development, e.g. autonomous navigation in the care home environment.

[2] https://www.robotis.us/turtlebot-3-waffle-pi/.

A 3D-printed cover with the design of an orange cat was mounted on top of the TurtleBot. This first prototype weighs around 4 kg, is 80 cm long from head to end, 40 cm wide and around 40 cm tall, so to be able to move under furniture, while avoiding contamination from the floor, as pointed by the hygiene expert. Moreover, the staff should be able to move it, if stuck in furniture and in case of malfunction. For research purposes, Sanne had a camera mounted behind her ears, so to record reactions of residents and staff (Fig. 2).

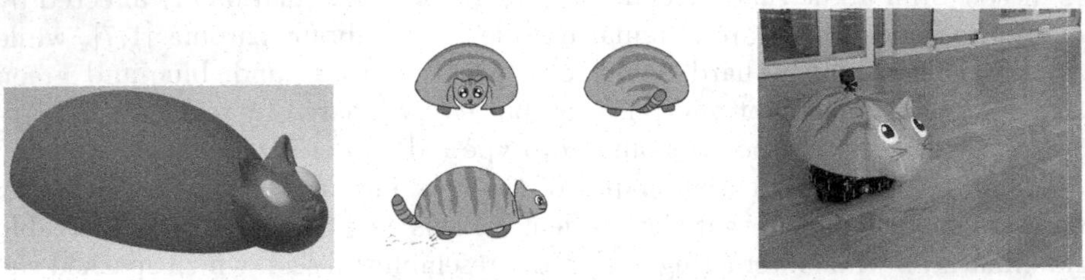

(a) 3D sketch of prototype (b) Animated prototype for videos (c) 3D-printed prototype used in the study

Fig. 2. Different stages of development of the Sanne prototype

Currently we are still experimenting with acceptable movement patterns, regarding speed and quality of movement when approaching residents, so to be seen, and to avoid scaring and intruding in residents' activities. In the tests, Sanne slowed down when approaching residents and moved faster when further away. In addition, a 'wiggling' movement was used when Sanne was close to residents, by driving back and forth and sideways, to make Sanne look playful and attract residents attention. This pattern was inspired by the clown's movement.

For the study, we utilised a Wizard of Oz setup, which is a common method used for exploring how humans react to autonomously moving objects and robots before having fully functioning prototypes [16,20]. This means that we remote-controlled the movement of Sanne, enabling us to flexibly react to emerging situations and adjust on-the-spot to the residents' needs.

4 The Study

The evaluation of our proof-of-concept prototype was conducted in the field, that is at our partner care home. Our study focused on the perception of Sanne, residents' acceptance towards our robotic prototype, and on movement patterns suitable for a care home. We tested the mentioned movement pattern while observing the residents' reactions in relation to their current activity level.

We conducted our test in two care homes of our partner institution, OK-Fonden, in 6 different house units. In total, 30 residents (16 females, 14 males) participated in our study. Their age and names were not recorded, as for our study the state and effects of the dementia disease were more relevant than personal information. The process of the study was approved by OK-Fonden's management. Informed consent was obtained from the patient's relatives for their participation. For presentation here, participants have been anonymized via drawings based on the recorded videos. Our tests took place on three days at different times and lasted 30 to 70 min. To investigate if and how the residents' activity level might influence their perception of Sanne, we showed them our prototype before and during lunch, which qualify respectively as low and high activity levels. In total, 2:50 h video footage were gathered in total. One camera was mounted on top of the robot's head, approximating Sanne's field of view, to record close-ups of the residents. A second camera was installed in the room, to record the space and document other eventual interactions between the residents and how Sanne might affect these.

As the researchers did not speak Danish fluently, a staff member of the care home was present to help communicating with the residents and intervene in any unexpected situation. The researchers wore a care staff uniform, to blend in and not raise too much attention. They also had to wear a face shield and keep distance from the residents, and were tested negative, due to hygienic restrictions related to the Covid-19 pandemic as shown in Fig. 1.

One researcher controlled the robot via a remote control, according to the Wizard-of-Oz method, to simulate that the robot was moving autonomously. This researcher stayed in the background and tried to hide the remote control, to avoid that the residents might notice it. A second researcher stayed close to the residents, to take notes of their reactions and their words Fig. 1. The present care staff were sitting or standing next to the residents, talking to them or supporting them in daily activities.

Later, we conducted a series of follow-up semi-structured interviews, the first with the staff of the care home and the second one with its management. Both interviews lasted 30 min and were recorded. These interviews focused on the tests and staff's regular daily practices and challenges. The aim of these interviews was to gain an understanding on whether the care givers noticed any unusual moods or reactions, caused by Sanne's presence in the home. Since Sanne is supposed to ease the daily work of the care staff in keeping the home clean, we asked them how they perceived Sanne, to comment on her potential and which difficulties they could foresee. The interview with care home management focused on the general concept of Sanne and how the user tests were experienced.

5 Findings

The recorded video footage provided the key data for our analysis. It was cut, labelled, translated, and categories were assigned to identified occurrences, such as: residents' reactions to Sanne, their activity level, and how they became aware of Sanne during the test. In total, 37 situations were identified, analysed (also referred to as reactions), and organised into a logbook. We focused especially on occurrences in which the residents noticed Sanne and were led to act in different ways than usual.

Fig. 3. Positive reaction, luring with hand

5.1 Reactions to Sanne

The residents' reactions were categorised into positive, neutral, negative, and non-reaction. *Positive reactions* towards the robot include situations in which the residents showed interest in Sanne by asking questions, talking about or to her, smiling at her and luring Sanne to come closer or touching her (Fig. 3). Situations where residents only noticed and visibly accepted her presence or commented briefly, but did not further interact or relate to Sanne, were categorised as *neutral reactions.* Negative verbal comments, a perceptibly worsening mood or a rejecting gesture were categorized as *negative reactions.* Situations, in which residents could not perceive Sanne because of their activity level or health condition, as well as situations where they did not show any interest, ignoring Sanne, were labelled as *non-reaction* (both types are counted as non-reaction as it is not always possible to tell whether Sanne was intentionally ignored or not visible from the point of view of the resident).

16 out of 37 reactions were positive, only one was negative. 11 residents reacted neutral, and in 9 situations, no reaction was discernible (Table 1).

The four reaction types were subcategorised according to the kind of reaction (Table 1). Residents who reacted positively, were either talking to or about Sanne, luring and/or touching her. In three situations, Sanne was touched by residents, they either scratched her head or touched her ears. Before every touching situation, the participants talked to Sanne or lured her. While talking to her, some participants altered their voice to reach a higher tone, reminding of the tone used while talking to children or pets. Luring the robot was done either by whistling, reaching with the feet towards Sanne, or via a hand luring gesture (Fig. 4).

Residents who showed neutral reactions either just observed Sanne or listened to a caregiver, or employee talking about her and agreed to what was said. In three of the 11 neutral situations the conversation sounded like this:

Caregiver: Look, the cat is coming over there.
Resident: What is it doing?
Caregiver: It's supposed to wash our floors, wouldn't that be nice?
Resident: Yes, of course!

Table 1. Occurrences of reactions to Sanne and sub-types of reactions

Reaction	Situations	Sub-type	Situations
Positive	16	Talking	5
		Talking and luring	5
		Luring	3
		Talking, luring and touching	2
		Talking and touching	1
Neutral	11	Observing	7
		Listening and agreeing	3
		Listening	1
Negative	1	Kicking	1
Non	9	Not interested	5
		Not possible	4

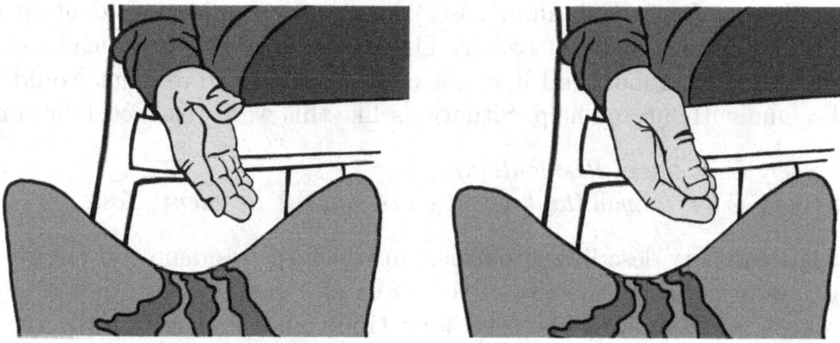

Fig. 4. Close up on lure gesture with hand

The one negative situation observed was labelled as such because the resident followed Sanne and kicked her (Fig. 5). Nevertheless this situation was ambiguous, as he did not show visible rejection, fear or anger and continued to follow Sanne. The resident appeared negative concerning our study in general, as he also kicked a researcher to clear his way. Kicking is usually done to show dislike or to keep something at distance, and was therefore categorised as negative.

In some cases, no reaction was observed, this happened typically when residents were focused on other activities and did not notice Sanne. Some seemed to see her, but did not appear interested, so that it was not possible to determine if they would accept her or not.

5.2 Attention

As another key finding, we consider how the residents became aware of Sanne's presence. During the user study, at least one caregiver or employee of the care home was present, which led to conversations about Sanne. To determine whether Sanne will be able to drive through the care home by herself without needing somebody to introduce her or to make the residents aware of her, we analysed how many people were able to perceive her without any help. There are four different categories of the attention level (Fig. 6).

From 37 situations, 26 residents were able to notice and reacted to Sanne *independently*. In those, no help was needed from a caregiver, employee, or other resident to perceive the robot and to react. *Semi-dependent* were residents who either needed help to shift their attention towards Sanne or to react. Only three residents needed this partial help.

1. *Caregiver: Look who is coming here!*
   Resident: Oh yes, is it walking on wheels?
2. *(Resident observing Sanne on the floor)*
   Caregiver: Do you think its cute?
   Resident: Yes.

The category *Dependent* summarises the situations where residents needed help to notice Sanne and react to her. The caregiver or employee lead the conversation about the robot, and it is not clear whether the resident would have noticed Sanne without any help. Situations like this were observed four times.

Caregiver: Look there! Resident: Ah.
Caregiver: What do you think about it, is it nice? Resident: Yes.

The last category describes situations, in which the residents did not pay any attention towards Sanne, in spite of the effort of a caregiver or other residents. This lack of attention was observed four times and assigned to the reaction category *Non* and subcategory "Not possible".

5.3 Influence of Activity Level

The third aspect of our analysis deals with whether the activity level of the residents might have influenced their reaction to Sanne. Activity levels were

Fig. 5. Negative reaction, kicking

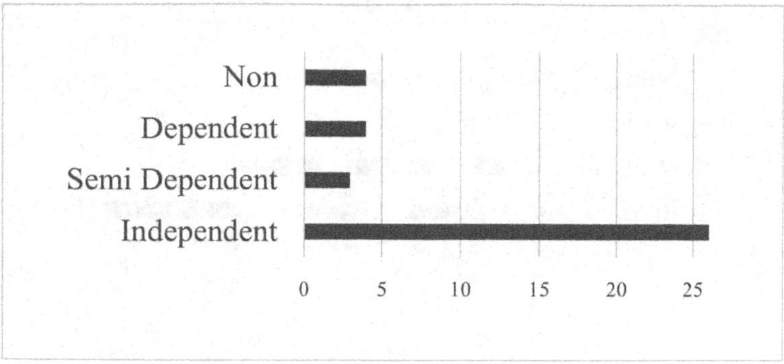

Fig. 6. Attention towards Sanne

categorised in low, middle, and high. A *high activity level* is represented by situations in which residents are busy during a meal, talking to somebody, or focused on an activity such as handicraft. Instances in which residents were watching TV, reading a magazine, walking through the care home, or having a small snack or drink, were categorised as a *middle activity level*, as these did not require intense focus from the residents. Situations where people were only sitting or standing somewhere were categorised as *low level activity*. The prototype was tested before lunch (low to middle activity level) and during lunch (high activity level). From 16 positive reactions to Sanne, only one resident had a high activity level, while 11 residents had a low level. Six of the 11 neutral reactions happened during high activity levels. In general most (19 of 37) situations were observed during the residents had a low activity level (Fig. 7), including also the largest number of positive reactions.

6 Discussion

A key finding from our study is that **73% of observed residents showed to have accepted Sanne**, which means that at its current state, our prototype was accepted and tolerated by most residents. Only one negative situation was observed and 24% of observed situations had no discernible reaction to the robot (non-reaction). These cases of no reaction were considered a positive finding, since the residents did not appear scared or annoyed, but simply went on with their activities, ignoring Sanne. The observed negative situation was, as reported by the caregivers, explainable with the fact that the resident never liked animals in his life. Moreover, by previously kicking one of the researchers, this resident indicated to be annoyed by anyone or anything standing in his way. Even though some residents might not like cats or the chosen colour for Sanne, we can argue that our prototype did not cause any fear, disturbance, or anxiety. Since Sanne is primarily intended to clean the floor, and only secondarily to provide an opportunity to interact or play with her, the residents do not necessarily have to respond and should be able to ignore her. Our research question *"Can a playful*

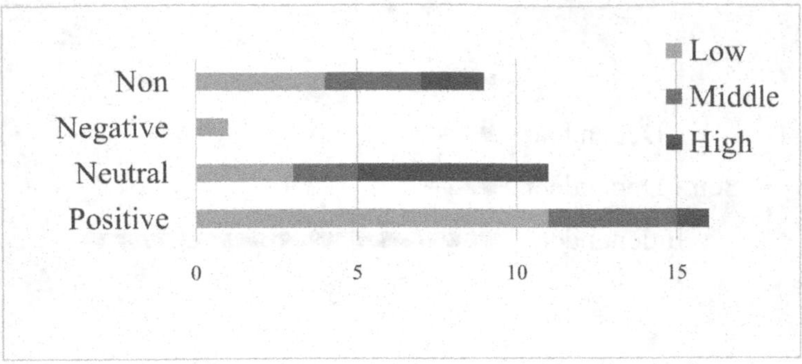

Fig. 7. Activity level

robotic vacuum cleaner, like Sanne, be accepted by people with dementia?" can, therefore, be answered positively at this current state of development.

Another key finding is that **Sanne is perceived as cat-like**, indicated by 11 out of 16 positive reactions ending with touching her. The behaviour of luring and touching could be counted an implicit behaviour, comparable to a playful interaction with pets. Nonetheless the residents clearly appeared to be aware that Sanne is not a real living cat, as some commented on her body being hard and knocking on her head, showing that the design of Sanne evokes behaviours that allude to cats as well as toy pets, without misleading people affected by dementia.

70% of the Residents Were Able to React to Sanne Independently. This shows that the robot could be used in an everyday situation, moving around the care home without needing help from caregiver to be introduced or be supervised during interactions. In this way, our prototype should be able to fulfil the purpose of keeping the floors clean and relieving care staff of this task, as the residents could perceive, accept, and some even liked to interact with Sanne, opposite to what happened with the previous commercial robotic vacuum cleaner.

58% of Residents with a Low Activity Level Reacted Positively to Sanne. The most significant reactions to Sanne occurred during low activity levels. When residents were focusing on a task and thus had a higher activity level, they only reacted neutral or very briefly to the robot. This shows that people can easily ignore Sanne, which might fit the purpose of cleaning the floors without causing unnecessary distraction. Finally this finding can provide clues for caregivers to find a suitable time to use the robot for actively cleaning the floor (for example during lunch or another activity) and for using it as an entertainment and talking point for residents.

6.1 Future Work

According to our study, Sanne might become a source of danger to those residents who have difficulties to attend to more than one thing at a time, or to anything that is not in their line of sight, a known issue for late stages of dementia [2]. In one instance, a resident was walking up and down the hallway and did not notice the robot on the floor, if the researchers would not have controlled the robot, a tripping incident might have occurred. Therefore, further investigation is required to develop a safety protocol for Sanne, fine tuning her movement pattern, establishing a safe distance and acceptable warning signals for residents in transit.

The observed negative situation revealed that Sanne should be able to react to residents' rejections. Actions like kicking or utterances like *"Go away"* can be interpreted as warning signals, which Sanne should be able to detect and to shut off or drive away in response, avoiding further annoyance.

At the current stage of our research, it is not possible to make any claims on the noise level of Sanne, as the tested prototype did not yet have a vacuum cleaning function. According to experiences reported by the caregivers with their previous cleaning robot, loud noise can negatively affect the residents, therefore, it is our plan to further investigate this aspect during in-situ workshops.

As the residents touched Sanne in 69% of the positive reactions, the tactile properties of the shell material should be further explored. Currently Sanne is made of 3-D printed plastic, which is not particularly pleasant, hence we aim to find a soft-feeling material, which invites touch but is also hygienic, so that it does not summon more work from the care staff for disinfecting the robot.

7 Conclusion

In our study, we explored the design of a non-threatening robotic vacuum cleaner for care homes, addressing in particular the needs of people affected by late stages of dementia. Our study was conducted through a Human Centred Design methodology. Therefore, we engaged in a close partnership with two care homes located in Odense, Denmark.

Our study demonstrates that people at late stages of dementia can accept a robotic vacuum cleaner, if it carries playful qualities in its appearance and movement pattern. Based on our conversations with staff, we gave our prototype, which we call Sanne, the appearance of an orange red-striped cat and a movement pattern, which supports visibility and predictability, avoiding fright and tripping.

Our results show that residents responded positively to our prototype, as most of them tried to engage with our prototype to play as if it was a pet or a cat-like toy. Only one negative response was observed, which was a rejection, but not accompanied by fright or accidents. Other residents simply ignored Sanne, as she was not in their field of view or they were engaged in activities. We consider non-responses as positive, as people are entitled to interact with Sanne or not according to their wish. These occurrences mean that there might be a risk of tripping, therefore, our next step in development will focus on exploring a safety protocol to avoid accidents while Sanne is cleaning the floor or simply sharing space with residents.

Acknowledgment. This research was supported by the project ReThiCare, funded by the VolkswagenStiftung. We thank the OK-Fonden staff and management, in particular the local leader Anne Mulberg Dahl and the clinical clown Lulu, and the residents.

References

1. September 2018. https://www.felgains.com/blog/seeing-red-dementia-care-colour-red-stimulate-appetite-not/
2. Borges, S.D.M., Radanovic, M., Forlenza, O.V.: Fear of falling and falls in older adults with mild cognitive impairment and Alzheimer's disease. Aging Neuropsychol. Cogn. **22**(3), 312–321 (2015)
3. Bozeat, S., Patterson, K., Hodges, J.: Relearning object use in semantic dementia. Neuropsychol. Rehabil. **14**(3), 351–363 (2004)
4. Carers, E.: Embracing the critical role of caregivers around the world. Darmstadt, Germany (2017)
5. Chrysikou, E.G., Giovannetti, T., Wambach, D.M., Lyon, A.C., Grossman, M., Libon, D.J.: The importance of multiple assessments of object knowledge in semantic dementia: the case of the familiar objects task. Neurocase **17**(1), 57–75 (2011)
6. Cox, C., Vassallo, M.: Fear of falling assessments in older people with dementia. Rev. Clin. Gerontol. **25**(2), 98 (2015)
7. Dewing, J.: Caring for people with dementia: noise and light. Nurs. Older People **21**(5), 34–38 (2009)
8. Alzheimer Europe: Dementia in Europe yearbook 2019: Estimating the prevalence of dementia in Europe. Alzheimer Europe (2019)
9. Guffroy, M., Nadine, V., Kolski, C., Vella, F., Teutsch, P.: From human-centered design to disabled user & ecosystem centered design in case of assistive interactive systems. Int. J. Sociotechnol. Knowl. Dev. (IJSKD) **9**(4), 28–42 (2017)
10. Harrison, B.E., Son, G.R., Kim, J., Whall, A.L.: Preserved implicit memory in dementia: a potential model for care. Am. J. Alzheimer's Disease Other Dementias® **22**(4), 286–293 (2007)
11. EIT Health: Rising need for elder care in Europe necessitates new paradigm for elder caregiving training: a landscape analysis. EIT Health - Innovative healthcare solutions of tomorrow, December 2017
12. OECD Indicators: Health at a glance 2011. OECD Indicators, OECD Publishing, Paris (2015). https://doi.org/10.1787/health_glance-2015-en. Accessed 15 Feb 2016
13. International-Standards-Organization: Ergonomics of human-system interaction-part 210: Human centred design for interactive systems, ISO 9241–210 (2010)
14. Jones, M., Marsden, G., et al.: Mobile Interaction Design, vol. 10. Wiley, New York (2006)
15. Latikka, R., Turja, T., Oksanen, A.: Self-efficacy and acceptance of robots. Comput. Hum. Behav. **93**, 157–163 (2019)
16. Martelaro, N., Ju, W.: Woz way: enabling real-time remote interaction prototyping & observation in on-road vehicles. In: Proceedings of the 2017 ACM Conference on Computer Supported Cooperative Work and Social Computing, CSCW 2017, pp. 169–182. Association for Computing Machinery, New York (2017). https://doi.org/10.1145/2998181.2998293

17. Riek, L.D.: Healthcare robotics. Commun. ACM **60**(11), 68–78 (2017)
18. Rimmer, E., Wojciechowska, M., Stave, C., Sganga, A., O'Connell, B.: Implications of the facing dementia survey for the general population, patients and caregivers across Europe. Int. J. Clin. Pract. **59**, 17–24 (2005)
19. Rogers, Y., Sharp, H., Preece, J.: Interaction Design: Beyond Human-Computer Interaction. Wiley, Hoboken (2011)
20. Sirkin, D., Mok, B., Yang, S., Ju, W.: Mechanical ottoman: how robotic furniture offers and withdraws support. In: Proceedings of the Tenth Annual ACM/IEEE International Conference on Human-Robot Interaction, HRI 2015, pp. 11–18. Association for Computing Machinery, New York (2015). https://doi.org/10.1145/2696454.2696461
21. Takeda, M., et al.: Laughter and humor as complementary and alternative medicines for dementia patients. BMC Complement. Altern. Med. **10**(1), 1–7 (2010)
22. World-Health-Organisation: World health organisation - dementia, June 2021. https://www.who.int/news-room/fact-sheets/detail/dementia

An Engineering Approach Towards Multi-site Virtual Molecular Tumor Board Software

Richard Henkenjohann[1], Benjamin Bergner[1], Florian Borchert[1], Nina Bougatf[2], Hauke Hund[2], Roland Eils[3], and Matthieu-P. Schapranow[1](✉)

[1] HPI Digital Healh Canter, Hasso Plattner Institute for Digital Engineering, University of Potsdam, Prof.-Dr.-Helmert-Str. 2-3, 14482 Potsdam, Germany
{richard.henkenjohann,benjamin.bergner,florian.borchert, schapranow}@hpi.de

[2] Heidelberg University Hospital, Im Neuenheimer Feld 672, 69120 Heidelberg, Germany
{nina.bougatf,hauke.hund}@med.uni-heidelberg.de

[3] Berlin Institute of Health, Kapelle-Ufer 2, 10117 Berlin, Germany
roland.eils@charite.de

Abstract. Molecular tumor boards are an emerging platform for multidisciplinary oncology care specialists to assess treatment options based on the patient's individual molecular tumor profile. However, they require complex manual preparation, e.g., data retrieval from widespread knowledge bases. We define clinical process models and a software prototype supporting the adoption of virtual molecular tumor boards across multiple clinical sites. Together with real-world experts, we created software prototypes to optimize the individual steps of preparing, conducting, and follow-up after molecular tumor boards. Thus, our Web-based prototype supports oncologists in selecting individual treatment options more effectively.

Keywords: Virtual tumor board · Molecular tumor board · Cancer therapy · IT-aided clinical processes · HiGHmed

1 Introduction

The heterogeneity of cancer diseases demands multidisciplinary collaboration and adequate software tool support for medical professionals in their daily routine [16,35]. The wide adoption of Tumor Boards (TBs) as the defacto standard for oncology decision-making shows the importance of joint medical expertise: A group of trained practitioners discusses each patient's cases individually by jointly assessing all available patient data to support the treating doctor in finding the best treatment option [15,21]. Recent advances in molecular diagnostics like Whole Genome Sequencing (WGS) make even more fine-grained molecular data available for oncologists enabling evidence-based decision finding [36].

E. Pissaloux et al. (Eds.): IHAW 2021, CCIS 1538, pp. 156–170, 2021.
https://doi.org/10.1007/978-3-030-94209-0_13

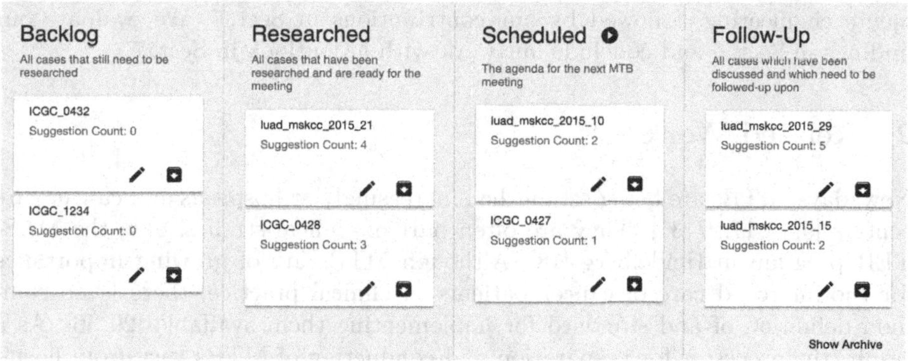

Fig. 1. Several patients arranged in the MTB dashboard using Kanban methodology. From left to right: The backlog contains non-annotated cases, followed by already researched molecular profiles, patients scheduled for an upcoming MTB, and those that require a follow-up. Each card represents an individual patient case.

However, at the same time, it is getting increasingly complex for oncologists to gain insights from this sheer amount of data due to the lack of adequate tool support. This work reports on observed challenges with conducting Molecular Tumor Boards (MTBs) that include the patient's molecular profile as an essential basis for personalized treatment recommendations [15]. We further contribute a prototype for software support for "Virtual MTBs" [4,24].

At the moment, TBs and MTBs among hospitals vary due to missing standardization, and, to the best of our knowledge, no standardized process models exist in the literature. Tools for MTB support are divided into two categories: Clinical Decision Support Systems (CDSS) and management support systems. CDSS focus on the preparation process and either leverage Artificial Intelligence (AI) to extract relevant information or store expert experiences such as variant-treatment combinations [32,34]. Annotation and publication databases play a crucial role in the preparation phase but need to be queried individually. Online services aim to link medical publications and data from disease-specific databases to support the information-seeking process for researchers and clinicians [30]. In contrast, the literature rarely reports management support systems, i.e., tools supporting look-up of patient data, tracking of case progress along the tumor board process, creating presentations, documentation, and follow-up of patients. Therefore, we contribute by our "MTB Assist" software tool to address these open issues. A screenshot of its dashboard is depicted in Fig. 1. Our work was created in the context of the HiGHmed consortium, one of the four consortia funded by the Medical Informatics Initiative of the German Federal Ministry of Education and Research [11].

The remainder of the work is structured as follows: After setting our work in the context of related work in Sect. 2, the methods of our involved engineering process are described in Sect. 3. Section 4 describes the results of the requirements engineering, followed by our contributions in Sect. 5. We evaluate our findings in Sect. 6 and conclude our work with an outlook in Sect. 7.

2 Related Work

Nowadays, MTBs are being established increasingly at hospitals and cancer care centers [9,15,17,21,31]. They are often part of clinical studies, e.g., the MASTER program in Heidelberg [18]. Although MTBs are of growing importance for the improved care of cancer patients in clinical practice, there is no common definition of and standard for implementing them available [29,36]. As a result, the processes for preparation and conducting of MTBs vary from hospital to hospital [3]. Thus, the reproducibility and quality of MTB findings may vary. To the best of the authors' knowledge, only informal descriptions of MTB implementations were published at the time of writing [12,15,23].

Therefore, we define a formal description of the process using Business Process and Notation (BPMN) in Sect. 5.1. Nowadays, patient data is typically stored across distributed data silos such as hospital information systems (HIS) or local workstations in a hospital setting, hindering collaborative real-time access and making manual data aggregation necessary [5,22]. Moreover, apart from essential meeting tools, dedicated software tools for preparation, conducting meetings, documentation, and follow-up are not reported in literature [14,27].

3 Methods

In the following, we share details about the incorporated methods and engineering approaches. For our work, we followed an engineering approach that incorporated the Design Thinking (DT) methodology. Design Thinking methodology is a method to identify and solve problems which includes an empathizing, ideation, prototyping, and testing phase iteratively [25]. Therefore, we conducted interviews with subject-matter experts from hospitals in Germany to identify current limitations and define a clinical process model for adopting MTBs in the clinical setting. Furthermore, we described specific requirements for software tools to enable beyond-hospital collaborations between oncologists to contribute to a shared clinical knowledge for genetic annotations.

Observations and Personas: We visited MTBs of two major German university hospitals and interviewed subject-matter experts to empathize with the practitioners. The interviewees (n = 8) were identified through purposive sampling. We were able to define three personas involved in our observed MTB processes: the treating physician, MTB research expert, and moderator. Personas are an instrument to help identify the user's needs and desires [7,25]. Based on the personas requirements, we defined clinical process models using Business Process Modeling and Notation (BPMN) version 2.0 for individual clinical steps as outlined in Sect. 5.1 [8]. The process models were evaluated several times together with subject-matter experts in oncology meetings within the HiGHmed consortium.

Rapid Prototyping: Prototyping is a powerful way to evaluate ideas at an early stage, which aids in proving underlying assumptions [10]. Therefore, we drafted whiteboard sketches to align ideas and present iterative software prototypes to selected medical experts. Based on their feedback, we designed a software tool supporting oncologists in preparing, conducting and following up MTB cases. Our interactive "MTB Assist" prototype is a Web application that allows easy access via Web browsers without local installations and configuration as part of AnalyzeGenomes.com [26,30]. The software consists of a graphical user interface (Angular 6), a backend server (Python-Flask), and an in-memory database management system (IMDB) to enable real-time data analysis.

Evaluation: "MTB Assist" was evaluated based on user tests with selected annotators (n = 2) from a major German cancer center with regular MTBs. The interviewees were identified through purposive sampling. The evaluation incorporated two iterations. Each test participant was first introduced to the purpose of the MTB support tool, then asked to simulate the whole MTB process. Along with the test, we adapted the Think-Aloud method to encourage the interviewees to talk about their impressions and actions [6].

4 Requirements Engineering

In the following, we share our observations from the DT empathizing phase.

4.1 Observations

For each participating patient in an MTB, treatment options are researched from different medical knowledge databases based on a list of genetic variants [3]. The annotation includes druggability options, drug evidence levels, and ongoing clinical studies [18,37]. MTB meetings are conducted in a conference room with external practitioners who receive feedback on their cases. Each case is introduced by summarizing the patient's medical history, then discussed, and treatment suggestions are written down. Due to the breadth of existing and unharmonized knowledge bases and primary literature, information seeking is tedious and may result in missed treatment recommendations. Historical cases are a valuable source; however, those cases often are not indexed and are difficult to retrieve. Also, it is hard to keep track of the current preparation state, i.e., "is annotated," "needs a follow-up" when preparing multiple cases. Once treatment recommendations are researched, presentation slides are assembled by copying results into an MS PowerPoint template. This time-consuming process needs to be repeated for each patient and tumor board. Often, multiple information systems are used to access data highlighting the need for a unified interface. The consultation of relevant data interrupts the meeting, although participants must focus on discussing the case. Whenever a question cannot be answered due to missing details, the patient's discussion is postponed to the next meeting. All MTBs attendees must be given the possibility to prepare each case to have rich discussions and fewer postponed meetings. Strong digital collaborations between the participants require differing permissions to a patient's case sub-resources.

4.2 Software Requirements

Based on our observations from Sect. 4.1, we derived the following functional software requirements for a Web-based software support tool [20].

F1 *Automatic Import of Patient Data:* Relevant case data shall be imported automatically from the respective HIS.
F2 *Visual Clinical Process Overview:* Provide a graphical overview of the preparation progress with a list of cases in the queue.
F3 *Variant Annotation:* Enable users to create and save annotations of genetic variants into a database with a unified structure including entries, sources, medication, evidence level, and appropriate reasoning.
F4 *Genetic Variants Ranking:* Calculate a relevance score for individual genetic variants based on their pathogenicity.
F5 *Parallel Entry Extraction:* Inform about the availability of entries in annotation sources for a genetic variant.
F6 *Similar Patient Case:* Identify similar cases based on their molecular profile.
F7 *Collaboration:* Case information such as annotations can be shared to obtain feedback from peer researchers and clinicians.
F8 *Case Presentation:* Automate the process of slide creation with a one-click solution containing relevant information per patient case for MTB discussion.
F9 *Documentation:* Provide a documentation system for treatment recommendations linked to the case.

In addition to the functional software requirements, we also identified non-functional requirements as follows:

N1 *Usability:* The software shall have a design being easy and intuitive to use by trained and non-trained medical end-users.
N2 *Maintainability:* For the IT staff, it shall be easy to add new components, e.g., data sources, enhance existing functions, e.g., calculation of relevance scores, and roll-out updates or bug fixes to all users promptly.
N3 *Minimal Setup Effort:* Medical professionals as users of the software should have minimum efforts to install, set up, and configure it before using it.

5 Contributions

In the following, we share our contributions, i.e., the clinical process models for conducting MTBs and the proposed software support prototype.

5.1 Clinical Process Model

Together with subject-matter experts from oncology, we defined clinical process models for MTBs to support their adaption in clinical settings. The process models aim to support the standardized implementation of MTBs in clinical settings and are available in the appendix. The process addresses the identified MTB processes: a) preparation of a case for the MTB, depicted in Fig. 3, and b) MTB meeting, depicted in Fig. 4.

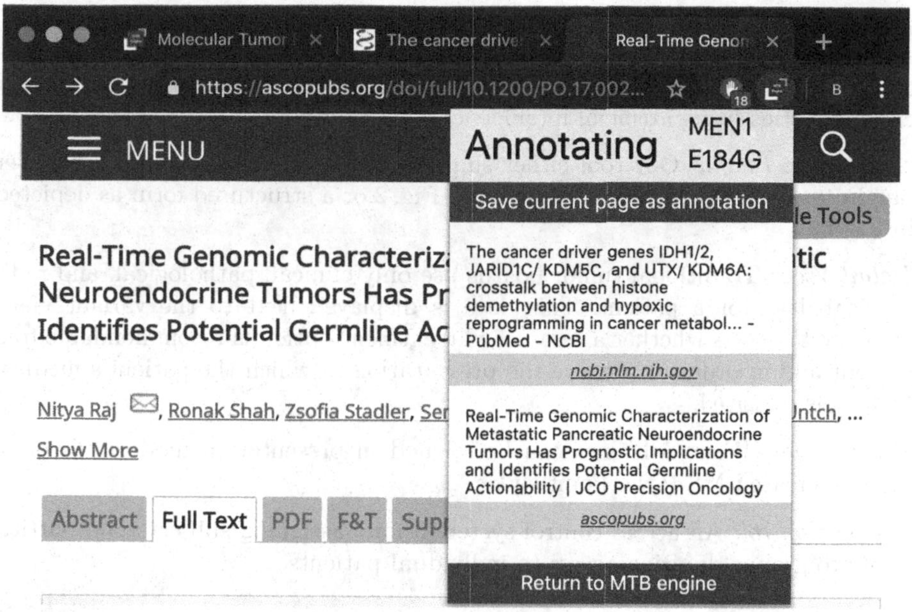

Fig. 2. The browser plugin assists in keeping track of annotations from arbitrary sources, which matches clinical practice.

5.2 Software Prototype

The clinical processes identified in Sect. 5.1 are supported by our prototype "MTB Assist" to address software requirements outlined in Sect. 4.2 as follows:

Import of Patient Case Data: Case data can be added to the system either manually (see Fig. 5) or by querying the local clinical data repository. Case-related data is stored in an in-memory database to enable real-time data analysis.

Patient Overview: The dashboard depicted in Fig. 1 implements the Kanban methodology to manage the current state of each case in the MTB process [1,2, 19]. Kanban is an agile method that improves communication and coordination, visualizes the work in progress, and reduces process times.

Variants View and Literature Sources: All functional genetic variants, gene locations, and affected proteins are shown in Fig. 7. Amongst others, the following knowledge sources are PubMed, ASCO, CIViC and historical cases.

Relevancy Scores: Mutations can be sorted by a relevance score calculated using functional analysis through hidden Markov models obtained by VarSome [33]. The score indicates the functional effects of protein missense mutations. Further scores may be implemented [13]. Interactive figures help to assess driver mutations as depicted in Fig. 8.

Similar Patients: Historical data enables reusing existing clinical knowledge, also from other hospitals. We defined three levels of patient similarity: Weak similarity is given by characteristics such as age, gender, diagnosis. In addition, similar patients can be matched by alterations occurring in the same gene. The third level of similarity is given with all available structured patient and tumor characteristics using artificial intelligence (AI) techniques [28].

Annotation Plugin: Our tool either supports the annotator through a browser plugin for Google Chrome as depicted in Fig. 2 or a structured form as depicted in Fig. 6.

Detail View: Traditional tumor boards use only clinical, pathological, and radiological data for a patient. This data is displayed next to the variant view, allowing to assess whether a researched treatment option is recommendable to a patient and in order to prepare the presentation in which the patient's medical history is revisited.

Presentation View: All cases can be opened in presentation mode in favor of manual-created MS PowerPoint slides.

Access Control: An access control system allows assigning subjects and participants to groups, limiting access to individual patients.

6 Evaluation and Discussion

In the following, we evaluate our findings and discuss their applicability with regards to multi-site virtual tumor boards.

Firstly, we need to consider how to establish the required clinical processes for such MTBs. Our defined MTB process models presented in Sect. 5.1 were created and validated with subject-matter experts from multiple German hospitals. Thus, they built upon best practices from hospitals conducting MTBs. Furthermore, subject-matter experts were able to provide feedback on how to adapt these processes. We found out that for some hospitals there will be selected specifics. Therefore, our clinical process models aim to be flexible and open to include these hospital specifics as well.

The models are open to participants from remote entities via a conferencing system. Inter-institutional information exchange is the basis for the identification of similar historic patient cases. Therefore, the search for selected non-identifiable attributes should be supported, such as gender, age group, primary diagnoses, selected genetic changes.

Our interviews revealed that the quality of an MTB highly depends on the work of the MTB research expert. By leveraging our software tool "MTB Assist", the burden on they are reduced in the long term because the system grows through multi-center use and allows the combination of annotation from all sites. Thus, we expect that the most time-consuming step, the research for patient-specific annotations, will reduce over time.

Our tool forms the foundation for building up a single multi-site knowledge base, which contains amongst others point-of-care data, annotations for molecular variants, assessed treatment options, and clinical trials enriched by selected clinical data. We consider it as a management support system that helps to implement standardized MTB processes.

The feedback from medical professionals revealed that our proposed "MTB Assist" provides suitable IT-aided process support for the preparation and conduction of tumor boards. For example, the linkage to primary annotation knowledge bases supports reproducible decision-making. Accessing public annotations from distributed databases for genetic variants via a single user interface was considered time-saving. Our interview partners highly appreciated the modular fashion of source inclusion for the annotation. However, the correct selection of sources remains challenging, and comprehensive tool support is missing [3]. The drug auto-complete option in the annotation view was considered helpful because it avoids inconsistencies. However, it lists only approved medications, and it does not contain recent drug candidates available from clinical trials. During our interviews, we found out that Microsoft Internet Explorer and Mozilla Firefox are the most common Web browsers in hospitals, which limits the functionality available for plugin development.

We consider the combination and sharing of clinical knowledge between medical experts – even across institutional borders – as an enabler for a more cooperative decision-making process in oncology. In addition, the idea of displaying selected data from similar patients has been perceived as a unique advantage because it is not available in clinical practice, yet. The ability to automatically turn assembled case data into a screen presentation was an essential feature. It releases medical professionals from composing slides using Microsoft PowerPoint and making additional time for medical investigation available.

7 Conclusion and Outlook

With the Design Thinking methodology, we assessed current limitations in conduction multi-site MTBs. We identified current state-of-the-art processes and defined clinical process models in BPMN. MTBs can be streamlined with IT support; thus, we designed a software support tool that addresses critical management challenges. Our contribution includes the clinical process models from Sect. 5.1 that can be used as a prototype for a standardized implementation of MTBs in hospitals across Germany. Finally, we demonstrate how software tools like our proposed MTB planning software prototype can support the IT-aided clinical process. Our prototype addresses oncologists' requirements and combines fragmented knowledge. The Web-based software tool supports more efficient and effective treatment planning. Our contributions open up opportunities for future work. For example, future work can assess the implementation of OpenEHR structures into an MTB management tool.

Acknowledgments. Parts of this work were generously supported by a grant from the German Federal Ministry of Research and Education (01ZZ1802).

A Appendix

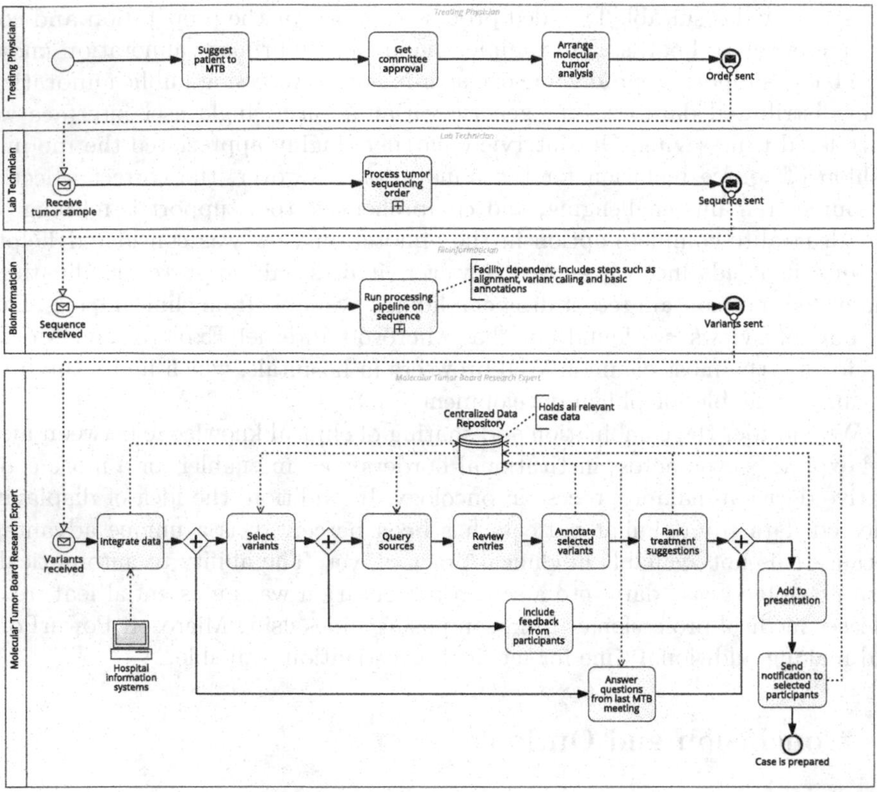

Fig. 3. Process model for MTB preparation. For inclusion to an MTB, a patient must be approved. Approval may be given when state-of-the-art therapies have failed. Next, molecular analysis is ordered, and lab technicians sequence the tumor to retrieve the list of genetic variants. The research expert then creates a case in the MTB tool by merging all relevant patient data from different sources. The identified genetic variants can be used to query similar cases. Variants are ranked based on their therapeutic relevance according to external sources like Var-Some. The research expert selects the most relevant variants and annotates them with identified therapies by literature review. Tool support is given by generating search queries automatically, leveraging named-entity recognition to highlight genes/drugs, and generating text summaries. The variant, drug, evidence level, source, and explanation are annotated to the case. Suitable therapy suggestions are ranked considering the medical history of the patient, the evidence level, and the feasibility of therapy. Additional information is drawn from historical cases to include existing clinical knowledge and improve preparation efficiency. The patient's de-identified case data can be made available to other researchers. The patient is scheduled for one of the upcoming MTB meetings, and the presentation view including all necessary information can be started right away.

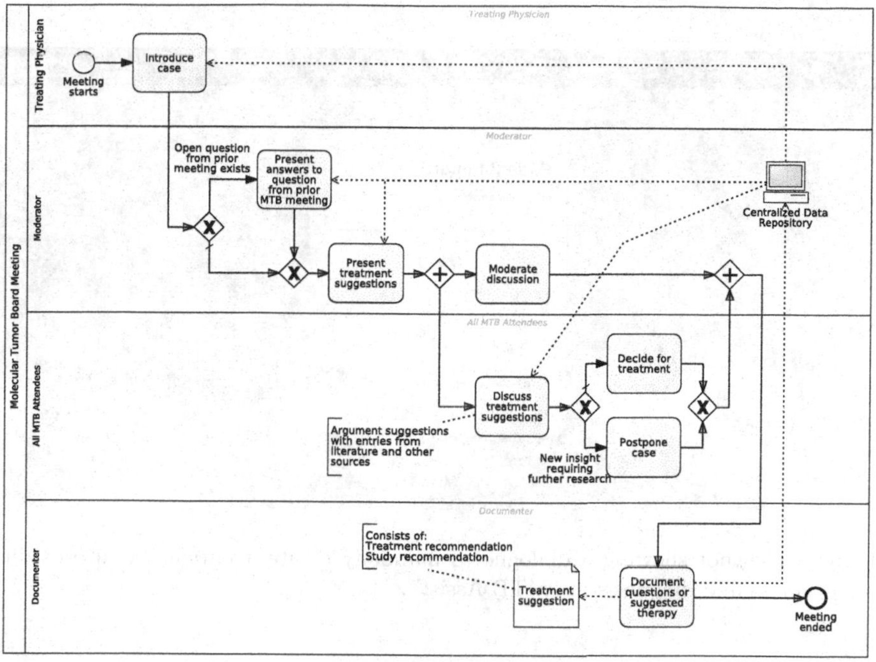

Fig. 4. Process model for MTB meeting. During the meeting process, a patient case is introduced, and its medical history is presented briefly. Consequently, the moderator starts to follow up on any open questions from the last MTB meeting. Next, the moderator presents a prioritized list of treatment suggestions and available studies, including eligibility criteria and location. Afterwards, all attendees are guided through the discussion and are invited by the moderator to comment on the case and provide more suggestions that influence the treatment decision. Successively, the group agrees on the most appropriate treatment recommendation, which will be documented.

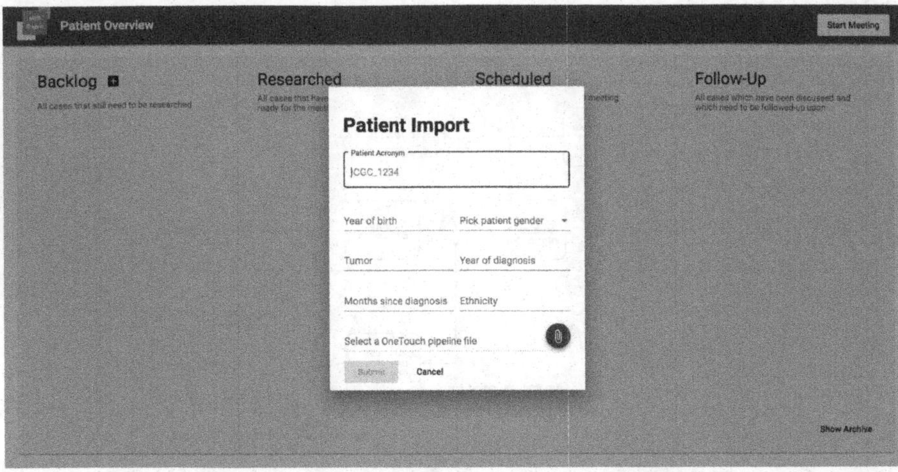

Fig. 5. Screenshot showing a dialogue to manually create a patient by an identifier, demographics and diagnosis in "MTB Assist".

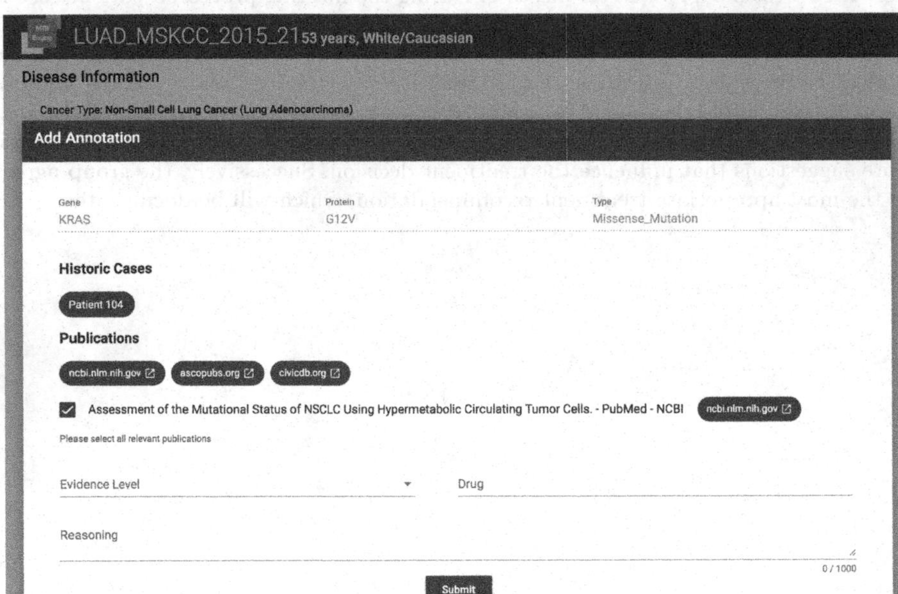

Fig. 6. Screenshot showing a modal form to add an annotation to a case. The dialogue adds a drug, evidence level and reasoning to the selected mutation.

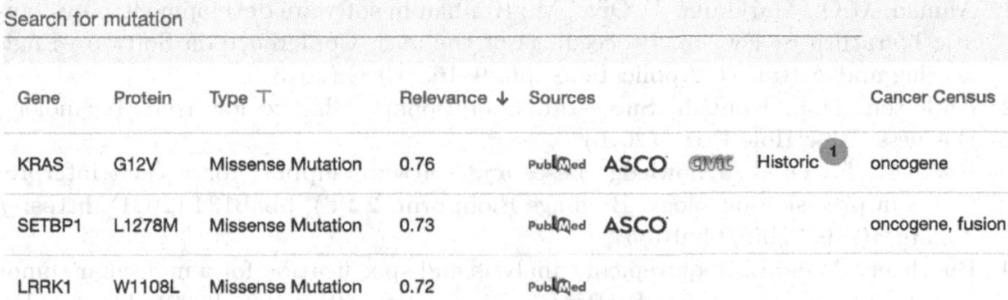

Search for mutation
Gene
Protein
Type
Relevance
Sources
Cancer Census
KRAS
G12V
Missense Mutation
0.76
ASCO
Historic
1
oncogene
SETBP1
L1278M
Missense Mutation
0.73
ASCO
oncogene, fusion
LRRK1
W1108L
Missense Mutation
0.72

Fig. 7. Variant view for a selected case. Amongst others, it depicts altered genes, e.g., KRAS, SETBP1, LRRK1, type of variant, relevance, primary sources, similar cases, and the role of the gene according to the Cancer Gene Census database.

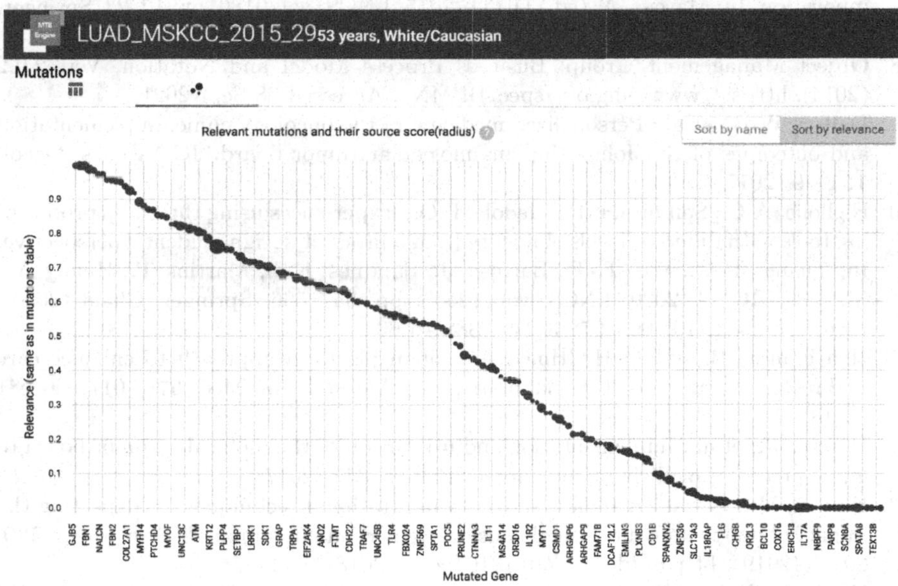

Fig. 8. Screenshot showing functional genetic variants sorted by their calculated relevance score. The graph shows the score that is calculated by the appearance of gene mutations in multiple sources: To account for source quality, we put a higher weight on specific sources, making those mutations stand out more by appearing higher up in the list and having a bigger circle inside the diagram. We value sources from CIViC higher since entries are most likely created by MTB research experts or equivalent professionals. Historical cases are valued highest since entries stem from known experts in the field.

References

1. Ahmad, M.O., Markkula, J., Oivo, M.: Kanban in software development: a systematic literature review. In: Proceedings of the 39th Conference on Software Engineering and Advanced Applications, pp. 9–16. IEEE (2013)
2. Anderson, D.J.: Kanban: Successful Evolutionary Change for Your Technology Business. Blue Hole Press (2010)
3. Borchert, F., et al.: Knowledge bases and software support for variant interpretation in precision oncology. Briefings Bioinform. **22**(6), bbab134 (2021). https://doi.org/10.1093/bib/bbab134
4. Buechner, P., et al.: Requirements analysis and specification for a molecular tumor board platform based on cBioPortal. Diagnostics **10**(2), 93 (2020). https://doi.org/10.3390/diagnostics10020093
5. Cases, M., et al.: Improving data and knowledge management to better integrate health care and research. J. Int. Med. **274**(4), 321–328 (2013)
6. Charters, E.: The use of think-aloud methods in qualitative research an introduction to think-aloud methods. Brock Educ. J. **12**(2), 68–82 (2003). https://doi.org/10.26522/brocked.v12i2.38
7. Chasanidou, D., Gasparini, A.A., Lee, E.: Design thinking methods and tools for innovation. In: Marcus, A. (ed.) DUXU 2015. LNCS, vol. 9186, pp. 12–23. Springer, Cham (2015). https://doi.org/10.1007/978-3-319-20886-2_2
8. Object Management Group: Business Process Model and Notation, Ver. 2.0.2 (2014). https://www.omg.org/spec/BPMN/. Accessed 28 Sept 2021
9. Dalton, W.B., et al.: Personalized medicine in the oncology clinic: implementation and outcomes of the Johns Hopkins molecular tumor board. JCO Precis. Oncol. **1**, 1–19 (2017)
10. Figliolia, A.C., Sandnes, F.E., Medola, F.O.: Experiences using three app prototyping tools with different levels of fidelity from a product design student's perspective. In: Huang, T.-C., Wu, T.-T., Barroso, J., Sandnes, F.E., Martins, P., Huang, Y.-M. (eds.) ICITL 2020. LNCS, vol. 12555, pp. 557–566. Springer, Cham (2020). https://doi.org/10.1007/978-3-030-63885-6_60
11. Haarbrandt, B., et al.: HiGHmed - an open platform approach to enhance care and research across institutional boundaries. Methods Inf. Med. **57**(S 01), e66–e81 (2018)
12. Harada, S., et al.: Implementation and utilization of the molecular tumor board to guide precision medicine. Oncotarget **8**(34), 57845 (2017)
13. Hassan, M.S., et al.: A review study: Computational techniques for expecting the impact of non-synonymous single nucleotide variants in human diseases. Gene **680**, 20–33 (2019). https://doi.org/10.1016/j.gene.2018.09.028
14. Hinderer, M., et al.: Supporting molecular tumor boards in moleculargaided decision-making-the current status of five German university hospitals. Stud. Health Technol. Inform. **236**, 48–54 (2017)
15. Hoefflin, R., et al.: Personalized clinical decision making through implementation of a molecular tumor board: a German single-center experience. JCO Precis. Oncol. **2**, 1–16 (2018)
16. Hollunder, S., et al.: Cross-sectional increase of adherence to multidisciplinary tumor board decisions. BMC Cancer **18**(1), 936 (2018)

17. Horak, P., et al.: Comprehensive genomic and transcriptomic profiling in advanced-stage cancers and rare malignancies: clinical results from the MASTER trial of the German Cancer Consortium. Ann. Oncol. **30**(Suppl. 7), vii24 (2019)
18. Horak, P., et al.: Precision oncology based on omics data: the NCT Heidelberg experience. Int. J. Cancer **141**(5), 877–886 (2017)
19. Huang, C.C., Kusiak, A.: Overview of Kanban systems. Int. J. Comput. Integr. Manuf. **9**, 169–189 (1996)
20. International Organization for Standardization: ISO/IEC/IEEE 24765:2017 - Systems and Software Engineering - Vocabulary (2017). https://www.iso.org/standard/71952.html. Accessed 28 Sept 2021
21. Luchini, C., et al.: Molecular tumor boards in clinical practice. Trends Cancer **6**(9), 738–744 (2020). https://doi.org/10.1016/j.trecan.2020.05.008
22. Nardi, E.A., et al.: Emerging issues and opportunities in health information technology. J. Natl. Compr. Canc. Netw. **14**(10), 1226–1233 (2016)
23. Patel, M., Kato, S.M., Kurzrock, R.: Molecular tumor boards: realizing precision oncology therapy. Clin. Pharmacol. Ther. **103**(2), 206–209 (2018)
24. Pishvaian, M.J., et al.: A virtual molecular tumor board to improve efficiency and scalability of delivering precision oncology to physicians and their patients. JAMIA Open **2**(4), 505–515 (2019)
25. Plattner, H., Meinel, C., Leifer, L.: Design Thinking: Understand - Improve - Apply. Springer, Heidelberg (2010)
26. Plattner, H., Schapranow, M.P.: High-Performance In-Memory Genome Data Analysis: How In-Memory Database Technology Accelerates Personalized Medicine. Springer, Heidelberg (2014)
27. Rankin, N.M., et al.: Implementation of a lung cancer multidisciplinary team standardised template for reporting to general practitioners: a mixed-method study. BMJ Open **7**(12), e018629 (2017)
28. Rao, S., et al.: Collaborative, multidisciplinary evaluation of cancer variants through virtual molecular tumor boards informs local clinical practices. JCO Clin. Cancer Inform. **4**, 602–613 (2020)
29. Rieke, D.T., et al.: Comparison of treatment recommendations by molecular tumor boards worldwide. JCO Precis. Oncol. **2**, 1–14 (2018)
30. Schapranow, M.-P., et al.: A federated in-memory database system for life sciences. In: Castellanos, M., Chrysanthis, P.K., Pelechrinis, K. (eds.) BIRTE 2015-2017. LNBIP, vol. 337, pp. 19–34. Springer, Cham (2019). https://doi.org/10.1007/978-3-030-24124-7_2
31. Schwaederle, M., et al.: Molecular tumor board: the University of California-San Diego Moores Cancer Center experience. Oncologist **19**(6), 631–636 (2014). https://doi.org/10.1634/theoncologist.2013-0405
32. Seva, J., et al.: Multi-lingual ICD-10 coding using a hybrid rule-based and supervised classification approach at CLEF eHealth 2017. In: CLEF (Working Notes) (2017)
33. Shihab, H.A., et al.: Predicting the functional, molecular, and phenotypic consequences of amino acid substitutions using hidden Markov models. Hum. Mutat. **34**(1), 57–65 (2013)

34. Somashekhar, S., et al.: Watson for oncology and breast cancer treatment recommendations: agreement with an expert multidisciplinary tumor board. Ann. Oncol. **29**(2), 418–423 (2018)
35. Strohschneider, T.: Opening address by Prof. Dr. Siewert at the 23rd Congress of the German Cancer Society 8 June 1998 in Berlin "Oncology in the tension field between reality and vision". Der Chirurg; Zeitschrift für alle Gebiete der operativen Medizin **70**(6), Suppl-156 (1999)
36. Van der Velden, D., et al.: Molecular tumor boards: current practice and future needs. Ann. Oncol. **28**(12), 3070–3075 (2017)
37. Zarin, D.A., et al.: The ClinicalTrials.gov results database: update and key issues. N. Engl. J. Med. **364**(9), 852–860 (2011)

ICT and Wellbeing

The Living-Lab Methodology for the Prevention of Falls in the Elderly

Jennifer N. C. Bassement[1](✉), Christine Selvez[1], Philippe Pudlo[2], Perrine D'Hont[1], and Fanny Blondiau[1]

[1] Living-Lab Label-Âge, Pôle de Gériatrie, Centre Hospitalier de Valenciennes, Valenciennes, France
bassement-j@ch-valenciennes.fr

[2] PRIMOH, Université Polytechniques des Hauts de France, Valenciennes, France

Abstract. The present work describes the initiative of the Centre Hospitalier de Valenciennes (CHV) and the Pôle de Recherche et Innovation en Mobilité et Handicap (PRIMOH) which create a joined Living-Lab for the prevention of falls in the elderly. Local authorities, social services and networks, companies, local associations, elderly structures, researchers, health practitioners and elderly people have started cooperating within the Living-Lab in order to propose new health protocol, new technologies, new methods to support the prevention of falls in the elderly population. This approach focuses on the real needs of the users, taking into account the experiences of each participant, professional or individual. Elderly people, physicians, nurses, helpers, services, experts discuss and share knowledge and feedbacks to improve the care associated with falling. The originality of the method is that users are involved from the very beginning of each project, they even decide which project the Living-Lab should carry out. The paper provides an overview of the methodology that was followed and describes the current projects centered on the reduction of fall in the elderly.

Keywords: Living-lab · Elderly · Prevention of fall

1 Introduction

Living-Labs have been described in the literature since 2006 and address a wide ranging variety of fields [1]. Various definitions can be found about Living-Lab but they mostly converge to a real world environment for research and innovation including end-users and stakeholders [2]. In the field of health, Living-Labs have been mainly used for testing new technologies and acceptability for the patients [3–5]. Only a few have other purposes such as education or specific training [6]. The method of Living-Lab has been documented and referenced in several books [7, 8].

In the field of fall prevention, many interventions have been tested and carried out to reduce the number of falls in the elderly. Results are sometimes found to be effective [9] and sometimes no proof can be shown for the reduction of the number of falls [10, 11]. To our knowledge, there is no study showing the use of Living-Lab methodology to

E. Pissaloux et al. (Eds.): IHAW 2021, CCIS 1538, pp. 173–178, 2021.
https://doi.org/10.1007/978-3-030-94209-0_14

design fall prevention programs, to improve the process of the diagnosis and treatment after falls or to encourage the elderly to participate in activities. We believe that including the elderly in projects aiming to keep them active, to reduce falls and use technologies that improve their quality of life may have a positive impact on their health and on their long-term involvement in the activities.

2 Living-Lab

Our Living-Lab is located in the city of Valenciennes in the Hauts-de-France region. It was funded over the first year by the Nord local council to develop innovative solutions for the mobility and the autonomy of senior citizens. It is now self-supported by the Centre Hospitalier de Valenciennes (CHV). The CHV has a large department of gerontology including residences with various levels of assistance and services, several health services such as a mobile geriatric team, day hospital and geriatric hospitalization unit, several type of geriatric consultations including cognitive impairment, oncogeriatrics, pre-surgery assessment etc. Therefore CHV geriatrics services is highly interested in improving the elderly people's care especially in the term of fall prevention, falls being one of the most common reasons for admissions and for dependency. The first partner of our Living Lab is PRIMOH which is a research group within the University Polytechnique Hauts-de-France with a main focus on developing innovation around mobility and disability. PRIMOH federates a large range of professionals including researchers, public and private health institutes, companies, local authorities and users.

Falling is a well-known issue throughout the world since global population is aging fast. Many scientific papers have been published on programs which aim at reducing the risk of falls. However in all of these the papers, the initiative comes from researchers, caregivers, health administration. It never comes from the elderly themselves. We have chosen to address the issue of falling from a different point of view, and we started by involving the elderly right at the beginning of the project. We think that if the elderly are actors of their own program and are personally involved in activities it may improves falls reduction and long term health.

Different phases are necessary to build a Living-Lab. The first one is to create a community of participants including stakeholders and users. The partners which have already joined the Living-Lab are: the teams of the CHV gerontology department, research laboratory (LAMIH UMR CNRS UPHF 8201), local geriatric networks, elderly residences, the regional network for autonomy (CLIC), local neighborhood association (Maison de Quartier), the Senior initiative of the city (Council of senior citizens), local associations for mobility as well as companies dealing with the development of technologies for seniors. The elderly are recruited within the partner residences, the associations and networks.

The second phase aims at organizing workshops with volunteers on the topic they feel concerned about and based on real-life issues. The purpose of the workshop is to set the participant in a creative and innovative environment. The collaboration between people with different backgrounds and experiences results in unexpected and interesting ideas. Involving the users and as many stakeholders as possible generates solutions with real possibilities of applications, taking in consideration the barriers, the life context, the needs and the expectations of the users.

The third phase consists in working on the ideas proposed by the community of users. That work includes organizing more workshops to select and define an idea and then discuss the possible actions and initiatives necessary for the implementation of this idea. It also includes broadening the spectrum of partners to reach out to more stakeholders and more end-users.

The Living-Lab currently encompasses those three phases. The upcoming phases will include the implementation of the selected ideas, testing and evaluating of the actions/initiatives and developing more projects.

3 Projects

The Living-Lab develops several axes within various project are emerging:

Axis 1 Fall Prevention
Axis 2 Technologies for senior citizens
Axis 3 Events for information, education and initiation
Axis 4 Local issues working group

3.1 Axe 1: Fall Prevention

Finding a way to progress and evolve in the field of fall prevention is at the core of the Living-Lab. Many publications demonstrate the effectiveness of interventions in laboratory settings. The idea is to transpose those interventions in real-life settings. We take into account the recommendations of the professionals and the needs, expectations and motivations of the elderly and we try to bridge the gap between what should be done theoretically and what is really done in daily life. We organize workshops twice a month with elderly people and with geriatric professionals to identify the issues, the barriers and the obstacles for the prevention of falls in order to work out ideas to improve prevention. As an example: one of the project developed in fall prevention was adapted physical activity. During the workshops, the seniors discussed about feeling a decrease in balance; being afraid of falling and willing to do something about it. Using the living-lab methodology, the seniors designed the program including walking and balance exercises but they suggested to use dance and social games. The performance were evaluated with clinical tests to acknowledge the progress. The covid 19 sanitary crisis interrupted the program and biased the tests results. However, an increasing number of seniors were taking part in the sessions and would enjoy pursuing the activity.

3.2 Axe 2: Technologies for Senior Citizens

This is the display of the Living-Lab: we can test and evaluate devices targeting seniors. We select the devices which seem interesting for improving their mobility and autonomy and we offer to test them within our community of users. Currently, four start-ups, centered on technologies for seniors are working with us on developing protocols for testing and evaluating their products (Fig. 1). Two types of assistive robots are being evaluated for their benefits in improving the cognitive and physical stimulation and improving social interaction in elderly. The cognitive stimulation with virtual reality is also being tested, the system is a capsule bringing additional inputs such as warmth cold and smell to the virtual experience. Finally, touch pads are used to propose computer experience to the elderly with social calls, games and internet search for information.

We also welcome start-ups and student projects to help them develop their products for seniors. Thanks to the close collaboration with the university (UPHF), the students can test their ideas in a real-life settings with feedbacks from real end-users. We organize demonstrations and initiations to technologies for seniors and caregivers every 3 months. If the technologies are accepted by the elderly and caregivers, the living-lab further develop the project either to evaluate the product or to evaluate the effects it has on users.

The projects of the living-lab offers innovative testing linked to research. The projects are set in real life which harden the data collection because it is not a controlled environment of a laboratory. Therefore, there is very few restriction for the inclusion of the population and the questionnaires and evaluations scales are extremely simplified to be quick and understood by everyone. The projects request a great deal of adaptations to stick to the rigor of research and fit in the real life environment.

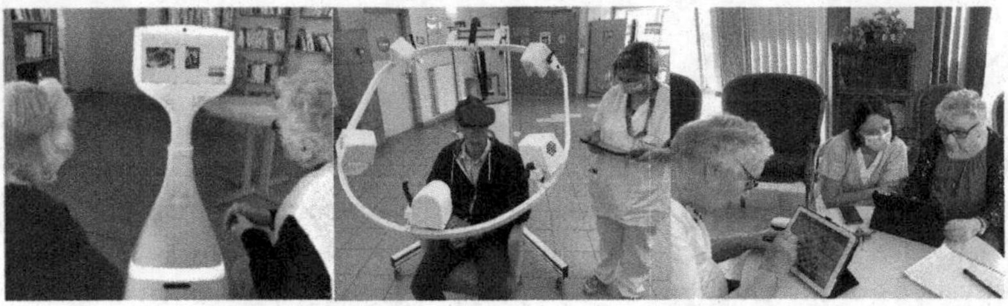

Fig. 1. Testing of technologies for seniors.

3.3 Axe 3: Event for Seniors

This is the "sharing" part of the Living-Lab, we offer the opportunity to try the innovations in real conditions, through events with demonstrations and initiations. Feedbacks and satisfaction questionnaires are collected after each event. For example, with the objective of mobility and autonomy, we are trying to keep the seniors active. An event is planned in the spring of 2022 to encourage the elderly to practice activities (Printemps de la Forme 2022). Conferences, workshops, initiations, activities, tests of technologies will be organized, according to the needs expressed by the elderly in the Living-Lab's workshops. Partners are associated for the organization of the event with the main objective of responding to the needs of the users. Others events are planned and will center on nutrition (Silver Fourchette) and inter-generational exchanges (Activités avec tes ainés).

3.4 Axe 4: Local Issues Working Group

This is the practical aspect of the Living-Lab. Research and innovation take time, several workshops and lots of background work are necessary to work out applicable solutions.

Several months are needed to fully develop an idea. Meanwhile, it is necessary for the elderly and for the caregivers to remain enthusiastic about joining the workshop. Being aware of the influence of their input on the evolution of the research, helps. Therefore, we organize monthly workshops to work out local issues. For example, in one of the residences, the library was closed for lack of users and staff to handle the book loan. The residents wish the library reopened and the workshops aim at preparing the re-opening and the management of that library. Other projects are planned such as re-thinking the organization of the animation of a residence and finding ways to reach out to isolated senior citizens.

All the project are ongoing, the Living-Lab has already organized over 50 workshops since its opening in September 2019.

4 Discussion

All the projects presented in this paper are currently running, therefore the results are not yet available, however the form of the results can still be discussed. The evaluations present challenges for several reasons: the health condition of the elderly is rapidly changing, and influences their participations and the results to the evaluations. The questionnaires and scales must be short and clear to keep them focused for the duration of the test. The data collection should fit the elderly capacities but should also remain meaningful for research purposes.

The Living Lab started on September 2nd 2019, it is thus relatively new. The initial funding ended after one year. However, the Living-Lab was able to continue its action by applying to other grants and finding partners to finance projects. The large amount of projects that have started and the number of partners who are interested in the Living-lab method are very encouraging for the long-term development of this Living-Lab.

The Living-Lab method already shows its efficiency in our projects regarding the amount of information gained in the workshops. It increases the collaboration between services and networks and it brings opportunities for education, formation and information to the participants. It allows the new services and technologies to reach a larger amount of people. It favors citizens' and professionals' involvement in projects, makes them leaders and actors of their health and it increases users' and stakeholders' satisfaction.

The motivation of the participants in the workshops shows the success of this Living-Lab. The workshops are organized according to the Living-Lab method: we create the environment and situations that favor creativity and innovation, we encourage the participation of anyone who feels concerned about the topic and is willing to share ideas. Together, they work on each other's ideas to complete and improve the propositions.

Specific attention is directed toward ethics and the protection of data. The results of the workshops belong to the participants throughout the community of the Living-Lab. The participants do not surrender their rights and intellectual property. They agree to share their ideas on behalf of the Living-Lab community and have access to the data that was generated.

Acknowledgments. The Living-Lab was funded the first year by the Hauts-de-France region: Projet Innovation AMI 2 Autonomie. We greatly acknowledge the partners for trusting us with launching the Living-Lab and for their participation in the workshops. Especially the residents of Fondation Duvant, the caregivers of La Rhonelle and EMIOG of the CHV who are highly enthusiastic and strongly support the workshops, demonstrations and events. Special thanks to Caroline Simon of UPHF for advices on the writing of this paper.

References

1. Schuurman, D., De Marez, L., Ballon, P.: Living labs: a systematic literature review. In: Open Living Lab Days 2015 (2015)
2. Følstad, A.: Living labs for innovation and development of information and communication technology: a literature review. Electron. J. Organ. Virtualness **10**, 99–131 (2008)
3. Swinkels, I.C.S., et al.: Lessons learned from a living lab on the broad adoption of eHealth in primary health care. J. Med. Internet Res. **20**(3), e83 (2018)
4. Liedtke, C., Welfens, M.J., Rohn, H., Nordmann, J.: LIVING LAB: user-driven innovation for sustainability. Int. J. Sustain. High. Educ. **13**(2), 106–118 (2012). https://doi.org/10.1108/14676371211211809
5. Vaziri, D.D., et al.: Exploring user experience and technology acceptance for a fall prevention system: results from a randomized clinical trial and a living lab. Eur. Rev. Aging Phys. Activity **13**(1), 6 (2016)
6. Blain, H., et al.: Living lab falls-MACVIA-LR: the falls prevention initiative of the European innovation partnership on active and healthy ageing (EIP on AHA) in Languedoc-Roussillon. Eur. Geriatr. Med. **5**(6), 416–425 (2014)
7. Dubé, P., Sarrailh, J., Billebaud, C., Grillet, C., Zingraff, V., Kostecki, I.: Le livre blanc des Living Labs. Montréal InVivo, UMVELT, 1st edn. (2014)
8. Stahlbrost, A., Holst, M.: The Living Lab Methodology Handbook. Plan Sju Kommunikation AB, Sweden (2012)
9. Gates, S., Fisher, J.D., Cooke, M.W., Carter, Y.H., Lamb, S.E.: Multifactorial assessment and targeted intervention for preventing falls and injuries among older people in community and emergency care settings: systematic review and meta-analysis. BMJ **336**(7636), 130–133 (2008)
10. Coussement, J., De Paepe, L., Schwendimann, R., Denhaerynck, K., Dejaeger, E., Milisen, K.: Interventions for preventing falls in acute-and chronic-care hospitals: a systematic review and meta-analysis. J. Am. Geriatr. Soc. **56**(1), 29–36 (2008)
11. Salminen, M., Vahlberg, T., Kivelä, S.L.: The long-term effect of a multifactorial fall prevention programme on the incidence of falls requiring medical treatment. Public Health **123**(12), 809–813 (2009)

Tackling the Sustainability of Digital Aging Innovations Through Design Thinking and Systems Thinking Perspectives

Mexhid Ferati[1](✉), Marco Bertoni[2], Fisnik Dalipi[1], Arianit Kurti[1], Päivi Jokela[1], Peter Anderberg[3,4], and Anita Mirijamdotter[1]

[1] Department of Informatics, Linnaeus University, Växjö & Kalmar, Sweden
{mexhid.ferati,fisnik.dalipi,arianit.kurti,paivi.jokela, anita.mirijamdotter}@lnu.se

[2] Mechanical Engineering Department, Blekinge Institute of Technology, Karlskrona, Sweden
marco.bertoni@bth.se

[3] Department of Health, Blekinge Institute of Technology, Karlskrona, Sweden
peter.anderberg@bth.se, peter.anderberg@his.se

[4] School of Health Sciences, University of Skövde, Skövde, Sweden

Abstract. The digitalization of society brings many opportunities and challenges, especially on how we organize the welfare society in the future. This becomes especially pertinent as we are heading toward a global increase of older people, which will strain healthcare and bring the challenge of building sustainable solutions. In this paper, we argue that the unsustainable solutions within healthcare are due to them being defined and 'solved' with a single approach or approaches used in silos. We advocate that a more sustainable solution could be achieved by combining systems thinking and design thinking perspectives throughout the entire process – from problem definition to solution offering. A benefit of such combined perspectives is the ability to develop a shared context among all stakeholders, which helps uncover unique tacit knowledge from their experience. This will serve as a solid foundation to generate unconventional ideas that will lead to sustainable and satisfactory solutions.

Keywords: Systems thinking · Design thinking · Healthcare · Sustainability

1 Introduction and Background

The ongoing evolution from an industrial to digital society leads to radical changes in the way we offer and organize the welfare society. In these settings, technological developments are converging with the demographic changes, thus we are heading toward a global increase of older people and vast technological innovation trends [1].

The average global life expectancy has increased by more than five years in the last two decades, according to the World Health Organization (WHO) [2]. Sweden has the highest life expectancy, 81 years for men and 84 for women [3]. It is estimated that by 2060, the life expectancy will increase by at least five years for both genders, meaning

E. Pissaloux et al. (Eds.): IHAW 2021, CCIS 1538, pp. 179–184, 2021.
https://doi.org/10.1007/978-3-030-94209-0_15

that one in four inhabitants will be 65 or older [4]. In addition, according to WHO, 15% of the entire world population [4] lives with some disability, which will increase the total number of people needing care in the future. Furthermore, Sweden's Social Service Act encourages older people and those with disabilities to live independent lives in their own homes, which puts a strain on healthcare [3].

Digitalization leads to profound changes in how we consider older adults as patients, citizens, and consumers. Digitalization is a process that creates new models and concepts that lead to new services and new ways of delivering services. It is characterized by digitizing already in use or new artifacts integrated into healthcare and daily life. For the aging population, this will lead to new opportunities but also new challenges. The ability to leverage the adoption rate of these technologies is to understand how older people are using (or not using) the digital tools today, the potentials and pitfalls in future development as well as how they can proactively participate in the design and innovation of digital tools and services they will be using. Especially since the older population is increasingly becoming adept at internet use [5].

Evidence shows, however, that despite investments done in using digital solutions in healthcare, relatively few solutions have been efficiently implemented into the welfare practices so far [6]. Most solutions within healthcare fail to progress and impact the real-life environment; they remain within the academic and research environment as a proof-of-concept [11, 12]. The sustainable adoption of interactive e-health technologies is a complex matter that must consider the healthcare sector's entire value chain, together with the well-being of the patient and the feasibility of the proposed technology [1]. This requires a holistic understanding of the context, actors involved, and understanding human needs and system requirements. To gain such understanding, in this paper, we argue that a combination of the Design Thinking (DT) and Systems Thinking (ST) approaches is a way forward for sustainable adoption. By applying such a combined perspective, we can research the broader implication of the innovation (through the means of ST) as well as their novelty and ease of use (through the means of DT) within the healthcare sector.

2 Current Challenges within Healthcare

A crucial challenge within healthcare is to constantly improve and maintain the health and well-being of older people by using interactive technologies mainly because the relation between the care of the older people and interactive technologies is linked to another challenge, which is how to influence this community to adopt innovation [7].

One of the main reasons for the lack of the adoption of digital technologies is the inability to consider the innovation from a holistic perspective and to account for its short- and long-term consequences for different stakeholders in the healthcare sector [8]. This challenge requires active users and stakeholders to map, analyze, and enhance the user experience with interactive technologies focusing on welfare, accessibility, and adoption. This is a matter of designing rewarding, multifaceted user experiences, which consider how a solution is used and how it is communicated, delivered, supported, and followed up.

Another challenge is how to manage the healthcare system (e.g., through governance models) to increase the efficiency of care and reduce inequity. The management of e-health systems plays a crucial role in their sustainable adoption and operation. The sustainable management of healthcare systems requires that we monitor and evaluate specific technologies' performance while ensuring that the implementation of technologies will also support the entire e-health system and lead to desired effects [9]. This presents a challenge since an efficient system should improve collaboration, alignment of work activities, and interoperability of different co-operating systems, thus ensuring the most prudent use of the limited human and technological resources [10].

3 The Need for Systems Thinking and Design Thinking

The described challenges indicate that the healthcare and well-being sector is a complex, diverse, and heterogeneous socio-technical system consisting of various stakeholders and technologies, numerous interactions between them, and different powers between stakeholders. Such a complex system is open, i.e., it interacts with its environment and responds to external changes. The diversity and versatility of a complex, open system are essential for system adaptability, but they also increase the system's uncertainty and interactions with the environment. Considering that an open system does not have an established equilibrium, new connections can continuously emerge. Moreover, the effects of the interactions are unpredictable, and can be non-linear. Therefore, small internal or external changes can lead to significant outcomes, or vice versa [10, 11].

Systems Thinking (ST) is a particular way of treating and approaching such complex situations. Based on foundational features of ST highlighted by [12], we can identify three generic imperatives of ST in practice: *understanding inter-relationships* (the holistic 'thinking'), *engaging with numerous perspectives* (joined-up thinking 'practice'), and *reflecting on boundary judgments* (thinking in practice). With ST in mind, managers, practitioners, and designers explore how the functionality of a system performs in wholeness and not how the parts perform independently. Furthermore, ST focuses very much on stakeholders and their interactions to gain a rich understanding of the context.

In combination with ST, we also need the Design Thinking (DT) perspective, which is defined as a human-centered approach to innovation that integrates people's needs with the potential of technology [13]. DT helps to understand the needs and redefine problems to identify alternative possibilities that might not be instantly apparent with our initial level of understanding, thus bringing novelty and innovation potential. Using DT, a researcher is encouraged to challenge the current context and assumptions by continuously extending the limits of what might be possible [14]. ST offers the ability to dissolve complex issues from a systemic worldview, whereas DT helps in looking at complex issues from various angles and perspectives.

4 Using ST and DT to Address Identified Challenges

Considering the complementing strengths of ST and DT, their combination could help in several aspects, such as (1) identifying relevant stakeholders and developing a shared context among them; (2) making better sense of the problems being addressed; (3) fostering a unique idea generation process; and (4) designing sustainable solutions.

4.1 Identifying Relevant Stakeholders and Developing a Shared Context

Within DT, stakeholders are typically observed by the researchers. Their needs and abilities are carefully studied along with the context where they conduct their activities. The researchers typically try to include a broad spectrum of stakeholders to gain a multiple angle understanding. Included stakeholders, however, are typically studied and observed separately, and the collected data is analyzed in parts [14]. This causes a struggle to see the interrelation and interdependence among stakeholders [13].

Another crucial and often forgotten aspect is the power balance among various stakeholders in the healthcare domain. Not all stakeholders carry the same power. For instance, there are often power imbalances between older care recipients and care professionals. Moreover, nurses could have the best knowledge in the day-to-day activities; however, they do not have the decision capacity that typically someone at a political and management level with a budget power has. Such disbalance needs to be handled appropriately in the design and development process by recognizing and leveraging the qualities and powers of all stakeholders involved.

At this point, ST facilitates researchers to combine the knowledge from all stakeholders and develop a shared context among them. This shared context should reside with the researcher and should be propagated further to all stakeholders to help them understand each stakeholder's role within the system. This is important, considering that stakeholders are also regarded as designers within the DT approach, and if they are going to develop ideas and designs, they should have access to all knowledge.

4.2 Making Sense of the 'Problem'

The main benefit related to the combination of ST and DT is that designing digital solutions in healthcare must deal with inherently 'wicked' problems. It is very seldom the case when the problem is apparent, and the solution is merely available through applying rules or technical knowledge. Creating a solution that fits in a more profound situational or social sense is often a complex task, and the 'problem' is often not understood until a solution (even preliminary) is developed and tested. Systems analysis lacks the ability for clear problem identification, but instead, DT, by implementing a fast-paced cycle of idea generation, prototyping, and evaluation, supports a process where problems are discovered through the iterative assessment and testing of solutions [15].

DT is a powerful tool when it comes to approaching a real problem from different perspectives to solve it most effectively. What makes DT suitable to be used in combination with ST is its highly non-linear and recursive process and the fact that this is intended to be initiated already in the fuzzy front-end of the innovation process. The intent is to support designers in 'failing sooner' to succeed sooner, by plotting several alternative courses of action, testing them, learning from failure, and iterating.

4.3 Fostering a Unique Idea Generation Process

A significant reason to combine ST and DT shall be found in the ability of the latter to stimulate a rather unconventional style of reasoning, which is abductive thinking. The underlying assumption for abductive thinking endeavors is that one cannot find a solution to problems with the similar thinking mindset that created them; the solution does not derive from the problem. Instead, designers shall constantly rethink and reconsider theory conjectures and transform them into opportunities.

As highlighted by Vianna et al. [16], human beings are design thinkers by nature, mainly because abductive thinking allows for the evolution of artifacts in our civilization: from primitive civilizations to vernacular design and traditional craftsmanship. The ability to foster this ancestral idea-generation process makes DT particularly useful to 'think outside the box' when generating solutions. Looking at how the problem is 'explored,' one also notices how DT differs from ST (or rather complements it) by adopting an abductive mental process. The questions posed by a DT team are not defined 'a priori' (i.e., being taken from a standard protocol) but rather formulated 'on the fly' (i.e., they differ for each interaction) using information gathered from the observation of the context pervading the problem.

4.4 Designing Sustainable Solutions

Ultimately, for a solution to be sustainable, it should be acceptable by its stakeholders. While ST helps in the identification of stakeholders in the broader sense, DT ensures their proper involvement in the design process of a solution. This contributes to stakeholders tolerating initial design flaws by helping them take ownership and consequently diminish resistance towards the emerging solution [17]. Also, the participatory design approach and rapid prototyping using agile development principles could help focus on value creation for the end-users [18]. These prototypes should be specially tailored to the specificities of the user contexts and their health and well-being. The aging population involved in these efforts will not be considered an end-user but rather a partner and co-designer in the project. The application of DT methods and tools helps mitigate the challenges that the aging population faces when adopting innovation and learn more about the expectations and requirements from the different solution stakeholders. While the ST approach tackles the interactions among the stakeholders through a holistic viewpoint, the DT brings problem restructuration to the solution space by considering these interactions to reach a sustainable innovation.

5 Conclusion

In this paper, we proposed a combination of Systems Thinking and Design Thinking perspectives to tackle current challenges within healthcare. As a complex and open socio-technical system, healthcare is characterized by high uncertainties due to unpredictable and non-linear development, which a creative and iterative design approach should address. We argued that the unsustainable solutions within healthcare are due to them being defined and 'solved' with a single approach or approaches used in silos. We advocate that a more sustainable solution could be achieved by combining and simultaneously using the Systems Thinking and Design Thinking approaches throughout the entire process – from problem definition to solution offering. This will establish a solid foundation for generating relevant and sometimes unconventional ideas that will lead to sustainable and satisfactory solutions.

References

1. Anderberg, P.: Gerontechnology, digitalization, and the silver economy. XRDS: Crossroads, The ACM Magazine for Students (2020)
2. World Health Organization. https://www.who.int/news/item/19-05-2016-life-expectancy-increased-by-5-years-since-2000-but-health-inequalities-persist. Accessed 27 Sept 2021
3. Elderly Care in Sweden. https://sweden.se/life/society/elderly-care-in-sweden. Accessed 27 Sept 2021
4. European Commission. https://ec.europa.eu/info/business-economy-euro/economy-finance-and-euro-publications_en. Accessed 27 Sept 2021
5. Anderberg, P., Skär, L., Abrahamsson, L., Berglund, J.S.: Older people's use and nonuse of the internet in Sweden. Int. J. Environ. Res. Public Health (2020). https://doi.org/10.3390/ijerph17239050
6. Van Velthoven, M.H., Cordon, C.: Sustainable adoption of digital health innovations: perspectives from a stakeholder workshop. J. Med. Internet Res. **21**(3), 1–8 (2019)
7. Hoque, R., Sorwar, G.: Understanding factors influencing the adoption of mHealth by the elderly: an extension of the UTAUT model. Int. J. Med. Inform. **101**, 75–84 (2017)
8. Melkas, H.: Effective gerontechnology use in elderly care work: from potholes to innovation opportunities. In: Kohlbacher, F., Herstatt, C. (eds.) The Silver Market Phenomenon, pp. 435–449. Springer, Heidelberg (2011). https://doi.org/10.1007/978-3-642-14338-0_32
9. Iqbal, S., Jokela, P.: Innovative approaches in health care: observational study of an elderly care unit in Japan. In: International Conference on Business, Technology & Innovation, Kosovo (2019)
10. Pekkarinen, S., Melkas, H., Hyypiä, M.: Elderly care and digital services: toward a sustainable sociotechnical transition. In: Toivonen, M., Saari, E. (eds.) Human-Centered Digitalization and Services. TSS, vol. 19, pp. 259–284. Springer, Singapore (2019). https://doi.org/10.1007/978-981-13-7725-9_14
11. Peters, D.H.: The application of systems thinking in health: why use systems thinking? Health Res. Policy Syst. **12**(1), 1–6 (2014)
12. Midgley, G.: Systems thinking for evaluation. In: Systems Concepts in Evaluation: An Expert Anthology, pp 11–34. EdgePress, Point Reyes (2007)
13. Brown, T.: Design thinking. Harv. Bus. Rev. **86**(6), 84 (2008)
14. Pourdehnad, J., Wexler, E.R., Wilson, D.V.: Integrating systems thinking and design thinking. Syst. Thinker **22**(9), 2–6 (2011)
15. Buchanan, R.: Systems thinking and design thinking: the search for principles in the world we are making. She Ji: J. Des. Econ. Innov. **5**(2), 85–104 (2019)
16. Vianna, M., Vianna, Y., Adler, I.K., Lucena, B., Russo, B.: Design Thinking. MJV Press, Rio de Janeiro (2012)
17. Rehm, R.: People in Charge: Creating Self Managing Workplaces. Hawthorn Press (1999)
18. Ferati, M., Babar, A., Carine, K., Hamidi, A., Mörtberg, C.: Participatory design approach to internet of things: co-designing a smart shower for and with people with disabilities. In: Antona, M., Stephanidis, C. (eds.) UAHCI 2018. LNCS, vol. 10908, pp. 246–261. Springer, Cham (2018). https://doi.org/10.1007/978-3-319-92052-8_19

Using Force-Feedback Haptic Effects to Develop Serious and Entertainment Games Accessible for Visually Impaired People

Simon L. Gay[1(✉)], Ngoc-Tan Truong[2], Katerine Romeo[2], and Edwige Pissaloux[2]

[1] LCIS, University of Grenoble Alpes, Grenoble, France
simon.gay@univ-grenoble-alpes.fr
[2] LITIS, University of Rouen Normandy, Mont-Saint-Aignan, France

Abstract. Nowadays, serious and entertainment games are developed with the latest technologies for sound and graphical content. However, they are often not accessible to Visually Impaired People (VIP) as they frequently are based on a visual interface. This paper proposes to overcome this limitation via the implementation of the force-feedback principle. The Force-feedback Tablet (F2T) is designed as a 2D actuated support with a mobile thumbstick mounted on it. F2T allows the exploration of a tactile environment with original haptic force feedback applied on the finger. Based on the advantages of these effects, F2T is used to create different 2D interactive environments such as paintings, maps, text and especially to develop unique gameplay elements, which may be combined with spatialized audio cues. As a result, this paper proposes to explore possibilities offered by a new force-feedback based device to develop serious and entertainment games accessible to VIP.

Keywords: Haptic · Tactile perception · Force feedback · Games · Visually impaired people

1 Introduction

In our current digital society, 2D and 3D e-data are becoming increasingly ubiquitous in culture and education. Accessing such information is difficult for Visually Impaired People (VIP) as it mainly relies on graphical content or image data without readily accessible textual descriptions with a screen reader.

Many electronic touch-stimulating devices have been developed to convey refreshable tactile information. However, most of these devices have some serious drawbacks, impeding their large scale adoption by VIP [1], for example

Research supported by the ANR, the FIRAH, the CCAH, the Normandy Region, the University of Normandy, NORMAStic/CNRS FR3638, and the Handicap Space of University of Rouen Normandy.

E. Pissaloux et al. (Eds.): IHAW 2021, CCIS 1538, pp. 185–197, 2021.
https://doi.org/10.1007/978-3-030-94209-0_16

their prohibitive cost [2], the lack of technological maturity (e.g. [3,4]), or the lack of efficient stimuli for tactile communication (e.g. [5,6]). To overcome some of those limitations, we propose the Force Feedback Tablet (F2T), an original force-feedback based haptic device which uses force-feedback effects to easily communicate digital and graphical content to VIP [7]. The F2T design is easily scalable, making possible to develop devices that can be attached to screens of different sizes (such as tablets or smartphones) and to explore the content of an image displayed on a screen.

The F2T control software uses a set of images containing different tactile properties that are used to control the force feedback on the device, allowing different kinds of mechanical resistance which are applied to end-user's finger/forearm.

Moreover, F2T can generate haptic and kinesthetic effects allowing interactive applications that can be exploited for serious and entertainment games. They are useful for serious and entertainment games. The domain of video games becomes to be an increasingly important part of cultural and educational development, but it is still difficult for VIP to access as it mainly relies on vision.

Several audio games were proposed for ludic (e.g. [8–10]) or educative [11] purposes for VIP, but they provide a limited experience of the environment. To increase the experience of the environment and raise the space awareness important especially for VIP autonomous mobility, several haptic and force feedback devices such as joysticks, robotic arms or haptic gloves, were proposed for serious and entertainment games. However, their high prices and specialized uses limit them for professional training serious games; general public devices only propose simple haptic effects such as gamepad vibrations [5].

Through a set of demonstration environments, this paper proposes the new methods to use the F2T tactile and kinesthetic effects for gameplay elements in serious and entertainment games. The use of F2T original haptic and kinesthetic effects can also provide new sensorial channels to sighted users and improve their experience of the virtual environment. Through some applications, the possibility to use the kinesthetic effects of the F2T is demonstrated for learning and motor rehabilitation.

The paper is organized as follows: Sect. 2 presents the tablet F2T. Section 3 presents different potential usages of the F2T to support serious and entertainment games. Section 4 presents the planned experiments. Finally, Sect. 5 recalls the main research contributions and offers some future development perspectives.

2 F2T: A Force Feedback Tablet

2.1 Related Works

Force feedback devices aim to simulate physical properties of virtual objects by applying a kinesthetic feedback to the user. This feedback can simulate virtual objects and their tactile properties. Nowadays, some applications of force feedback devices are available on the market (aiming video games, 3D design and virtual reality training,...). These devices are made for 3D exploration of virtual objects and often take the form of robotic arms, 3D mice or gloves which make them cumbersome, expensive and unpractical for 2D data access. Several solutions are proposed to develop haptic screens based on this principle.

Solis et *al.* proposed a 2D system using a 2 degrees-of-freedom arms integrated to a desktop which allow interacting with screen's content [12]. Besides, many 2D haptic systems use a pantograph architecture [13,14]. The arm's position is determined by measuring motor angles. Each system requires a high backdrivability to manipulate easily the devices' arms. This backdrivability implies no reduction gears and high-torque motors. The position is estimated using encoders on motor axes, requiring the end effector to move to get the user's intentions. This approach limits the possibilities of interactions with the user. Moreover, this device cannot provide a consistent maximum force and velocity on the usable surface, and the complex control model is necessary to move arms properly. Generally, the specific pantograph arms architecture makes these devices bulky for a limited available surface. It cannot be considered as an alternative for a portable system used by the VIP. Saga and Raska proposed a 2D version of the SPIDAR architecture, that consist of a mobile element moved by actuated pulleys and tensed wires [15]. Despite being less cumbersome than pantographs, this architecture requires at least four motors and still requires measuring movement from the user, limiting the interaction possibilities of the device.

Consequently, we present a novel force feedback architecture, named F2T, which provides edge and texture effects, high interactive capabilities, and a high resolution dynamic display of 2D data in Sect. 2.2.

2.2 F2T Principle

The Force Feedback Tablet (F2T) uses the force feedback principle to convey haptic and kinesthetic information deduced from images [16]. A prototype implementing F2T architecture is shown in Fig. 1. The F2T consists of a 2D frame with a mobile support actuated through two orthogonal motorized axes, allowing the support to be moved on the X and Y axes. The thumbstick is controlled in speed to follow user's movements, while measuring the user's intended movement independently from the actual movement of the support. Two encoders measure the thumbstick position in the frame (Fig. 2a). According to the current position of the thumbstick, the device gets haptic properties at the same position from images, and it generates offsets in the motion control to induce force feedback simulating haptic effects from image extracted property, while the user explores the surface (Fig. 2a & b). The already implemented haptic effects are presented in Sect. 2.3.

2.3 Haptic Effects

We implement and test a set of five haptic effects that can be used to represent elements displayed of a surface. They are: friction, edge and relief, flow, rail, and

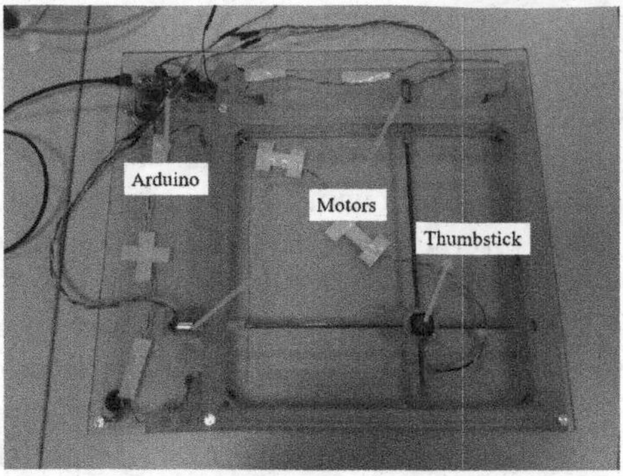

Fig. 1. Prototype of the F2T. The thumbstick is actuated with two high-torque electric gearmotors, and its position is obtained using magnetic encoders mounted on the motor's axes

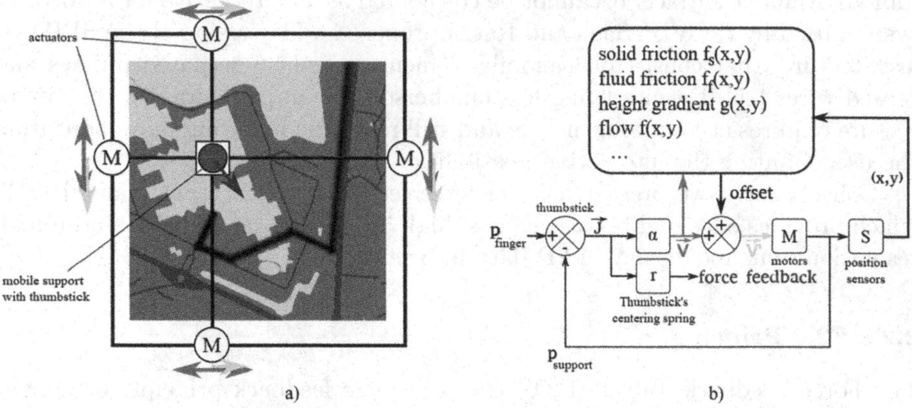

Fig. 2. a) Thumbstick position on an image (here, a map), b) The haptic properties at the current position are obtained from the image to add offsets in the motion control.

attractors. The design of the F2T also allows building a guiding system, which can move the user's finger through a predefined path.

- ***Friction*** effect reduces the finger's speed according to friction coefficients. Solid and fluid friction can be simulated to represent rough or viscous areas (Fig. 3a-b).
- ***Edge and relief*** effects represent object's edges and height variations (Fig. 3c). When the slope of the object's edge is small, the user's finger will be either slowed down or accelerated depending on the direction of the image gradient. This effect can be used to explore a bas-relief or to guide the users along a trench, maintaining their finger on a path. Besides, when the gradient is strong enough, the movement will stop. In that case, the user's finger can slide along the object's edge which makes that the user easily recognizes the object's shape. This effect also allows representing walls separating areas.

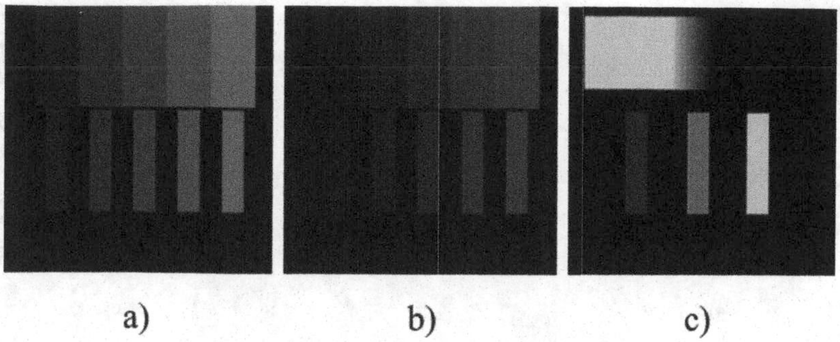

Fig. 3. Examples of color-coded representations of the haptic effects are used to simulate image properties. a) fluid friction, b) solid friction, c) elevation (Color figure online)

- ***Flow effect*** adds an offset to the finger's movement. The offset value and direction can be defined at each point of the surface. It is thus possible to represent dynamic environments with mobile parts (e.g. vehicles or conveyors) or dynamic physic elements (e.g. wind, water flow) as shown in Fig. 4a.
- ***The rail*** is an effect with no equivalent in the real natural world (Fig. 4b). This effect is based on a vector field defining a predefined direction in each point, reducing the component of the movement that is perpendicular to the direction defined at the current touched point. Therefore, movements following the direction are not modified while movements in other direction will be more or less slowed down (depending on the direction and the norm of the vector).
- ***Attractors*** are areas or points generating an attractive or repulsive force on the user's finger (Fig. 4c). The force strength, profile, and range can be predefined for each attractor. This effect can be used to simulate magnetic paths, holes, bumps, or even gravity fields.

These different effects are cumulative and can be combined to simulate complex haptic properties.

The force feedback principle also allows a guiding system to move the user's finger through a predefined path. This specific mode guides the user through the surface to help understanding its spatial structure.

The current F2T software also allows generating spatialized and contextual sounds. The sounds can be localized around the user's position, and they can be enabled when moving over a predefined area or by fulfilling predefined conditions. The localized sound sources use the open 3D sound library OpenAL [17] to modify sound properties according to the relative position of the user.

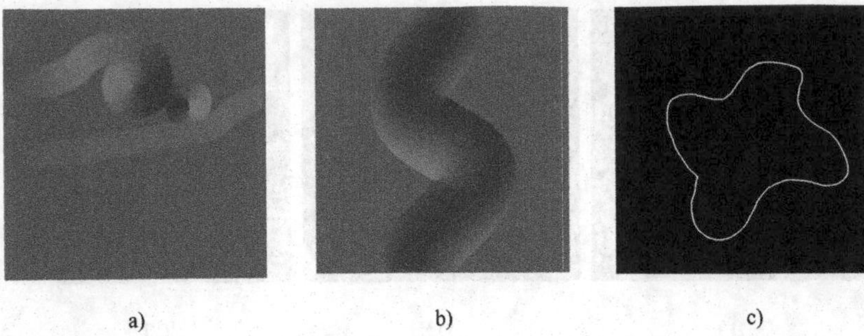

Fig. 4. a) and b) images encoding vector fields that can be used for flow and rail effects, c) attractor image

3 Development of Serious and Entertainment Games for VIP

Based on the F2T's effects, we can define the elements to develop serious and entertainment game for VIP. They are: environment description (in Sect. 3.1), gameplay effects (in Sect. 3.2), localized and contextualized sounds (in Sect. 3.3), guiding system (in Sect. 3.4), multi-player interactions (in Sect. 3.5) and examples of applications and environments (in Sect. 3.6).

3.1 Environment Description

The visual experience is fundamental for shaping space awareness [1] and mobility experience; therefore the design of the environment allows acquiring such fundamental knowledge.

The different haptic effects can be combined to represent an environment that can be explored through touch and sound.

The edge effects can be used to set walls and non-flat surfaces, and thus to model indoor and outdoor environmental structures. This effect can also be used to dig a 'trench' keeping the user's finger in the center of a path to help following it (e.g. for rehabilitation purposes).

The friction effects allow setting surfaces of different nature to differentiate areas, and to use these properties in gameplay mechanisms: fluid friction can slow the user down when moving in viscous areas or deep water. Solid friction can indicate cluttered areas, the lower speed simulating the difficulties for the user to move in such areas.

3.2 Gameplay Effects

Gameplay effects are based on the active effects of the F2T: flow, rail, and attractors. They can be integrated to define the dynamic properties of the environment.

Flow effect can be used to define dynamic properties of the environment, such as water flow of a river or strong wind, or mobile parts of elements, such as vehicles or conveyors. This effect can be enhanced by using appropriate sounds to help identifying the mobile elements intuitively.

Rail effect helps the user to keep its direction and orientation, or on the contrary, be used as an invisible force pulling away the user of its objective.

The F2T also provides distance effects through attractors. These elements generate an attractive or repulsive force within a predefined range of distance. Such elements can be used as obstacles or traps that can be detected from a distance using this force. An attractor with a long-range and weak force can also help the user to localize an element in the environment through the direction and intensity of the force that it generates.

Moreover, the actuation of the mobile support also allows directly modifying the movements and behaviors of the thumbstick. Modifying the thumbstick movements makes it possible to simulate physical properties of the controlled avatar, such as its mass, aerodynamics, and inertia. It can also modify the avatar speed, such as slowing it down when manipulating or carrying a heavy object, or to simulate tiredness or wounds, and increasing the avatar speed when using a vehicle or specific equipment.

3.3 Localized and Contextualized Sounds

Sound is one of the important elements to understand the environmental context and object's location around VIP. Therefore, the F2T software uses localized and contextualized sounds to develop audio-haptic applications. The specific sound can help to identify elements perceived through haptic effect by providing an audio context. Localized sounds are punctual sound sources placed in the environment; they allow the creation of an immersive sound environment. Contextualized sounds are background sounds that are played when entering a predefined area of the surface, that helps the users to localize themselves or to change the ambiance at certain points of the game.

3.4 Guiding System

The guiding system can be used as a narrative tool when combining with synchronized audio-description, which presents the story and the spatial organization of the environment. It can also be used to define automatic movements generated by the environment. Automatic movements can be exploited in different ways for games and gameplay mechanisms:

- Set the actual position of the player when changing area, in the case of a fixed-screen game. In this kind of game, the player moves in a fixed area that changes when the player reaches a border of the screen. The player's position is updated to match with the new area. This mechanism allows the development of multi-screen games and avoiding positioning problems.

- Game-conducted movements, such as teleportation, or physical effects (e.g. jumping and falling).
- Proprioceptive effects added to the player's movements (e.g. vibrations).

3.5 Multi-player Interactions: Collaborative or Competitive Haptic Games

A multiplayer game (Fig. 5) allows building an individual network. This can help VIP to improve social interaction capacity. To do that, the F2T actuation offers original features for multi-player games as the position and movement of the thumbstick are known for each player. It is possible to set a shared motion control on multi-devices, allowing players to manipulate their thumbstick as if they manipulate the same object. This feature allows new possibilities for collaborative haptic games.

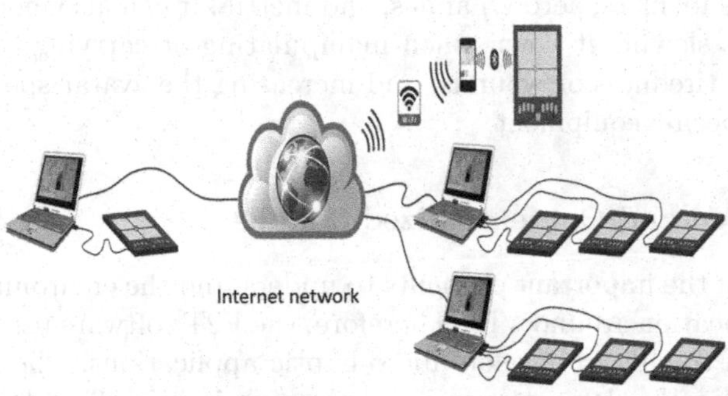

Fig. 5. Multi-player system through local or internet network. A single computer can control multiple F2T devices, making multiple player to interact with the same environment in local multiplayer games, in a similar way than a game console with multiple connected gamepads. A local or internet network enables online games.

3.6 Applications and Environments of Serious and Entertainment Games

After presenting the important elements to develop a serious and entertainment game for VIP, this section proposes demonstration interactive environments to illustrate the possibilities of the F2T: a maze, a trapped area, and an adventure game panel environment.

In the *maze* environment (Fig. 6), walls are encoded using the edge effect. The walls cannot be crossed. Instead, the thumbstick of the F2T can slide along the walls, allowing the user to discover and explore the structure of the maze. The user can freely (or in guided mode) explore the maze, using the position of their finger from the tablet's corners to localize themselves.

Fig. 6. Maze environment. Green areas are walls that cannot be crossed. It is however possible to slide along these walls to explore the maze. The blue line indicates the movements of the thumbstick over the explorable surface of the F2T. (Color figure online)

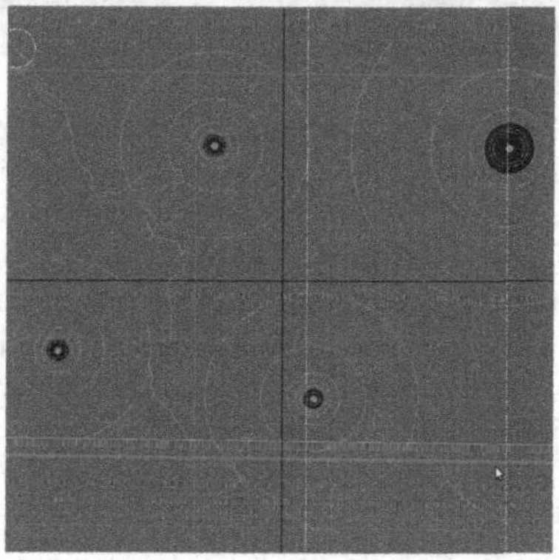

Fig. 7. Trapped environment. The punctual attractors and their influence areas are displayed as concentric circles. The blue discs indicate the areas where the attraction force is too strong to move away (event horizon). The cyan line (thumbstick movements) shows how the points attract the finger. The player has to quickly react before it is too late. (Color figure online)

The *trapped environment* (Fig. 7) is an area covered with attractor points with different range areas and attraction profiles. However, the attraction force is defined such that below a certain distance to a point (event horizon), the attraction force is strong enough to capture the player. The player's aim is thus to find its way to cross the surface without falling into a trap, by feeling the attraction force before it becomes strong.

The adventure game panel (Fig. 8) represents a subsection of the global map of a top-view fixed-screen display adventure game, where the players can move from one subsection to the other by walking to the boundaries of the current one, like the first "The Legend of Zelda" game. This subsection represents a path crossing the area from West to East, with a crossroad leading to the south. These paths are encoded using the rail effect, helping the players to orientate themselves. On the north, a river is represented with fluid friction simulating the avatar moving in water. On the south, a forest is represented with solid friction, indicating that it is difficult to move in these areas. Tree trunks are modelized with edge discs, constituting obstacles of the forest. Localized sounds of rivers and birds help the players to orientate and identify the surrounding elements.

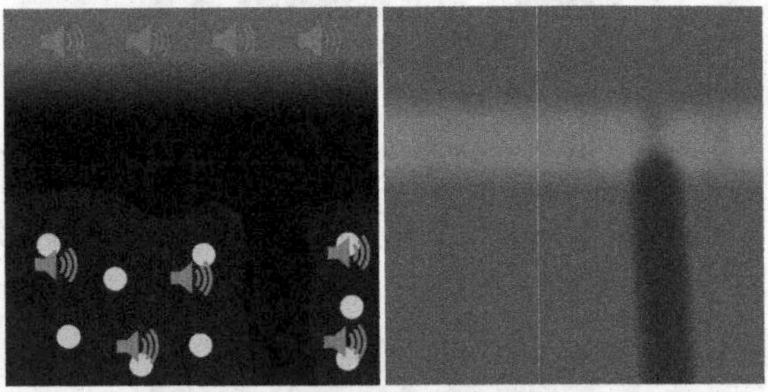

Fig. 8. Adventure game panel, with a path and an intersection, a river in the north, and a forest environment in the south. Left image encodes haptic properties: red encodes fluid friction, with higher friction while the river becomes deeper, blue encodes solid friction to simulate the difficulties of moving in a forest environment, and green encodes edges of tree trunks. Right image encodes rails of the paths, making them easier to follow. Each pixel encodes the rail direction through red and green channels' values. River and forest localized sounds are added to help the player to spatialize and identify the surrounding environment. (Color figure online)

We also propose *an educational/rehabilitation example* application based on handwriting. This application uses the F2T guidance and interactive functionalities to help the users drawing shapes (e.g. letters). Such an application can help children to facilitate handwriting and reading learning (e.g. assistance to children with dyslexia). Moreover, it can help in successful motor rehabilitation and to relearn synchronizing arm movements (Fig. 9). This application uses three effects:

- Guiding mode to indicate the drawing movement,
- Rail effect to partially guide the user while drawing the letter,
- Edges variations and conditional sounds to let the users draw the letter by themselves while indicating them when the finger is moving away far from the true drawing.

In these applications, we use the thumbstick cap to play. However, the thumbstick cap can be easily replaced by other interface elements, such as a stylus with the tip attached to the pin of the thumbstick. Such stylus can be used for educational and/or motor rehabilitation applications, or for applications requiring a

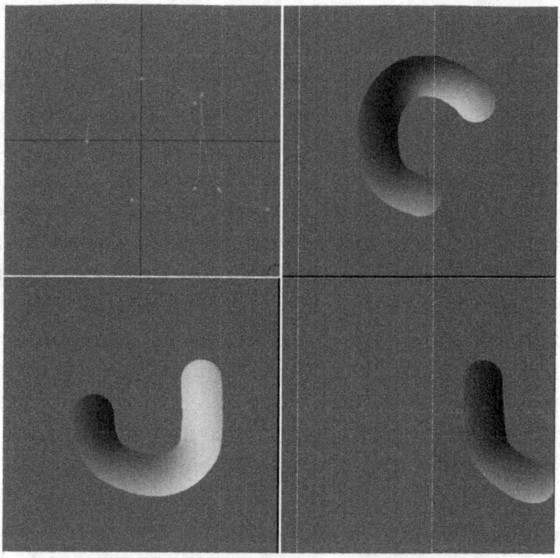

Fig. 9. Top left image shows the path used by the guiding system to draw the letter 'a'. The three other images encode the rails that are successively loaded while the users are drawing with their finger. The rails image are successively loaded to constrain their movements to match with the correct movements.

high precision. After introducing the applications of serious and entertainment games for VIP, Sect. 4 presents the planning of experiments to validate these applications.

4 Planning of Experiments

To obtain feedback from the users trying a video game, some experiments are planned. The goal of these experiments is to verify the impact of haptic perception in the tested environment. The evaluation is done with semi-structured questionnaire to check for global satisfaction and the added value for the following points:

- learning gestures,
- quality of haptic simulation of the environment,
- quality of realistic perception of the environment,
- contribution of haptic and kinesthetic effects,
- gaming experience.

The experiments are intended to be inclusive so the tests will be done with persons visually impaired or not. The questionnaire will be the same for everybody.

5 Conclusion

The F2T is an inexpensive and versatile device for general e-data accessibility. This versatility could facilitate the dissemination of the device to VIP as well as sighted public, and then allow the development of game applications.

The haptic effects produced by the F2T make it possible to perceive virtual environments through sensory channels, that are not used in traditional video games. Haptic and kinesthetic channels make these virtual environments accessible to VIP, and enhance the experience of these environments for sighted people. Moreover, the kinesthetic effects also bring valuable help in learning environments for training motor and cognitive rehabilitation.

It is possible to give an insight on how to move in a given environment. One can imagine applications in scenography and choreography. Moreover, one can learn drawing gestures and acquire experience and speed practicing on F2T.

In future work, we will improve the game engine of the F2T software to add mobile elements, similar to sprites in visual games, to make it possible to use mobile elements and non-playable characters in the games. We also intend to develop interfaces with the existing popular game engines to facilitate the development of games. All the proposed games will be tested with visually impaired participants.

References

1. Gori, M., Cappagli, G., Tonelli, A., Baud-Bovy, G., Finocchietti, S.: Devices for visually impaired people: high technological devices with low user acceptance and no adaptability for children. Neurosci. Biobehav. Rev. **69**, 79–88 (2016)
2. Prescher, D., Borschein, J., Khlmann, W., Weber, G.: Touching graphical applications: bimanual tactile interaction on the HyperBraille pin-matrix display. Univ. Access Inf. Soc. **1**(19), 391–409 (2017). https://doi.org/10.1007/s10209-017-0538-8
3. Phung, H., et al.: Interactive haptic display based on soft actuator and soft sensor. In: IEEE/RSJ International Conference on Intelligent Robots and Systems (IROS), pp. 886–891 (2017)
4. Velázquez, R., Pissaloux, E.E., Hafez, M., Szewczyk, J.: Tactile rendering with shape memory alloy pin-matrix. IEEE Trans. Instrum. Measur. **57**(5), 1051–1057 (2008)
5. Amberg, M., Giraud, F., Semail, B., Olivo, P., Casiez, G., Roussel, N.: STIMTAC, a tactile input device with programmable friction. In: 24th ACM Symposium on User Interface Software and Technology, pp. 7–8 (2011)
6. Bernard, F.: Conception, fabrication et caractérisation d'une dalle haptique base de micro-actionneurs piézoélectriques. Ph.D. University of Grenoble (2016)
7. Gay, S., Rivière, M.-A., Pissaloux, E.: Towards haptic surface devices with force feedback for visually impaired people. In: Miesenberger, K., Kouroupetroglou, G. (eds.) ICCHP 2018. LNCS, vol. 10897, pp. 258–266. Springer, Cham (2018). https://doi.org/10.1007/978-3-319-94274-2_36
8. audiogames.net. http://www.audiogames.net/. Accessed Jan 2020
9. A Blind Legend. http://www.ablindlegend.com/. Accessed Jan 2020

10. Smith, B.A., Nayar, S.K.: The RAD: making racing games equivalently accessible to people who are blind. In: ACM Conference on Human Factors in Computing Systems (CHI) (2018)
11. Allain, K., et al.: An audio game for training navigation skills of blind children. In: IEEE 2nd VR Workshop on Sonic Interactions for Virtual Environments, pp. 1–4 (2015)
12. Solis, J., Marcheschi, S., Portillo, O., Raspolli, M., Avizzano, C.A., Bergamasco, M.: The haptic destop: a novel 2D multimodal device. In: 13th IEEE International Workshop on Robot and Human Interactive Communication, pp. 521–526 (2004)
13. Campion, G., Wang, Q., Hayward, V.: The pantograph MkII: a haptic instrument. In: 2005 IEEE/RSJ International Conference on Intelligent Robots and Systems, IROS, pp. 723–728 (2005)
14. Martinez, M.O., Campion, J., Gholami, T., Rittikaidachar, M.K., Barron, A.C., Okamura, A.M.: Open source, modular, customizable, 3-D printed kinesthetic haptic devices. In: 2017 IEEE World Haptics Conference, WHC 2017, pp. 142–147 (2017)
15. Saga, S., Raskar, R.: Simultaneous geometry and texture display based on lateral force for touchscreen. In: World Haptics Conference (WHC), pp. 437–442 (2013)
16. Gay, S., Pissaloux, E., Romeo, K., Truong, N.T.: F2T: a novel force-feedback haptic architecture delivering 2D data to visually impaired people. IEEE Access, 1–11. https://doi.org/10.1109/ACCESS.2021.3091441. Print ISSN 2169–3536, Online ISSN 2169–3536
17. OpenAL. https://www.openal.org/. Accessed Jan 2020

A Rehabilitation Wearable Device to Overcome Post-stroke Learned Non-use. Methodology, Design and Usability

J. De la Torre Costa[1,2](✉), B. R. Ballester[1], and P. F. M. J. Verschure[1,3]

[1] Laboratory of Synthetic, Perceptive, Emotive and Cognitive Systems (SPECS, IBEC), Barcelona, Spain
paul.verschure@upf.edu

[2] Universitat Pompeu Fabra (UPF), Barcelona, Spain

[3] Institució Catalana de Recerca i Estudis Avançats (ICREA), Barcelona, Spain

Abstract. After a stroke, a great number of patients experience persistent motor impairments such as hemiparesis or weakness in one entire side of the body. As a result, the lack of use of the paretic limb might be one of the main contributors to functional loss after clinical discharge. We aim to reverse this cycle by promoting the use of the paretic limb during activities of daily living (ADLs). To do so, we describe the key components of a system composed of a wearable bracelet (i.e., a smartwatch) and a mobile phone, designed to bring a set of neurorehabilitation principles that promote acquisition, retention and generalization of skills to the home of the patient. A fundamental question is whether the loss in motor function derived from learned–non–use may emerge as a consequence of decision–making processes for motor optimization. Our system is based on well-established rehabilitation strategies that aim to reverse this behaviour by increasing the reward associated with action execution and implicitly reducing the expected cost of using the paretic limb, following the notion of reinforcement–induced movement therapy (RIMT). Here we validate an accelerometer-based measure of arm use and its capacity to discriminate different activities that require increasing movement of the arm. The usability and acceptance of the device as a rehabilitation tool is tested using a battery of self–reported and objective measurements obtained from acute/subacute patients and healthy controls. We believe that an extension of these technologies will allow for the deployment of unsupervised rehabilitation paradigms during and beyond hospitalization time.

Keywords: Stroke · Wearables · Learned non-use · Hemiparesis · ADLs

1 Introduction

Stroke is currently the third cause of death and the main cause of adult disability worldwide. The massive health cost associated, especially under the scope of a global financial crisis, and recent research on post-stroke recovery dynamics, calls for the need for new strategies that can extend and reduce the charge of rehabilitation approaches [1]. The

E. Pissaloux et al. (Eds.): IHAW 2021, CCIS 1538, pp. 198–205, 2021.
https://doi.org/10.1007/978-3-030-94209-0_17

dramatic loss of neural tissue following a stroke leaves up to 70% of patients experiencing persistent cognitive and motor impairments, such as hemiparesis [2, 3]. Importantly, some patients seem to show a substantial decline in function after six months [4]. Several studies suggest that this deterioration might be driven by a lack of use of the paretic limb at home despite residual capabilities, which results in a long–term cycle of ceased neural representation, and thus, a loss of motor function, known as learned non–use (LNU) [5]. LNU might emerge as a consequence of decision–making processes for motor optimization [6] dependent on factors determining hand selection, such as the expected cost and the probability of success of using either effector (i.e., paretic or non-paretic limb). Han proposed a functional model in an attempt to understand the relationship between use and function (i.e., recovery) after stroke [7, 8]. A key prediction from the model was that if spontaneous recovery, or training, or both, bring performance beyond a certain threshold, the repeated spontaneous use of the arm instantiates a virtuous cycle in the form of motor learning that promotes performance and future spontaneous use.

Building on this basis, different strategies have tried to overcome LNU by promoting the use of the paretic limb during Activities of Daily Living (ADLs). For instance, Constrained–Induced Movement Therapy (CIMT) proposes to restrict the use of the patient's less affected arm by impairing its movement (e.g., by using a mitt) [9]. On the other hand, recent approaches such as Reinforcement–Induced Movement Therapy (RIMT) aim to invert the strategy by decreasing the *expected cost* and increasing the *probability of success* of using the paretic effector [10], which brings reduced demands and inconveniences for the patient, offering positive reinforcement. Despite the promising results, these treatments are still limited to short intervention sessions, and the generalization to the performance during ADLs is yet poorly understood. Although conventional rehabilitation strategies (i.e., Occupational Therapy) aim to embed recovery into ADLs, it often results in the acquisition of compensatory strategies to gain independence. Given this situation, reviews on the outcomes of conventional therapy are discouraging, suggesting that recovery outcomes five years post-stroke resemble those after two months [11]. However, recent interventions that capitalize on neurorehabilitation principles [12] show that patients are still sensitive to treatment beyond one year [13]. In this context, we could consider post-stroke recovery a re-learning process in which the enhanced spontaneous biological recovery that follows the lesion [14] might be helped by activating experience-dependent plasticity mechanisms to promote the neural representation of behaviours that enhance the functionality and independence of the patient. Limited resources, together with a poor understanding of recovery dynamics, call for the need for 1) continuation of therapy at home and 2) longitudinal monitoring that can take place beyond healthcare facilities.

The application of wearable devices to the rehabilitation field offers several advantages to these ends. Their design allows for a personalized gamified intervention and the deployment of frequent and spaced delivery of multimodal feedback during the performance of ADLs, which may facilitate the shift of attention towards the affected limb, thus biasing the effector selection to the weaker arm. Previous results suggest that monitoring the amount of arm use and providing knowledge of progress promotes the integration of the paretic limb in the performance of ADLs [15]. This effect might emerge by increasing the value of using the paretic effector and permitting the patient to set implicit goals. However, those approaches are not suitable for real-world environments (e.g., patients using it at home regularly), as they rely on bi– or tri–axial [16] accelerometer–derived measurements to obtain a robust assessment of upper–extremity activity. Here, we argue that these strategies are unsuitable for an effective deployment at the home of patients and present results from a system based solely on a smartwatch, including a personal phone to present positive reinforcement, embedding recovery into ADLs. To do so, we infer the body activity that was gathered using additional sensors [15, 16] using a novel approach that takes into consideration a normalized account of the steps recordings. Moreover, our approach relies on commercial wearable solutions in opposition to specialized accelerometry sensors which are costly for general use (Table 1).

Table 1. Comparison of system features with Price's review [16] on stroke arm monitoring, previous [15] and current work.

	Price et al. 2014	Ballester et al. 2015	De la Torre et al
Minimal requirements	2 Wrist 1 hip (N = 3) 2 Wrist (N = 2)	2 Wrist (tri-axial)	1 Wrist (tri-axial)
Time/day	4–60 h	10–19 h	10 h
Storage	2–15 s epochs	60 s epochs	6 s epochs
Sampling	~32 Hz	50 Hz	50–100 Hz

2 Methods

2.1 Equipment

The wearable Rehabilitation Gaming System (RGS–Wear) is a wearable system for the continuous monitoring and reinforcement of arm use in hemiparetic stroke patients. The components of the system are a smartwatch (i.e., Fossil Gen 5) and a smartphone (i.e., Android personal phone of the patient). Data recordings are sent through Bluetooth to the paired smartphone, which communicates with a dedicated SQL database via Wi-Fi. The watch is worn in the paretic limb. The accelerometer and gyroscope data are sampled at 100 Hz for each directional component (x, y, z).

2.2 Measurements

The system provides two different kinds of measurements: 1) Arm Use Evaluation: a longitudinal behavioural indicator on paretic limb's *use* during ADLs, allowing to provide feedback to the patient and set personalized goals (i.e., treatment). 2) Exercise for Arm Function Evaluation. to assess the degree of motor *function* along different recovery stages (i.e., monitoring), supposed to correlate with clinical scales [17].

Arm Use: To extract a meaningful quantification on the isolated use of the arm, we compute the mean squared sum of the acceleration over a six-seconds window.

$$\beta = \sqrt{a_x^2 + a_y^2 + a_z^2}$$

$$\alpha = \beta - \delta$$

$$AU = \frac{\sum_0^N a_n}{N} \quad (1)$$

Arm Use (AU) calculation from accelerometer recordings.

In Eq. 1, β represents a rough proxy of the amount of movement of the paretic limb. As this movement might be partially attributed to confounding causes (e.g., whole–body movements, swing, walking), it requires some corrections. Thus, δ represents a proxy of the whole body activity (i.e., not attributed to the functional movement of the arm) extracted from the steps and normalized after a calibration for each individual. N represents the number of recordings per log, stored 24/7 every two minutes. We transform Arm Use (AU) data into Arm Points (APs) to provide a comprehensive measure to the patient. To do so, the transformation works as follows:

$$APcost_{initial} = \frac{\sum_n^N AU_i}{k}$$

$$if \sum AU_{count} > AP_{cost} : AP{+}= 1, AU_{count} = 0 \quad (2)$$

Arm Use is transformed into Arm Points to provide a comprehensible metric to the patient.

Where $APcost_{initial}$ represents the amount of Arm Use to score one Arm Point and is updated depending on user's performance. AU_{count} represents the amount of AU up to that timestamp and is restarted each time the user achieves an AP.

Exercise: Based on [17], we implemented a *circle drawing* exercise that the patients must complete every two days. The exercise consists of six horizontal and six vertical circles, three clockwise and three anti-clockwise in each block. The rationale behind this activity is to obtain an assessment of motor function that can predict clinical scores (i.e., Fugl Meyer Assessment of Motor Recovery for upper limb). The exercise takes a total of two minutes on average. We use the magnetometer and gyroscope data to correct for potential sensor drifts.

Feedback: The RGS–Wear provides hourly feedback on Arm Points (Eq. 2) and steps as a percentage of the same time interval during the previous day. This information is shown accompanied by haptic stimulation. The patient also has access to the history of APs and steps in the smartphone interface of the app.

2.3 Participants

For the validation of the accelerometer-based measurement of AU, we recruited eight right-handed volunteers without neurological impairments (5 males, 3 females, mean age $= 30 \pm 8.25$). To explore the usability of the system in stroke population, we recruited four stroke patients (three from the rehabilitation department of Hospital Sant Joan de Déu, one from INA Memory Center, Barcelona; 2 males, 2 females, mean age $= 64 \pm 10.13$) with mild–to–moderate upper limb hemiparesis and absence of any major cognitive impairment. All the participants signed informed consent.

Validation and Usability: To test the capacity of the system to isolate arm activity, we instructed participants to perform a battery of ADLs. Each activity was performed for five minutes, with resting periods of two minutes in between. Participants had to perform each activity twice: 1) wearing the smartwatch on the Dominant (D) Arm 2) wearing the smartwatch on the Non–Dominant (ND) arm. Bimanual execution was encouraged. We divided the battery of proposed ADLs depending on their level of demand: **1) Low**. Using phone and laptop, **2) Med**. Brushing teeth and dishes **3) High.** Organizing shelves and brooming. We expected to distinguish between these levels based on our AU measure. Moreover, we expected to see a low AU during walking due to the subtraction of body activity from Eq. 1. Otherwise, measurements during walking, without actively using the arm, would resemble high–intensity activity scores.

To assess the usability of the device in stroke population, we designed a user-experience battery to quantify the degree of independence of patients when interacting with the system (i.e., wearing the watch, navigating the app, understanding graphs…). The UX consisted of 10 statements that were reported using a 5–point Likert Scale, ranging from Strongly Disagree to Strongly Agree.

3 Results

We found a significant difference ($p = 0.0002$) in AU between low– ($\mu = 0.46$u, std $= 0.32$) and med–intensity ADLs ($\mu = 1.15$u, std $= 0.33$). This difference was also significant ($p < 0.01$) between med– and high– ($\mu = 1.62$u, std $= 0.4$) intensity activities. Importantly, the AU registered while walking ($\mu = 0.73$u, std $= 0.18$) was significantly lower than med– ($p < 0.05$) and high–intensity ($p < 0.01$) ADLs. The system was able to detect D vs. ND-Arm differences in the high–intensity activities such as *Brooming* (D Arm $\mu = 1.68$, std $= 0.17$, ND Arm $\mu = 1.077$, std $= 0.23$ $p < 0.05$) or *Organizing Shelves* (D Arm $\mu = 2.1$, std $= 0.18$, ND Arm $\mu = 1.64$, std $= 0.39$ $p < 0.05$). We suspect that a higher sample would have allowed reporting significant differences in all the ADLs battery, as the rest of the activities follow this trend. We used mannwhytney-u tests (Fig. 1).

Overall, the patients' ratings were above 3 (neutral), suggesting that the design was generally accepted. We noticed that the ratings that refer to the interaction with the hardware (i.e., navigating or opening the app in the watch) were notably lower. However, the system was specifically designed so that patients' don't need to access the watch except for exercise performance. We thus believe that the system will still be effective in encouraging and monitoring Arm Use during ADLs in patients that are not familiar with digital technologies in future interventions.

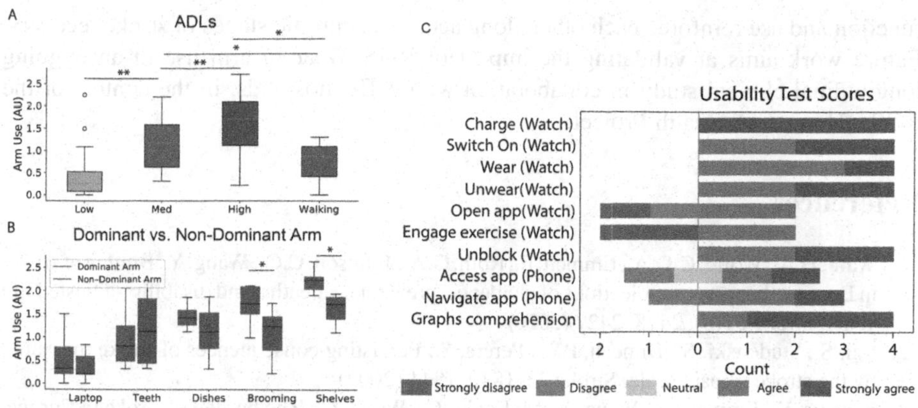

Fig. 1. Left. A. Arm Use in different ADLs classified depending on the level of demand. B. Differences in AU between the Dominant and Non-Dominant Arm in the most demanding ADLs. Right. C. Usability Questionnaire results for the 10 items regarding patients' perceived difficulty when using the RGS-Wear system. Responses range from 1 (Strongly disagree) to 5 (Strongly agree).

4 Conclusion and Discussion

In previous studies, we have shown that frequent exposure to direct feedback about Arm Use promotes the incorporation of the parctic limb into activities of daily living in stroke population [15]. However, this approach was limited by the need of using two simultaneous bracelets and phone measures during the recording time. As we aim to record the use of the arm during ADLs through long periods of time (i.e., chronic stages), the solution should be as noninvasive as possible. This is important given the fact that patients might struggle with the formation of new habits and feel overwhelmed with the introduction of new technologies [19]. Thus, the optimal strategy should include just one smartwatch for the recording of activity, and not depend on recordings of the phone, which they might not carry the whole time (e.g., leaving it at the table, sofa, etc.). Here, we show how the use of a unique smartwatch can provide with specific information on the use of the arm during different ADLs, which opens the way for the integration of these interventions beyond healthcare facilities. Based on a grounded computational model of motor recovery [7, 10], we suspect that hand selection in the performance of ADLs might be modulated by two parameters: 1) expected success and 2) cost of using either effector. Through our system, we can integrate adaptive difficulty theory knowledge to boost the use of the paretic effector in two ways: 1) providing *explicit* goals and feedback (i.e., positive reinforcement) to the and 2) *implicitly* adapting the cost of achieving these goals by modulating specific parameters to provide an optimal level of challenge [18], which might promote user's adherence and, in turn, functional recovery.

The adoption of wearable–based approaches might help us to provide an innocuous alternative of Reinforcement–Induced Movement Therapies that is naturally implanted in patients' life. Moreover, the continuous monitoring of a behavioural indicator (i.e., Arm Use as a case of study) might help us to empirically test the hypothesis whether function and use reinforce each other along acute and chronic stages of stroke recovery. Future work aims at validating the impact of RGS–Wear in arm use in an ongoing longitudinal clinical study in collaboration with 3 EU hospitals, in the context of the RGS@Home EIT Health Project.

References

1. Wafa, H.A., Wolfe, C.D.A., Emmett, E., Roth, G.A., Johnson, C.O., Wang, Y.: Burden of stroke in Europe: thirty-year projections of incidence, prevalence, deaths, and disability-adjusted life years. Stroke **51**(8), 2418–2427 (2020)
2. Lai, S., Studenski, S., Duncan, P.W., Perera, S.: Persisting consequences of stroke measured by the stroke impact scale. Stroke **33**, 1840–1844 (2002)
3. Stevens, E., Emmett, E., Wang, Y., McKevitt, C., Wolfe, C.: The burden of stroke in Europe, vol. 53, no. 9 (2017)
4. Uswatte, G., Taub, E.: Implications of the learned non-use formulation for measuring rehabilitation outcomes: lessons from constraint-induced movement therapy. Rehabil. Psychol. **50**(1), 34–42 (2005)
5. Lai, S.M., Studenski, S., Duncan, P.W., Perera, S.: Persisting consequences of stroke measured by the stroke impact scale. Stroke **33**(7), 1840–1844 (2002)
6. Wolpert, D.M., Landy, M.S.: Motor control is decision-making. Curr. Opin. Neurobiol. **22**(6), 996–1003 (2012)
7. Han, C.E., Arbib, M.A., Schweighofer, N.: Stroke rehabilitation reaches a threshold. **4**(8) (2008)
8. Hidaka, Y., Han, C.E., Wolf, S.L., Winstein, C.J., Schweighofer, N.: Use it and improve it or lose it: interactions between arm function and use in humans post-stroke, **8**(2) (2012)
9. Miltner, W.H.R., Bauder, H., Sommer, M., Psych, D., Dettmers, C., Taub, E.: Patients with chronic motor deficits after stroke. Clin. Psychol. 586–592 (1999)
10. Ballester, B.R., et al.: Counteracting learned non-use in chronic stroke patients with reinforcement-induced movement therapy. J. Neuroeng. Rehabil. 1–15 (2016)
11. Meyer, S., et al.: Functional and motor outcome 5 years after stroke is equivalent to outcome at 2 months: follow-up of the collaborative evaluation of rehabilitation in stroke across Europe. Stroke **46**(6), 1613–1619 (2015)
12. Maier, M., Ballester, B.R., Verschure, P.F.M.J.: Principles of neurorehabilitation after stroke based on motor learning and brain plasticity mechanisms. Front. Syst. Neurosci. **13**(December), 1–18 (2019)
13. Rubio, B.B., et al.: A critical time window for recovery extends beyond one-year post-stroke. J. Neurophysiol. (2019)
14. Pekna, M., Pekny, M., Nilsson, M.: Modulation of neural plasticity as a basis for stroke rehabilitation. Stroke **43**(10), 2819–2828 (2012)
15. Ballester, B.R., Lathe, A., Duarte, E., Duff, A., Verschure, P.F.M.J.: A wearable bracelet device for promoting arm use in stroke patients. In: NEUROTECHNIX 2015 - Proceedings of 3rd International Congress Neurotechnology, Electronics Informatics, no. August 2017, pp. 24–31 (2015)
16. Noorkõiv, M., Rodgers, H., Price, C.I.: Accelerometer measurement of upper extremity movement after stroke: a systematic review of clinical studies. J. Neuroeng. Rehabil. **11**(1), 144 (2014)
17. Krabben, T., Molier, B.I., Houwink, A., Prange, G.B.: Circle drawing as evaluative movement task in stroke rehabilitation: an explorative study. J. Neuroeng. Rehabil. **15**(March), 1–11 (2011)

18. Ahmed, S.: Theory of sustained optimal challenge in teaching and learning. In: Proceedings Human Factors and Ergonomics Society Annual Meeting, vol. 2017-Octob, pp. 407–411 (2017)
19. Hughes, A.M., et al.: Translation of evidence-based assistive technologies into stroke rehabilitation: users' perceptions of the barriers and opportunities. BMC Health Serv. Res. **14**(1) (2014). https://doi.org/10.1186/1472-6963-14-124

What Are IBD Patients Talking About on Twitter?

Maya Stemmer(✉), Yisrael Parmet, and Gilad Ravid

Ben-Gurion University of the Negev, P.O.B. 653, 8410501 Beer-Sheva, Israel
mayast@post.bgu.ac.il

Abstract. In recent years, social networking sites and online communities have served as alternate information sources for patients, who use social media to share health and treatment information, learn from each other's experiences, and provide social support. This research aimed to investigate what patients with Inflammatory Bowel Disease (IBD) are talking about on Twitter and to learn from the experimental knowledge of living with the disease they share online. We collected tweets of 337 IBD patients who openly tweeted about their disease on Twitter and used the Natural Language Understanding (NLU) module by IBM Cloud to apply category classification and keywords extraction to their tweets. To evaluate the results, we suggested a method for sampling the general population of Twitter users and forming a control group. We found statistically significant differences between the thematic segmentations of the patients and those of random Twitter users. We identified keywords that patients frequently use in the contexts of health, fitness, or nutrition, and obtained their sentiment. The results of the research suggest that the personal information shared by IBD patients on Twitter can be used to understand better the disease and how it affects patients' lives. By leveraging posts describing patients' daily activities and how they influence their wellbeing, we can derive complementary knowledge about the disease that is based on the wisdom of the crowd.

Keywords: Thematic analysis · Inflammatory Bowel Disease (IBD) · Twitter · Natural Language Understanding (NLU) · Sentiment analysis

1 Introduction

1.1 Overview

In recent years, social networking sites and online communities have served as alternate information sources for patients. Patients everywhere use social media to share health and treatment information, learn from each other's experiences, and provide social support. Particularly chronically ill patients, who use online environments to support daily self-management, exchange experiential knowledge about their disease that extends far beyond medical care. Mining these informative conversations may shed some light on patients' ways of life and support the research of chronic conditions.

E. Pissaloux et al. (Eds.): IHAW 2021, CCIS 1538, pp. 206–220, 2021.
https://doi.org/10.1007/978-3-030-94209-0_18

Inflammatory Bowel Disease (IBD) is a chronic condition that affects patients' lives daily. IBD patients are forced to adhere to strict dietary regimes and maintain a calm routine. Changes in nutrition or physical activity, currently tested by trial and error, result in a long and excruciating process for the patients [1–4]. By collecting and analyzing patients' data on social media, we can learn from their personal experience and support existing medical knowledge regarding the disease.

This research aimed to investigate what patients with IBD are talking about on Twitter and to learn from the experimental knowledge of living with the disease they share online. We wished to identify lifestyle-related treatments IBD patients endure to maintain their disease and to determine their sentiments towards them. We collected and analyzed tweets by IBD patients in the purpose of identifying lifestyle-related keywords and their influence on the patients.

We used Twitter API to collect tweets of 337 IBD patients who openly tweeted about their disease on Twitter. Using the Natural Language Understanding (NLU) module by IBM Cloud [5] we applied category classification to the tweets and identified themes discussed by IBD patients on Twitter. To account for the general Twitter population, we compiled a control group of random Twitter users and compared their thematic segmentation with the one of the IBD patients. Our analysis showed statistically significant differences between the thematic segmentations of two groups: while IBD patients talked more about health, fitness, and nutrition in comparison to the general population, the latter increased to refer politics and society.

Based on the thematic segmentation, we derived a collection of patients' tweets related to health, fitness, or nutrition, and investigated the index terms they contained. We used the keywords extraction feature of the NLU module to extract keywords from the tweets and calculate their sentiments within the text. We performed several text cleaning procedures to refine the extracted keywords and obtained the aggregated sentiment of each keyword. Visualizing the keywords and their mean sentiment with word-clouds showed that patients' sentiment turned more negative when they talked about their disease.

To adhere to ethical norms and maintain user privacy, we only publish aggregated results that do not reveal the specific users. The examples containing direct quotes from tweets are presented in this research after obtaining informed consent from their authors.

The study suggests that the personal information shared by IBD patients on Twitter can be used to understand better the disease and how it affects patients' lives. By applying text mining and statistics to patients' tweets, we can learn about the different treatments they try and identify helpful treatments. For example, one might expect that sentiment towards a relaxing activity like yoga will be positive, while sentiment towards alcohol, which can irritate the stomach, will be negative. Therefore, findings from such research can provide complementary knowledge about the disease that is based on the wisdom of the crowd.

1.2 Related Work

Twitter and Health. Twitter is a powerful tool for disseminating health-related information and an accessible platform for patients in need of immediate social support or relief [6]. Health-related tweets range from a simple toothache to more severe and chronic diseases such as diabetes, asthma, or cancer [7–9]. Even a sensitive disease like the Human Immunodeficiency Virus (HIV) is being discussed on Twitter [10–13]. Communication patterns regarding who tweets about what and why vary by disease [7].

During the past years, text mining and social network analysis have been used to detect mentions of health on Twitter [13, 14] or to track the spread of the covid-19 pandemic and its symptoms [15, 16]. Regarding chronic conditions, previous research has focused on analyzing patients' tweets and uncovering their Twitter community [17–19]. While relatively large amount of research was dedicated to diabetes or cancer, research regarding IBD is only just starting to consolidate.

Inflammatory Bowel Disease and Its Social Implications. Inflammatory Bowel Disease (IBD) is a chronic inflammation condition of the digestive system characterized by flares and remission states. The two primary diseases identified with IBD, Crohn's Disease (CD) and Ulcerative Colitis (UC), are usually diagnosed in young patients (in the age range of 15–30 years). The incidences of IBD are rapidly increasing, and it has evolved into a global disease [20–23].

There are no medications or surgical procedures that can cure IBD. Treatment options can only help with symptoms, and they affect each patient differently. They involve not only prescription drugs but also lifestyle change solutions, such as diets and therapies. Symptoms include abdominal pain, diarrhea, and fatigue; severe cases may result in hospitalization or surgical interventions [4, 24]. As chronic bowel diseases, both CD and UC require a day-to-day care of drug consumption and special nutrition.

Patients describe IBD as an embarrassing disease, which causes immediate disruption of daily activities. They experience difficulties adjusting to the changes it entails and consider themselves different from their peers. Since IBD is identified with frequent bowel movements, people do not hasten to share their disease with others [1–4]. According to IBD patients, part of the embarrassment can be attributed to a lack of public awareness. Outsiders cannot see that a person's stomach hurts or that his bowels are scarred. The disease is invisible, and others might doubt that it exists [25, 26].

Twitter and IBD. Exploring the entities that engage in IBD-related discussions on Twitter reveals that IBD patients are the most common type of users who talk about IBD on Twitter [27, 28]. IBD patients use Twitter for sharing personal experiences and for seeking social support. They exchange thoughts about symptoms and medications and recommend treatments to one another [29]. By sharing their disease on Twitter, patients fight disease invisibility and raise public awareness about IBD [30].

The embarrassment caused by IBD and the need to confide in people who undergo similar experiences help explain the creation of IBD-related communities on Twitter. By overcoming space and distance, Twitter users form a community that disregards physical boundaries or immobility. The sense of common ground can help break down barriers and enable conversation, increasing a person's willingness to share [31, 32]. It may be is easier to consult other patients who can relate and better understand the situation based on personal experience. One can identify more closely with users' stories like herself and embrace their advice more easily [33]. When people disclose health information on Twitter, they expose themselves to a large variety of opinions and reduce uncertainty about their disease [34].

Studying the social structure of different chronic patients on Twitter reveals that IBD patients tend to be more emotional and negative than other patients [35]. A topic analysis of tweets posted by IBD patients shows that patients usually express a negative sentiment when they talk about the disease and its symptoms but address more positively the diets and drugs that help maintain them [36]. Analyzing the sentiment of tweets posted by UC patients shows a strong correlation between the frequency of support tweets and overall positive sentiment tweets. Patients who provide and receive social support are more likely to post positive tweets [37].

2 Methods

2.1 Data Collection and Preparation

Patients' Group. In previous research [38], aiming to identify patients with IBD on Twitter, we identified 337 IBD patients, who publicly declared their disease on Twitter in a tweet written in English. On November 12th, 2020, we used Twitter Search API to collect the Twitter timelines of those patients. The Search API allows one to collect up to 3,200 of a user's latest tweets. If the user has less than 3,200 tweets, one may collect their full timeline using the API, but if the user tweets frequently and has more than 3,200 tweets, one may only collect their latest. We wanted to investigate the original content shared by patients, so excluded retweets (RTs) from the search. The process resulted in a collection of 628,301 tweets by IBD patients, sporadically written since the creation of Twitter in 2006.

To enable further analysis of the tweets, we cleaned their text by removing all screen-names (identified by the @ character) and URLs and turning all text to lowercase. We chose not to omit emojis, special characters or punctuation, since they were valuable for sentiment analysis. Examples of the cleaning process can be found in Table 1.

The purpose of the analysis was to understand what IBD patients are talking about on Twitter, to identify the lifestyle-related treatments they endure to maintain their disease and to determine the patients' sentiments towards them. We chose to use the Natural Language Understanding (NLU) module by IBM Cloud [5] to apply category classification and keywords extraction to the clean tweets. After text cleaning, 78,140 (12.4%) of the tweets contained less than three words and were therefore too short for language processing. The remaining dataset of 550,161 longer tweets was given as input to the NLU module for category classification.

Control Group. To evaluate the results, we wished to form a control group of Twitter users that will enable to compare the results of the patients with those of the general Twitter population. Since demographic data are not available on Twitter, we used Twitter's Sampled Stream API to collect a group of random users to account for the general population.

Twitter's Sampled Stream API streams about 1% of all tweets in real time [39]. We used it to stream users who wrote new content in English (and not just retweeted), over three days (Sunday May 23rd, 2021; Tuesday May 25th, 2021; and Thursday May 27th, 2021) and three day-periods (7AM, 12PM, 8PM UTC) to account for different daytimes/working hours over the world. We filtered out organizations and spammers and reached a control group of 57 private accounts of random English speakers from all over the world.

We repeated the process we applied for the patients and performed a similar category analysis for the control group: we collected their timelines (97,439 tweets overall), cleaned all the tweets, removed those with less than three words after cleaning, and used the NLU module to classify the 78,665 remaining tweets into categories.

Table 1. Three examples of text cleaning and category classification.

	Original text	Text after cleaning	Text category, likelihood
1	As soon as I can eat reliably and have energy I'm making a couple cheesecakes.	as soon as i can eat reliably and have energy i'm making a couple cheesecake s.	/food and drink, 0.717184 /society/social institution/divorce, 0.671966 /food and drink/food, 0.650148 /society/social institution/marriage, 0.618626 /pets, 0.578122 /family and parenting, 0.549967 /family and parenting/children, 0.537206 /health and fitness/weight loss, 0.533751 /food and drink/vegetarian, 0.530938 /food and drink/cuisines, 0.527833
2	@bottomline_ibd great poll. I do have the odd binge, but IBD has changed what I can drink. No more red wine or ale 😔	great poll. i do have the odd binge, but ibd has changed what i can drink. no more red wine or ale 😔	/food and drink /beverages /alcoholic beverages /cocktails and beer, 0.84566 /health and fitness /disease /ibs and crohn's disease, 0.80538 /food and drink /beverages /alcoholic beverages /wine, 0.80134 /food and drink /beverages /non alcoholic beverages /soft drinks, 0.54913 /food and drink /food allergies, 0.53412
3	I am living proof that yoga can help #uchi-	i am living proof that yoga can help #uchicagoibd #stu-	/society /senior living, 0.922317 /religion and spirituality /hinduism, 0.902807

2.2 Category Classification

Patients' and Control Group. The category classification of the NLU module aims to identify the theme of the text. Given a text, the NLU module provides a list of possible categories and subcategories and their corresponding likelihood. The likelihood score represents the confidence of the classification, and only those with confidence level higher than 0.5 are returned. The module uses a predefined list of 23 high-level categories with a different number of subcategories in each group, to which it classifies the text, if applicable. The returned list of possible classifications is sorted based on their likelihood, from largest to smallest (see examples in Table 1).

We used the module to apply category classification to each tweet in our dataset. For the sake of our analysis, we only addressed the module's first and most likely classification and returned all classifications to their high-level categories (they are marked with grey background in Table 1). We repeated the process for all the tweets in our dataset and aggregated the results. We obtained a segmentation of the themes discussed by patients, over the 23 categories, and a similar segmentation for the control group. In each group, we derived a segmentation for all the users together and for each of them separately.

Comparing the Groups. After obtaining a segmentation of the categories discussed in each group (patients vs. control), we used a Dirichlet regression [40] to compare the segmentations of the two groups. The Dirichlet regression approach was suitable for the compositional data we gathered [41].

For each user, we obtained their category segmentation and an annotation of the group they belonged to patients or control. Using the 'DirichletReg' package in R [42], we fitted a Dirichlet regression model to the data: the dependent variable was the segmentation of each user over the 23 categories and the independent variable was the group membership – whether the user belonged to the patients' group or to the control one.

Aiming to test whether the group membership influenced the category segmentation, we trained the model twice and compared two statistical models: the full model (with the group indicator as an explanatory variable) and the null model (without the group indicator). In the full model, each of the 23 categories was represented by an intercept and by the group variable, resulting in 46 parameters overall. In the null model, each category was represented only by an intercept, and it therefore contained 23 parameters overall. Finally, we used a likelihood-ratio test (LRT), Akaike information criteria (AIC) and Bayesian information criteria (BIC) to compare the results of the two obtained models.

2.3 Keywords Extraction

The next goal was to identify the lifestyle-related treatments patients endure to maintain their disease and to determine their sentiments towards them. Since we were interested in keywords that reflected on patients' lifestyles, we utilized the obtained segmentation from the **Category Classification** stage to focus our analysis on keywords related to health and nutrition. We grouped together all tweets that were categorized by the NLU module as related to "health and fitness" (53,598 tweets) or "food and drink" (30,747 tweets) and added all other tweets that explicitly mentioned IBD by containing at least one of the keywords: *crohn*, *colitis* or *#IBD* (additional 1,228 tweets). Overall, 85,573 tweets were selected for further analysis of keywords extraction.

The keywords extraction feature of the NLU module recognizes words and phrases that are of high importance within the text and calculates their sentiments. Given a text, the NLU module returns a list of keywords, sorted by diminishing relevance to the text, and their corresponding sentiment. For each keyword, the module provides a score on the closed line segment $[-1, 1]$ representing the keyword's sentiment within the text: -1 for extremely negative sentiment and 1 for extremely positive sentiment; A score of 0 means that the keyword was mentioned in a neutral context.

As can be seen in the examples in Table 2 below, the extracted keywords can be very specific and may include adjectives. We wished to group together different variations of similar keywords and obtain their aggregated sentiment. Therefore, we performed several steps to refine the keywords and achieve this goal:

1. **Articles and Pronouns:** we omitted definite and indefinite articles, demonstrative adjectives and pronouns and possessive pronouns from all keywords.
2. **Quantity:** we erased the beginning of keywords containing the combination "_____ of _____" to reflect on quantity (e.g., "300g of almonds" or "3 cups of coffee") and kept the part following the "of" (resulting in almonds and coffee, respectively).
3. **Adjectives:** we wished to include phrases like "red wine" or "sweet potato" for which the adjectives define their meanings, but to avoid phrases like "amazing cake" or "yummy chocolate" for which the adjectives should be considered in sentiment calculation only. Notice how the first word in all four examples is an adjective, and therefore Part of Speech tagging was not suitable to perform the differentiation between the phrases. Rather, we combined lists of adjectives from several sources and created a designated adjective list, suited for our unique task. Based on the list we eliminated adjectives that reflected on the quality or quantity of the objects (like awful, big, yummy, etc.) and kept the ones that altered the meaning of the objects and were therefore crucial for our analysis (like hot, spicy, red, green, etc.).
4. **Lemmatization:** we used spaCy library for NLP in python to apply lemmatization to the text and return the keywords to their basic form.

After completing the keywords refinement, we grouped together identical keywords and calculated the average sentiment for each of them. We wanted to avoid rare keywords that hardly appeared in our dataset, so we chose to include only keywords that were mentioned at least ten times. We also wanted to avoid a single patient sealing a keywords' fate by praising it or denigrating it, so we only included keywords that were mentioned by at least five different patients.

We examined the frequently mentioned keywords used by patients in four different groups: keywords from all tweets, keywords from tweets related to health and nutrition, keywords from tweets related to food and drink, and keywords from tweets related to IBD. There was an overlap between the "health and fitness" category and the tweets related to IBD, as 88.8% of the tweets that explicitly mentioned IBD were classified by the NLU module as related to health and fitness. For each group we generated a word-cloud that visualized the frequent keywords within the group. We obtained the 25 most frequent keywords in each group and compared the results using six Independent Samples t-tests, one for every two groups.

3 Results

3.1 Category Classification

Patients' Group. The NLU module was used for category classification over 550,161 tweets written by IBD patients. 7,964 of the tweets were ignored by the NLU module since they did not contain enough data for category classification and another 4,830 tweets were classified as written in languages other than English. Overall, a category was successfully retrieved for 537,367 tweets (97.7%).

Table 2. Two examples of keywords extraction and refinement.

	Text after cleaning	Extracted keyword, sentiment	Fixed keyword, sentiment
1	as soon as i can eat reliably and have energy i'm making a couple of cheesecakes.	couple of cheesecakes, 0.86 energy, 0.86	cheesecake, 0.86 energy, 0.86
2	great poll. i do have the odd binge, but ibd has changed what i can drink. no more red wine or ale 😔	odd binge, -0.45 red wine, -0.83 great poll, 0.96 ibd, -0.45 ale, -0.83	binge, -0.45 red wine, -0.83 poll, 0.96 ibd, -0.45 ale, -0.83

15.8% of the categorized tweets were classified as "art and entertainment", which turned out to be the most frequent category. 11.9% were classified as "society", 10.0% as "health and fitness", and 9.6% were classified as "sports". The classification continued with the category "law, govt and politics", which accounted for 7.9% of the tweets, followed by "family and parenting" with 5.7%, "food and drink" with 5.7%, and "technology and computing" with 5.0% of the tweets. The next four categories: "style and fashion", "automotive and vehicles", "business and industrial", and "pets" accounted for 4.0%, 3.3%, 3.2% and 3.0% respectively. The rest of the tweets were classified into 11 small categories (of size ranging between 0.2% to 2.5%), that accounted together for 15% of the tweets. All the 23 high-level categories suggested by IBM were detected within the patients' tweets, and the full category segmentation can be found here.

In the context of lifestyle, it is interesting to examine three categories: "health and fitness", which captures tweets related to diseases or physical activity; "food and drink", which captures tweets related to nutrition; and "religion and spirituality", which captures tweets related to spiritual, relaxing activities like yoga and meditation. The "health and fitness" category turned out to be the third largest category discussed by patients. The segmentation show that they talk about these subjects 10% of the time. "Food and drink" was also a dominant category, holding 5.7% of the tweets as the 7th largest category. The "religion and spirituality" category, on the other hand, was one of the smaller categories with only 2.5% of the tweets.

Control Group. The NLU module was used for category classification over 78,665 tweets written by users from the control group. After eliminating tweets that did not contain enough data or those classified as written in languages other than English, a category was successfully retrieved for 73,817 tweets (93.8%).

Comparing to the patients' group, the two largest categories of the control group were again "art and entertainment" and "society", which accounted for 16.3% and 14.7% of the tweets, respectively. Even though the classification stayed the same, both categories increased in the control group's segmentation.

Continuing to the third largest category, we noticed a difference between the groups in the classification itself: holding 10% of the patients' tweets, "health and fitness" was the third largest category within the patients' group; with only 4.8% of the random users' tweets, the same category dropped to the 6th place in the control group's segmentation.

The third largest category within the control group was "law, govt and politics", which held 10.8% of the tweets.

The "Food and drink" category dropped three places in comparison to the patients' group: from the 7th place with 5.7% of the patients' tweets to the 10th place with only 3.9% of the random users' tweets. The findings show that patients talk more about health and fitness in comparison to the control group, who talk more about politics and society. The full category classification of the control group's tweets can be found here.

Comparing the Groups. Observing the differences between the categories discussed by patients and those discussed by random users, we used a Dirichlet regression to check whether these differences were statistically significant. We obtained a category segmentation per user and tested whether the group of the user (patients or control) was a statistically significant explanatory variable.

The group indicator was found to be statistically significant by three different statistical measures: the likelihood-ratio test ($\chi^2(23) = 218.93$) comparing the two statistical models showed $P < .01$ and both AIC and BIC were smaller for the model with the group variable. Table 3 presents the analysis of deviance between the two statistical models we compared: model 1 (the full model), containing the group of the user as an explanatory variable and an intercept, and model 2 (the null model) containing an intercept only.

Table 3. Analysis of deviance table between the two regression models: model 1 with the group indicator as an explanatory variable and model 2 without.

Model	Deviance	N. parameters	Difference (LRT)	df	Pr (>Chi) (P-value)
1 – full	−46766	46			
2 – null	−46546	23	219.83	23	< 2.2e-16***

Figure 1 and Fig. 2 visualize the results of the Dirichlet regression we performed. Figure 1 shows the predicted category segmentation for each group: the patients' predicted probabilities are represented by green circles and those of the control group by red triangles. Already we can notice the difference between the two groups when it comes to health and fitness, as the predicted probability for this category within the patients' group is higher than the equivalent within the control one. We can see that the control group, on the other hand, talk more about politics and society comparing to the patients' group. Figure 2 shows the scaled difference between the predicted values of the patients' group and the predicted values of the control group, in each category. Again, we can see how patients talk more about health and fitness or even food and drink and less about politics and society, in comparison to the control group.

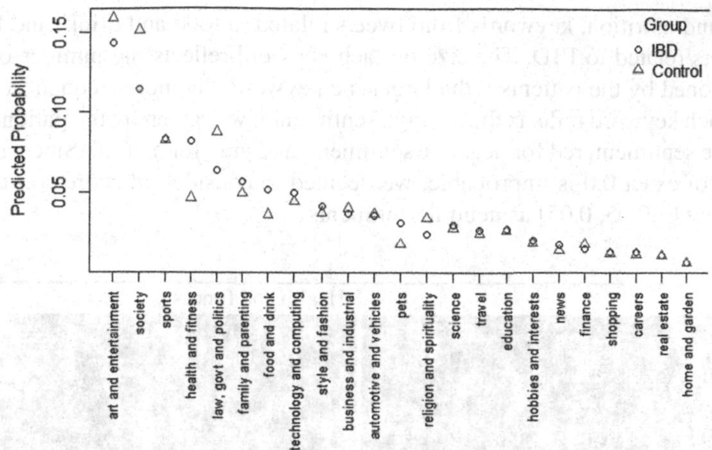

Fig. 1. Predicted probability of each category, by group: patients' group is marked with green circle and the control group with red triangle. (Color figure online)

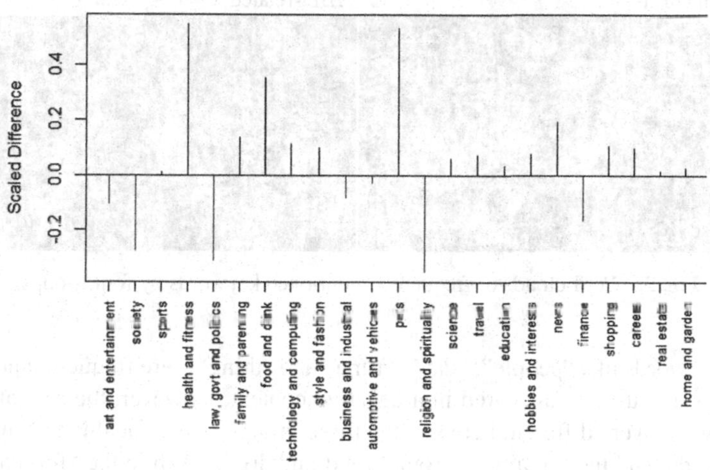

Fig. 2. Scaled differences between the predicted values of the patients' group and the predicted values of the control, in each category.

3.2 Keywords Extraction

Out of the 85,573 patients' tweets that were selected for keywords extraction, the NLU module was able to identify keywords in 82,778 tweets (96.7%), and a total of 218,592 keywords was extracted. After completing the refinement process and aggregating similar keywords, 64,020 different keywords were found. However, only 2,553 keywords were mentioned at least ten times in our data base, and only 2,335 keywords were also mentioned by at least five different patients.

Figure 3 shows four word-clouds of frequently mentioned keywords that were generated over four different groups: keywords from all tweets, keywords form tweets related to health and nutrition, keywords from tweets related to food and drink, and keywords from tweets related to IBD. The size of each keyword reflects the number of times it was mentioned by the patients – the larger the keyword, the more frequent it was. The color of each keyword reflects the average sentiment it was given by the patients – green for positive sentiment, red for negative sentiment, and gray for neutral. Since an average sentiment of exact 0.0 is improbable, we decided to consider all scores on the closed line segment [−0.05, 0.05] as neutral sentiments.

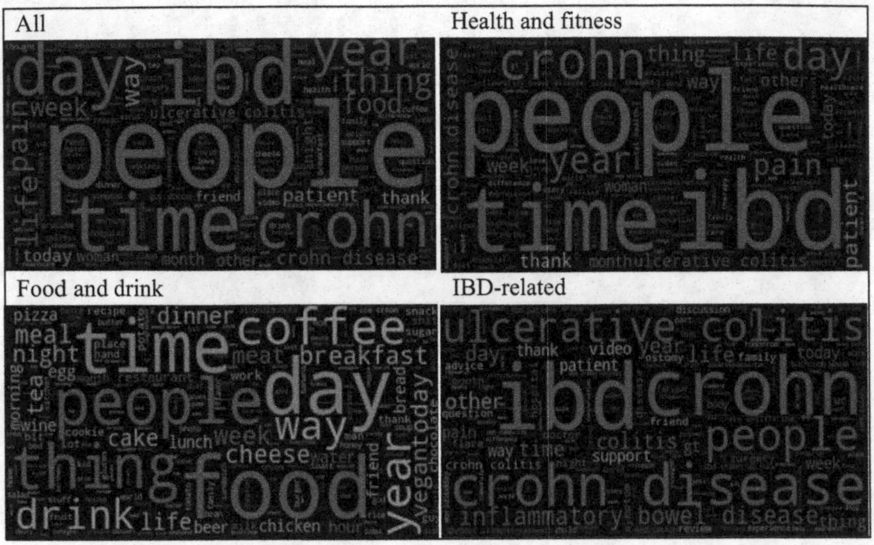

Fig. 3. Word-clouds of frequently mentioned keywords by four groups.

General words like "people", "day", "time" and "thing" were frequent among all the four groups and usually appeared in a negative context. However, the rest of the most frequent words were different between the three groups "All", "health and fitness" and "IBD-related", and the remaining group "food and drink". While the "food and drink" group captured words related to nutrition in a positive sentiment, all the other three groups captured phrases related to IBD that mainly had a negative sentiment.

The Independent Samples t-tests between the average sentiments of the "food and drink" group and those of the other groups showed that the sentiment in the "food and drink" group was indeed more positive compared to the other groups (all three tests showed $P < .01$). No statistical differences were found between the average sentiments of the other three groups.

Looking at the clouds in Fig. 3, we can see that the "food and drink" cloud is composed of relatively many green keywords, while the other three clouds are much redder. Words related to IBD are dominant in all three of them and they appear in red. It means that patients tend to use a negative sentiment when they talk about their disease.

4 Discussion

4.1 Principal Results

This research aimed to discover what IBD patients are talking about on Twitter and to learn from the personal experience they share in their tweets. A collection of tweets written by IBD patients was obtained and classified into thematic categories using the NLU module by IBM Cloud. It was found that the segmentation of topics discussed by IBD patients differ from the one discussed by the general population of Twitter users. While the random Twitter users frequently referred to politics and social affairs in their tweets, the IBD patients dedicated a considerable amount of their tweets (10%) to health and fitness. Only a small fraction (2.5%) of the patients' tweets related to religion or spirituality, which is surprising since relaxing physical activities like yoga, meditation or mindfulness are considered helpful to maintaining the disease.

To further investigate patients' discussion on Twitter, keywords extraction with sentiment analysis was applied to all tweets related to health, fitness, or nutrition. Using the NLU module, keywords from lifestyle-related tweets were identified and classified as positive, negative, or neutral, to reflect on the way patients deal with their disease. The analysis showed that the keywords were used in a more negative sentiment when the patients talked about their health.

Unlike previous research related to patients' sentiment on Twitter [35–37], we focused our research on entity sentiment rather than the sentiment of the entire tweet. The entity sentiment analysis can be used for characterizing patients' sentiment towards the different treatments they try. In our previous research [38] we investigated the sentiments towards lifestyle-related keywords from a predefined list which only contained single words. In this research we extended the analysis to index terms of both words and phrases that were extracted directly from the text.

This research suggests that there is room for collaboration between physicians and engineers regarding the understanding of chronic diseases. Due to the chronic nature of the disease and the fact that it involves bowel movements, IBD patients are compelled to follow a special nutrition and maintain a calm routine. By collecting and analyzing patients' personal experiences on social media, we can monitor patients' lifestyles and support medical knowledge regarding IBD. We can identify and assess complementary treatments of diets and physical activity and maybe ease patients' processes of finding the right treatments for them. Although such analysis should not strive to replace doctors or draw conclusions of clinical nature, it may provide complementary recommendations for healthy lifestyles based on the wisdom of the crowd.

4.2 Limitations and Future Work

The NLU module by IBM Cloud was used in this research for category classification and keywords extraction as a proof of concept. We did not evaluate its results, nor did we compare them to similar tools available in the market like the Natural Language AI by Google Cloud. Future research should consider performing similar analysis with different natural language processing tools and comparing their results. Even training designated algorithms on data from lifestyle-related tweets, like those used in this research, can benefit the analysis.

The control group used in this research was composed of only 57 random users, while the test group was larger and contained 377 IBD patients. The use of Twitter Streaming API is free, and one can quickly collect many random users to increase the control group. However, the rest of the analysis – collecting all their tweets and using the NLU module to extract keywords from each one – is time consuming and costly. In future work, we intend to continue the process and increase the control group to at least 100 users.

The collection of timelines for the patients' group was done in November 2020, while the collection of timelines for the control group was done in May 2021. The periodic gap between the collected data may affect the category segmentations. Another adjustment needed to balance the two groups is to collect the users' timelines over the same time periods.

4.3 Conclusions

This research provided thematic analysis and keywords identification in tweets by patients with IBD. The analysis showed that patients differ in the content they share on Twitter from other users, and that the information they share can be used to derive insights regarding their disease.

The methods presented in this research, that were applied to IBD, can also help to explore other medical conditions. Research of other diseases involving strict dietary guidelines, like Celiac Disease or diabetes, can use the analysis of patients' tweets to better understand patients' difficulties with adhering to their new lifestyles. Research of diseases considered embarrassing, like HIV, can use such analysis to learn more about the constant struggle of patients living with the disease.

Therefore, the contribution of this research is twofold: It provides an analytical contribution to the fields of text mining and social media and a practical contribution by better understanding chronic conditions and promoting a healthy lifestyle of chronic patients.

Acknowledgements. This study was supported by a grant of the ERA-Net Cofund HDHL-INTIMIC (INtesTInal MICrobiomics) under the umbrella of Joint Programming Initiative "A healthy diet for a healthy life".

References

1. Devlen, J., Beusterien, K., Yen, L., Ahmed, A., Cheifetz, A.S., Moss, A.C.: The burden of inflammatory bowel disease: a patient-reported qualitative analysis and development of a conceptual model. Inflamm. Bowel. Dis. **20**(3), 545–552 (2014)
2. Brydolf, M., Segesten, K.: Living with ulcerative colitis: experiences of adolescents and young adults. J. Adv. Nurs. **23**(1), 39–47 (1996)
3. Hall, N.J., Rubin, G.P., Dougall, A., Hungin, A., Neely, J.: The fight for 'health-related normality': a qualitative study of the experiences of individuals living with established inflammatory bowel disease (IBD). J. Health Psychol. **10**(3), 443–455 (2005)
4. Norton, B., Thomas, R., Lomax, K.G., Dudley-Brown, S.: Patient perspectives on the impact of Crohn's disease: results from group interviews. Patient Prefer Adherence **6**, 509–520 (2012)

5. Docs ICA: Natural Language Understanding. Natural Language Understanding (2020)
6. De Choudhury, M., Morris, M.R., White, R.W.: Seeking and sharing health information online: comparing search engines and social media. In: Proceedings of the SIGCHI Conference on Human Factors in Computing Systems (2014)
7. Chulis, K.: Data mining Twitter for cancer, diabetes, and asthma insights. Purdue University (2016)
8. Heaivilin, N., Gerbert, B., Page, J.E., Gibbs, J.L.: Public health surveillance of dental pain via Twitter. J. Dent. Res. **90**(9), 1047–1051 (2011)
9. Tsuya, A., Sugawara, Y., Tanaka, A., Narimatsu, H.: Do cancer patients tweet? Examining the twitter use of cancer patients in Japan. J. Med. Internet Res **16**(5), e137 (2014)
10. Adrover, C., Bodnar, T., Salathé, M.: Targeting HIV-related medication side effects and sentiment using twitter data. arXiv preprint arXiv:1404.3610 (2014)
11. Sioula-Georgoulea, I.: Approaching Twitter sociologically: a case study of the public humiliation of HIV-positive women. Επιθεώρηση Κοινωνικών Ερευνών **144**(144), 103–128 (2015)
12. Odlum, M., Yoon, S.: HIV/AIDS and the millennium development goals: a public sentiment analysis of world AIDS day twitter chat. Int. J. AIDS Res. **3**(9), 129–132 (2016)
13. Karisani, P., Agichtein, E.: Did you really just have a heart attack? Towards robust detection of personal health mentions in social media. In: Proceedings of the 2018 World Wide Web Conference (2018)
14. Yin, Z., Fabbri, D., Rosenbloom, S.T., Malin, B.: A scalable framework to detect personal health mentions on Twitter. J. Med. Internet Res. **17**(6), e4305 (2015)
15. Jahanbin, K., Rahmanian, V.: Using Twitter and web news mining to predict COVID-19 outbreak. Asian Pac. J. Trop. Med. **13**(8), 378 (2020)
16. Lopreite, M., Panzarasa, P., Puliga, M., Riccaboni, M.: Early warnings of COVID-19 outbreaks across Europe from social media. Sci. Rep. **11**(1), 1–7 (2021)
17. Gabarron, E., Dorronzoro, E., Rivera-Romero, O., Wynn, R.: Diabetes on Twitter: a sentiment analysis. J. Diabetes Sci. Technol. **13**(3), 439–444 (2019)
18. Beguerisse-Díaz, M., McLennan, A.K., Garduño-Hernández, G., Barahona, M., Ulijaszek, S.J.: The 'who' and 'what' of# diabetes on Twitter. Digit. Health **3**, 2055207616688841 (2017)
19. Sugawara, Y., Narimatsu, H., Hozawa, A., Shao, L., Otani, K., Fukao, A.: Cancer patients on Twitter: a novel patient community on social media. BMC. Res. Notes **5**(1), 1–9 (2012). https://doi.org/10.1186/1756-0500-5-699
20. Kaplan, G.G.: The global burden of IBD: from 2015 to 2025. Nat. Rev. Gastroenterol. Hepatol. **12**(12), 720–727 (2015)
21. Loftus, E.V.: Clinical epidemiology of inflammatory bowel disease: incidence, prevalence, and environmental influences. Gastroenterology **126**(6), 1504–1517 (2004)
22. Roccetti, M., Marfia, G., Salomoni, P., Prandi, C., Zagari, R.M., Kengni, F.L.G., et al.: Attitudes of Crohn's disease patients: infodemiology case study and sentiment analysis of Facebook and Twitter posts. JMIR Public Health and Surveill. **3**(3), e51 (2017)
23. Trivedi, I., Keefer, L.: The emerging adult with inflammatory bowel disease: challenges and recommendations for the adult gastroenterologist. Gastroenterol. Res. Pract. **2015**, 260807 (2015)
24. Rubin, D.T., Dubinsky, M.C., Panaccione, R., Siegel, C.A., Binion, D.G., Kane, S.V., et al.: The impact of ulcerative colitis on patients' lives compared to other chronic diseases: a patient survey. Dig. Dis. Sci. **55**(4), 1044–1052 (2010)
25. Frohlich, D.O.: The social construction of inflammatory bowel disease using social media technologies. Health Commun. **31**(11), 1412–1420 (2016)
26. Kemp, K., Griffiths, J., Lovell, K.: Understanding the health and social care needs of people living with IBD: a meta-synthesis of the evidence. World J. Gastroenterol. **18**(43), 6240–6249 (2012)

27. Khan, A., Silverman, A., Rowe, A, Rowe, S., Tick, M., Testa, S., et al.: Who is saying what about Inflammatory Bowel Disease on Twitter? (2018)
28. Rowe, A., Rowe, S., Silverman, A., Borum, M.L.: P024 Crohn's disease messaging on twitter: who's talking? Gastroenterology **154**(1), S13–S14 (2018)
29. Roccetti, M., Casari, A., Marfia, G.: Inside chronic autoimmune disease communities: a social networks perspective to Crohn's patient behavior and medical information. In: 2015 IEEE/ACM International Conference on Advances in Social Networks Analysis and Mining (ASONAM). IEEE (2015)
30. Frohlich, D.O., Zmyslinski-Seelig, A.N.: How uncover ostomy challenges ostomy stigma, and encourages others to do the same. New Media Soc. **18**(2), 220–238 (2016)
31. Becker, K.L.: Cyberhugs: creating a voice for chronic pain sufferers through technology. Cyberpsychol. Behav. Soc. Netw. **16**(2), 123–126 (2013)
32. Wiese, J., Kelley, P.G., Cranor, L.F., Dabbish, L., Hong, J.I., Zimmerman, J.: Are you close with me? Are you nearby?: investigating social groups, closeness, and willingness to share. In: Proceedings of the 13th International Conference on Ubiquitous Computing. ACM (2011)
33. Paek, H., Hove, T., Ju Jeong, H., Kim, M.: Peer or expert? The persuasive impact of YouTube public service announcement producers. Int. J. Advert. **30**(1), 161–188 (2011)
34. Lin, W., Zhang, X., Song, H., Omori, K.: Health information seeking in the Web 2.0 age: trust in social media, uncertainty reduction, and self-disclosure. Comput. Hum. Behav. **56**, 289–294 (2016)
35. Gloor, P.A., Maddali, H.T., Margolis, P.A.: Comparing online community structure of patients of chronic diseases. Int. J. Organ. Des. Eng. **4**(1–2), 113–136 (2016)
36. Pérez-Pérez, M., Pérez-Rodríguez, G., Fdez-Riverola, F., Lourenço, A.: Using twitter to understand the human bowel disease community: exploratory analysis of key topics. J. Med. Internet Res. **21**(8), e12610 (2019)
37. Cohen, E.R., Spiegel, B.M., van Oijen, M.G.: Tu1068 Twitter offers insight into health related quality of life (HRQoL) in ulcerative colitis. Gastroenterology **144**(5), S-751-S-752 (2013)
38. Stemmer, M., Ravid, G., Parmet, Y.: A framework for identifying patients on twitter and learning from their personal experience. ECIS (2020)
39. Twitter I. Sampled stream (2021). https://developer.twitter.com/en/docs/twitter-api/tweets/sampled-stream/api-reference/get-tweets-sample-stream
40. Maier, M.: Dirichlet Regression in R. Version 0.4-0.R Foundation for Statistical Computing, Vienna, Austria (2012)
41. Maier, M.J.: DirichletReg: Dirichlet regression for compositional data in R (2014)
42. Maier, M.J., Maier, M.M.J.: Package 'DirichletReg' (2015)

The Design of Novel Cellular Biomedical Technologies: Implications for Responsibility, Transparency and Patient Wellbeing

Beth Strickland Bloch(✉)

University of Kentucky, Lexington, KY 40506, USA
beth.s.bloch@uky.edu

Abstract. There are many novel cell-based technologies currently under development in university laboratories across the United States. These technologies include genetic engineering, synthetic biology, and nano-sized drug delivery, and are intended to treat patients at the cellular level. The early-stage designers of these technologies are often researchers working in laboratory groups associated departments of biomedical engineering. Although these groups play a critical role within the context of healthcare, they are rarely considered as having a fiduciary relationship with patients and a duty to provide trustworthy technologies. In this short paper, part of the results of a laboratory ethnography of cellular biomedical engineers is presented. Based on observations, interviews, and document analysis, the design practices of laboratory developing novel cellular technologies is considered. Using the conceptual tenets of Value Sensitive Design (VSD), the values of responsibility, transparency, and wellbeing are implicated in this analysis. The principles of translational medicine are also found to strongly influence cellular biomedical engineering laboratory activities.

Keywords: Biomedical technology · Values in design · Translational medicine

1 Introduction

There are many novel cellular technologies currently under development in university laboratories across the United States. These technologies often fall under the labels of genetic engineering, synthetic biology, and nano-sized drug delivery. All of these tools are designed with the intent to eventually treat patients at the cellular level. One important group of designers of these novel technologies are biomedical engineers who work in laboratory groups affiliated with academic biomedical engineering departments [1]. Although many types of novel technologies are developed in these spaces, this project only focuses on groups which develop cell-based technologies, and are referred to here as cellular biomedical engineering laboratories.

Little is known about how novel cellular technologies will ultimately impact the wellbeing of patients once they are regularly used. Although the implicit assumption is that developing these technologies will result in better care for patients, what we do not know is how much cellular biomedical engineers actually think about potential negative

E. Pissaloux et al. (Eds.): IHAW 2021, CCIS 1538, pp. 221–226, 2021.
https://doi.org/10.1007/978-3-030-94209-0_19

impacts early in the design process. Could possible future problems be controlled for at the R&D stage?

Researchers in the areas of human-computer interaction (HCI), values and design, and social informatics, all draw attention to the importance of understanding how values influence technological design practices [2, 3]. Where *values* can be thought of as those things people regard as important in their life, and have a type of *moral import* in how they relate to what is considered right and wrong (i.e., ethical) within a particular context [4]. Scholars concerned with values and design think about not only the use of technologies impacting society, but also how social and technical dynamics influence the design of technologies well before they are ever used in society. This approach is based on position that humans have values that shape their design practices, and that the resulting technologies come to embody those values [5]. The implication of this is that the way a technology is designed ultimately enables certain uses and actions; all of which have consequences whether they be positive or negative.

The designers of technology centered in this study are cellular biomedical engineering laboratories whose members engage in a complex network of scientific activity [6]. This complexity comes from a set of social and technical elements, at both the institutional and individual levels, and where the network is comprised of multiple actors in constantly shifting relationships [7]. Although university-based biomedical engineers are not commonly seen as actors within the context of healthcare, they do play an important role to develop safe and secure novel cellular technologies to use with patients.

The results of this study begin an overdue conversation about the role cellular biomedical engineering laboratories have in the design of novel technologies intended for clinical application. This paper focuses specifically on how values active within laboratory spaces influence the design of cellular technologies long before they are ever used to treat patients. This study uses VSD to examine how the values of responsibility, transparency, and wellbeing are implicated in laboratory design practices. This paper also considers the principles of translational medicine to inform part of the analysis.

2 Methodology

The results of this study come from hundreds of hours of observing the R&D practices of biomedical engineering laboratories located at universities in the United States. Each laboratory was in the process of developing a type of cell-based novel technology related to genetic engineering, synthetic biology, and/or nano-sized drug delivery platforms. A representative sample of semi-structured interviews were conducted, and the content of hundreds of documents were analyzed. Data were coded using NVivo qualitative software and analyzed using a modified grounded theory approach [8].

2.1 Data Gathering

Laboratories were targeted for recruitment based on information about their research agendas as indicated on their university-supported group websites. Those contacted met two criteria: the technology in development was designed for use at the cellular level; the technology was intended for future clinical use. A total of 8 cellular biomedical engineering laboratories from 5 publicly-funded R1 institutions agreed to participate. Over 250 h of observation were completed. Interviews took place at the end of the study and 26 members (from a possible 56) agreed to be interviewed. Observation notes, reflection memos, and interview transcripts were coded using NVivo. Two existing conceptual frameworks emerged as important for inclusion in this study (making for a *modified* grounded theory approach) and play a critical role in the findings.

2.2 Conceptual Frameworks

The Roadmap of Translational Medicine
Cellular biomedical engineering laboratories express a strong desire to make their projects *translational.* This is in reference to the notion of translational medicine which seeks to move scientific knowledge from "bench-to-bedside" [9]. This concept highlights the desire to translate early-stage R&D projects from the basic science stage, to a stage of care providing positive impacts on society. Part of the reason cellular biomedical engineers care about translation is because the National Institutes of Health (NIH) value translational goals. The NIH invests $37 billion annual in medical research, and more than 80% is disbursed to universities, medical schools, and other research institutions [10]. In 2003, the NIH created a conceptually linear five-stage translational roadmap based on the principles of translational medicine [11] (See Fig. 1).

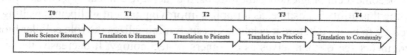

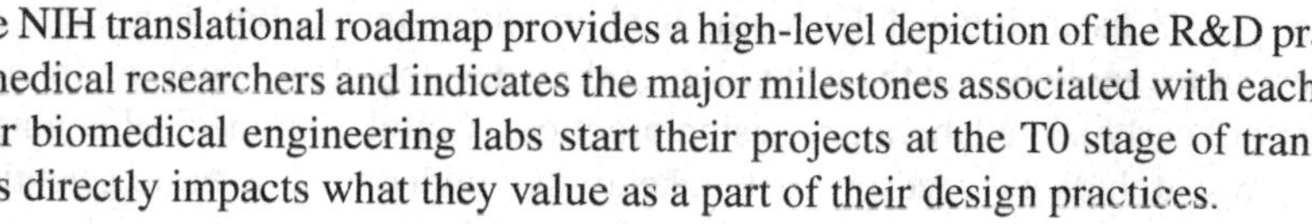

Fig. 1. NIH translational roadmap (simplified and adapted) [12]

The NIH translational roadmap provides a high-level depiction of the R&D practices of biomedical researchers and indicates the major milestones associated with each stage. Cellular biomedical engineering labs start their projects at the T0 stage of translation and this directly impacts what they value as a part of their design practices.

Value Sensitive Design
VSD emerged from the fields of HCI and information systems design. It provides a systematic way to study sociotechnical systems to discover, analyze, and operationalize values within the context of particular design projects [13]. Rather than just focus on how the use of a technology implicates certain values, this perspective argues values must also be considered as a critical component in their design process [14]. This approach validates the sociotechnical nature of technological design and realistically accounts for constraints while attempting to avoid potential negative future-use impacts.

Emerging cellular biomedical technologies are not yet regularly used within clinical settings; therefore, using VSD as a conceptual approach at this early stage of development grounds an initial assessment of the values active within these spaces. The use of a values heuristic is advocated by some VSD scholars [15] and includes: human welfare, ownership & property, privacy, environmental sustainability, universal usability, trust, autonomy, informed consent, accountability, freedom from bias, and identity.

Using this heuristic provides a starting point to consider which values may be implicated when designing a novel technology and should not be thought of as fixed nor exhaustive but rather serves as an analytical guide [16].

3 Findings and Values Implications

The purpose of this section is to identify the values implications found within university-based biomedical engineering laboratories as they design cell-based novel biomedical technologies. The wellbeing of future patients will be better protected if the values implications found here become routinely considered by members of cellular biomedical engineering laboratories.

3.1 Implication #1: Applying the Technology Label

The results of this study reveal that cellular biomedical engineers resist the label of "technology" to describe their novel technological developments. Although they recognize, to some extent, that their laboratory design activities contribute to the making of new biomedical technologies, the boundary for when something becomes a technology is often drawn around the laboratory walls. Specifically, laboratory developments are said to become technologies once they are used to achieve clinical objectives. Although providing this utility is positive, as it implies improving patient wellbeing, waiting for a technology to be used before it is labeled as such minimalizes the role cellular biomedical engineers see of themselves as designers of technology. It decreases the amount of *responsibility* these researchers perceive to have to design ethical (i.e., not harmful) biomedical technologies, and it supports the notion that negative impacts should be assessed once a technology is used outside the laboratory context.

The type of distancing cellular biomedical engineers invoke between themselves as designers of technology and the technologies they develop also reflects an internalized devaluing of early-stage laboratory design practices. Cellular biomedical engineers are stage T0 researchers engaged in what stakeholders understand as basic scientific laboratory activities. However, university-based biomedical engineering laboratories are located within colleges of engineering. This results in value clashes between basic versus applied research activities; the latter of which better align with engineering practices. Cellular biomedical engineers come to internalize this value hierarchy due to their stage T0 lab location along the translational roadmap, and it reinforces their perception as non-critical actors in developing ethical novel biomedical technologies.

3.2 Implication #2: The Meaning of Translation

The way in which the concept of translational medicine is used within biomedical engineering communities also supports the basic versus applied hierarchal values system. For example, in interviews with members of cellular biomedical engineering laboratories, they often described their laboratories as being *translational.* Using this term in this capacity was ultimately found to serve more as a stand-in for the term *applied* than it did as a representation for the provision of clinical care. Although a subtle distinction, it demonstrates how university-based biomedical engineers get trained to think about their work within the translational framework. This implicitly encourages laboratories engaged in basic scientific practices to aim for the production of tangible products. The goal of translation for basic biomedical research should be the result of positive patient health impacts at the end of the development process, but the expectation becomes that biomedical innovations should be made marketable as quickly as possible. This expectation motivates some laboratories to describe their research as translational, and sends the message that cell-based laboratories are committed to producing tangible outcomes based on their research projects.

Cellular biomedical engineers, as stage T0 researchers, have yet to engage with the necessary clinical stakeholders (e.g., hospital personnel, patients) who can usher biomedical technologies into the clinic. Describing a cellular biomedical engineering laboratory as a translational misidentifies the actual stage of technological development happening within the lab. These laboratories do not consider patient impacts in the way that using the term "translation" suggests. They instead prioritize the wants and needs of translational intermediaries, like the FDA or manufacturers, which get involved in the development process well before clinical actors. The term translation gets conflated to mean the design of a "product" rather than the provision of "healthcare". The pressure laboratories experience to ensure that their novel technologies are marketable and can be upscaled adversely impacts their relationship with translation. The term translation is ultimately used in a way that hinders the *transparency* of its intended meaning.

3.3 Implication #3: The Invisibility of Patients

The results of this study found that the eventual patient use of novel cellular technology is not what serves as the primary driver for a particular project. The specifics of how a novel technology will be used by physicians to treat patients in clinical settings is largely unknown. Cellular biomedical engineering laboratories are removed from the clinical context both physically and epistemologically. Cellular biomedical engineers do not work with patients given their stage T0 locations along the translational roadmap. The perception that cellular biomedical engineers have of who serves as the imagined end user of their novel technologies is adversely impacted by their distance from clinical realities.

Cellular biomedical engineers often see industry partners and governmental regulators as the actors responsible for considering how a novel cell-based technology will ultimately be used. This perception defaults to an implicit assumption among researchers that intermediaries are responsible for managing any potential negative impacts from their use. More importantly, this assumption also serves to distance the relationship that cellular biomedical engineers believe they have to worry about potential social impacts. The reality is that these groups of researchers, as designers of technology, have a *responsibility* to design novel cell-based technologies where patients are the intended primary user. Designing novel biomedical technologies for the needs of patients will help avoid potentially negative social impacts related to their use.

4 Conclusion

The results of the study presented here provide some initial insights into the laboratory activities and design practices of biomedical engineers as they develop novel cellular technologies. This paper serves as an entry point into a conversation about the role values play in the earliest stages of biomedical technological development. Although the values of responsibility, transparency, and patient wellbeing were considered here, a more comprehensive analysis of the values implications found in all kinds of biomedical engineering laboratories should be examined in future studies. Such studies should also focus on suggesting specific values interventions which could be integrated into laboratory design practices. These proposed interventions should provide holistic solutions and address challenges at both the laboratory level and institutional level. Although potential solutions go beyond what a single laboratory or even a single institution can achieve on their own, if all actors within the broader network work on issues collectively, this will better protect the wellbeing patients in the future.

References

1. Taktak, A., Ganney, P., Long, D., Axell, R.: Clinical Engineering: A Handbook for Clinical and Biomedical Engineers. Academic Press, Cambridge (2019)
2. Shilton, K.: Values and ethics in human-computer interaction. Found. Trends Human-Comput. Interact. **12**(2), 107–171 (2018)
3. Kling, R.: What is social informatics and why does it matter? Inf. Soc. **23**(4), 205–220 (2007)
4. Manders-Huits, N.: What values in design? The challenge of incorporating moral values into design. Sci. Eng. Ethics **17**(2), 271–287 (2011). https://doi.org/10.1007/s11948-010-9198-2
5. Winner, L.: Do artifacts have politics? Daedalus, 121–136 (1980)
6. Latour, B.: Science in Action: How to Follow Scientists and Engineers Through Society. Harvard University Press, Cambridge (1987)
7. Law, J.: Notes on the theory of the actor-network: ordering, strategy, and heterogeneity. Syst. Pract. **5**(4), 379–393 (1992). https://doi.org/10.1007/BF01059830
8. Geertz, C.: Thick description: toward an interpretive theory of culture. In: The Interpretation of Cultures: Selected Essays, pp. 3–30. Basic Books, New York (1973)
9. Wehling, M.: Principles of Translational Science in Medicine: From Bench to Bedside. Academic Press, Cambridge (2015)
10. National Institutes of Health, Appropriations. https://www.nih.gov/about-nih/what-we-do/nih-almanac/appropriations-section-1. Accessed 24 June 2020
11. Zerhouni, E.: The NIH roadmap. Science **302**, 63–72 (2003)
12. Liverman, C., Schultz, A., Terry, S.: The CTSA Program at NIH: Opportunities for Advancing Clinical and Translational Research. National Academies Press, Washington DC (2013)
13. Helen Nissenbaum Homepage. http://www.nyu.edu/projects/nissenbaum/vid/about.html. Accessed 10 Dec 2017
14. Knobel, C., Bowker, G.: Values in design. Commun. ACM **54**(7), 26–28 (2011)
15. Friedman, B., Kahn, P., Borning, A., Huldtgren, A.: Value sensitive design and information systems. In: Doorn, N., Schuurbiers, D., van de Poel, I., Gorman, M.E. (eds.) Early Engagement and New Technologies: Opening Up the Laboratory. PET, vol. 16, pp. 55–95. Springer, Dordrecht (2013). https://doi.org/10.1007/978-94-007-7844-3_4
16. Friedman, B., Kahn, P., Borning, A.: Value sensitive design and information systems. In: HCI in Management Information Systems, pp. 348–372. ME Sharpe, Armonk (2006)

AI Hears Your Health: Computer Audition for Health Monitoring

Shahin Amiriparian[1] and Björn Schuller[1,2(✉)]

[1] Chair of Embedded Intelligence for Health Care and Wellbeing, University of Augsburg, Augsburg, Germany
{shahin.amiriparian,bjoern.schuller}@uni-a.de
[2] GLAM – Group on Language, Audio, & Music, Imperial College London, London, UK

Abstract. Acoustic sounds produced by the human body reflect changes in our mental, physiological, and pathological states. A deep analysis of such audio that are of complex nature can give insight about imminent or existing health issues. For automatic processing and understanding of such data, sophisticated machine learning approaches are needed that can extract or learn robust features. In this paper, we introduce a set of machine learning toolkits both for supervised feature extraction and unsupervised representation learning from audio health data. We analyse the application of deep neural networks (DNNs), including end-to-end learning, recurrent autoencoders, and transfer learning for speech and body-acoustics health monitoring and provide state-of-the-art results for each area. As show-case examples, we pick three well-benchmarked examples for body-acoustics and speech, each, from the popular annual Interspeech Computational Paralinguistics Challenge (ComParE). In particular, the speech-based health tasks are COVID-19 speech analysis, recognition of upper respiratory tract infections, and continuous sleepiness recognition. The body-acoustics health tasks are COVID-19 cough analysis, speech breath monitoring, heartbeat abnormality recognition, and snore sound classification. The results for all tasks demonstrate the suitability of deep computer audition approaches for health monitoring and automatic audio-based early diagnosis of health issues.

Keywords: Computer audition · Digital health · Health monitoring

1 Introduction

Diagnosis of disease, ideally even before symptoms are noticeable to individuals, facilitates early interventions and maximises the chance of successful treatments, especially for mental health. Whilst early diagnosis cannot enable curative treatment of all possible diseases, it provides the considerable chance of averting irreversible pathological changes in organ, skeletal, and nervous systems, as well as

E. Pissaloux et al. (Eds.): IHAW 2021, CCIS 1538, pp. 227–233, 2021.
https://doi.org/10.1007/978-3-030-94209-0_20

chronic pain and psychological stress [8]. Research in machine learning for audio-based digital health applications has increased in recent years [6]. Substantial contributions have been made to the development of audio-based techniques for the recognition of various health conditions, including neurodegenerative diseases such as Alzheimer's or Parkinson's [20], psychological disorders such as bipolar disorder [16], neurodevelopmental disorders such as Fragile X, Rett-Syndrome, or Autism Spectrum Disorder [17], and contagious diseases such as COVID-19 [15]. In the proceeding section of this paper, we first introduce seven health-related corpora for speech and acoustic health monitoring tasks (Sect. 2). In Sect. 3, we then introduce a set of contemporary computer audition methods and analyse their performance for various early digital health diagnosis and recognition tasks. The last section concludes our paper and discusses future work.

2 Speech and Acoustic Health Datasets

In this section, we introduce seven health related speech and audio datasets which have been used in recent editions of the INTERSPEECH Computational Paralinguistics ChallengE (COMPARE) [18,19,22]. We further provide information about the important characteristics of each dataset and the used partitions for the machine learning experiments (cf. Table 1).

Cambridge COVID19 Sound Database – Speech & Cough. This dataset which was used for a sub-challenge in the 2019 edition of the INTERSPEECH ComParE contains two speech and cough subsets from the Cambridge COVID-19 Sound database [3,11]. The audio files were resampled (in some cases, upsampled) and then converted to 16 kHz and mono/16 bit, and further normalised recording-wise to eliminate varying loudness. For the COVID-19 Cough (C19C), 725 recordings (one to three forced coughs) from 343 participants were provided, in total 1.63 h. For the COVID-19 Speech (C19S), 893 speech recordings from 366 individuals were used, in total 3.24 h.

Upper Respiratory Tract Infection Corpus (URTIC). This corpus is provided by the Institute of Safety Technology, University of Wuppertal, Germany, and consists of recordings of 630 subjects (382 m, 248 f, mean age 29.5 years, std. dev. 12.1 years, range 12-84 years), made in quiet rooms with a microphone/headset/hardware setup (sample rate 44.1 kHz, downsampled to 16 kHz, quantisation 16 bit). To obtain the state of health, each individual reported a binary one-item measure based on the German version of the Wisconsin Upper Respiratory Symptom Survey (WURSS-24), assessing the symptoms of common cold. The global illness severity item (on a scale of 0 = not sick to 7 = severely sick) was binarised using a threshold at 6.

Düsseldorf Sleepy Language (SLEEP) Corpus. This corpus [21] contains speech recordings of 915 individuals (364 f, 551 m) at different levels of sleepiness (1–9 KSS, 9 denotes extreme sleepiness). The participants performed various pre-defined speaking tasks and read out text passages. Moreover, spontaneous speech is collected in the form of elicited narrative content. The sessions which

Table 1. Number of instances per class in the all partitions for each dataset.

#	Training	Development	Test	Σ
Speech-based datasets for health monitoring				
COVID-19 Speech (C19S) Corpus [3,11,23]				
No COVID-19	243	153	189	585
COVID-19	72	142	94	308
Σ	315	295	283	893
Upper Respiratory Tract Infection Corpus (URTIC) [19]				
C	970	1 011	895	2 876
NC	8 535	8 585	8 656	25 776
Σ	9 505	9 596	9 551	28 652
Düsseldorf Sleepy Language (SLEEP) Corpus [21]				
1–9 (Karolinska Sleepiness Scale (KSS))	5 564	5 328	5 570	16 462
Acoustic datasets for health monitoring				
COVID-19 Cough (C19C) Corpus [3,11,23]				
No COVID-19	215	183	169	567
COVID-19	71	48	39	158
Σ	286	231	208	725
UCL Speech Breath Monitoring (UCL-SBM) Corpus [18]				
Speakers	17	16	16	49
Heart Sounds Shenzhen (HSS) Corpus [22]				
Normal	84	32	28	144
Mild	276	98	91	465
Moderate/Severe	142	50	44	236
Σ	502	180	163	845
Munich-Passau Snore Sound Corpus (MPSSC) [19]				
Velum (V)	168	161	155	484
Oropharyngeal lateral walls (O)	76	75	65	216
Tongue (T)	8	15	16	39
Epiglottis (E)	30	32	27	89
Σ	282	283	263	828

lasted roughly one hour per participant were further held between 6 am to 12 pm in order to acquire high variability in the levels of perceived sleepiness. Using this dataset, the sleepiness of a speaker can be assessed as regression problem. Continuous recognition of sleepiness is of high relevance for sleep disorder monitoring.

UCL Speech Breath Monitoring (UCL-SBM) Corpus. This corpus contains spontaneous speech recordings that took place in a quiet office space, and recordings from a piezoelectric respiratory belts worn by the subjects. All signals were sampled at 40 kHz; speech was downsampled to 16 kHz and breath belts to 25 Hz in post-processing [18]. All 49 speakers (29 f, 20 m) reported English as a primary language ages range from 18 to approximately 55 years old (mean age 24 years; std. dev. ~10 years). Breathing patterns also provide medical doctors vital information about an individual's respiratory and speech planning [4].

Heart Sounds Shenzhen (HSS) Corpus. The HSS corpus, provided by the Shenzhen University General Hospital, contains heart sounds gathered from 170 subjects (55 f, 115 m; ages from 21 to 88 years (mean age 65.4 years, std. dev. 13.2 years) with various health conditions, such as coronary heart disease, heart failure, and arrhythmia. The acoustic signals were recorded using an electronic stethoscope with a 4 kHz sampling rate and a 20 Hz–2 kHz frequency response. Three types of heartbeats (normal, mild, and moderate/severe) have to be classified Table 1. Automatic machine learning based approaches could help monitoring patients with unclear symptoms of heartbeat abnormalities.

Munich-Passau Snore Sound Corpus (MPSSC). The MPSSC is introduced for classification of snore sounds by their excitation location within the upper airways. The corpus contains audio samples of 828 snore events from 219 subjects (cf. Table 1). The number of recordings per class in the corpus is unbalanced, with 84% of samples from the classes Velum (V) and Oropharyngeal lateral walls (O), 11%, Epiglottis (E)-events, and 5% Tongue (T)-snores. This is in line with the probability of occurrence during normal sleep [12].

Table 2. Results for all seven introduced corpora. The **official challenge baselines** and the winners of each sub-challenge are provided. UAR: Unweighted Average Recall. PCC: Pearson's correlation coefficient. ρ: Spearman's correlation coefficient. *: [2] was a separate submission and not as a part of the sub-challenge.

	Speech-based health monitoring						**Acoustic health monitoring**							
Approach	**C19S** UAR [%]		**URTIC** UAR [%]		**SLEEP** PCC		**C19C** ρ		**UCL-SBM** UAR [%]		**HSS** UAR [%]		**MPSSC** UAR [%]	
	Dev	Test	Dev	Test	Dev	Test	Dev	Test	Dev	Test	Dev	Test	Dev	Test
Baseline systems of the ComParE [23, 19, 21, 22, 2]														
openSMILE	57.9	**72.1**	64.0	70.2	.251	.314	61.4	65.5	.244	.442	50.3	46.4	40.6	58.5
End2You	70.5	68.8	59.1	60.0	N/A		61.8	64.7	.507	.731	41.2	37.7	40.3	40.3
auDeep	62.2	64.2	N/A		.257	.321	67.6	67.6	N/A		38.6	47.9	44.8	61.3
Deep Spectrum	56.0	60.4	N/A		N/A		63.3	64.1	N/A		44.1	46.1	44.8	67.0*
Fusion of Best	–	71.1	–	71.0	–	.343	–	73.9	–	.621	–	**56.2**	–	55.8
Winners of each sub-challenge from left to right: [10, 14, 9, 5, 13]														
	baseline won		**65.8**	**72.0**	**.367**	**.383**	**69.9**	**75.9**	**.640**	**.763**	**baseline won**		–	**64.2**

3 State-of-the-Art Methodologies and Results

This section provides results from the winners of each sub-challenge (cf. Table 2). Further, the results are compared with the performance of four machine learning and deep learning baseline systems of ComParE, namely openSMILE[1] [7], End2You[2] [24], auDeep[3] [1], and Deep Spectrum[4] [2]. Each of baseline system utilises a different methodology to extract or learn features from the audio signals. In particular, openSMILE is designed to extract expert-designed features such as pitch, energy, and prosody for specific speech and audio tasks. The End2You approach utilises an end-to-end learning paradigm to extract features from raw audio with a convolutional network and then performing the final classification using a subsequent recurrent network. auDeep makes use of recurrent sequence-to-sequence autoencoders for unsupervised representation learning, and Deep Spectrum applies transfer learning techniques with pre-trained image convolutional networks for deep feature extraction from audio plots.

4 Conclusions and Future Work

We have carefully selected seven (three speech-based and three body-acoustics-based plus one 'inbetweener' – breathing) medical datasets for audio-based early diagnosis of various health issues (cf. Sect. 2), and demonstrated the suitability of (deep) computer audition methods for all introduced tasks (cf. Sect. 3). For data of a more complex nature (e. g. SLEEP or C19C), we showed that unsupervised learning of representations provides better results compared to other baselines. For the regression task UCL-SBM, End2You (composed of convolutional and recurrent blocks) outperforms other systems showing its suitability for modelling time-continuous data. Further, we recommend the application of transfer learning approaches (e. g. Deep Spectrum) for audio health monitoring tasks where the data is scarce as such models are pre-trained on larger datasets. As a next step, more holistic views on audio-based health monitoring will be needed that do not focus on 'healthy' vs 'sick', but target the big picture of health state synergistically. With this and more data or data-efficient strategies, audio-based health monitoring in every-day life appears around the corner.

References

1. Amiriparian, S., Freitag, M., Cummins, N., Schuller, B.: Sequence to sequence autoencoders for unsupervised representation learning from audio. In: Proceedings of DCASE 2017, Munich, Germany, pp. 17–21 (2017)

[1] https://github.com/audeering/opensmile.
[2] https://github.com/end2you/end2you.
[3] https://github.com/auDeep/auDeep.
[4] https://github.com/DeepSpectrum/DeepSpectrum.

2. Amiriparian, S., et al.: Snore sound classification using image-based deep spectrum features. In: Proceedings of Interspeech 2017, Stockholm, Sweden, pp. 3512–3516 (2017)
3. Brown, C., Chauhan, J., Grammenos, A., et al.: Exploring automatic diagnosis of COVID-19 from crowdsourced respiratory sound data. In: Proceedings of KDD, San Diego, CA, pp. 3474–3484 (2020)
4. Capellan, A., Fuchs, S.: The interplay of linguistic structure and breathing in German spontaneous speech. In: Proceedings of Interspeech, Lyon, France (2013)
5. Casanova, E., Candido Jr., A., Fernandes Jr., R.C., et al.: Transfer learning and data augmentation techniques to the COVID-19 identification tasks in ComParE 2021. In: Proceedings of Interspeech 2021, pp. 446–450 (2021)
6. Deshpande, G., Schuller, B.: An overview on audio, signal, speech, & language processing for COVID-19. arXiv preprint arXiv:2005.08579 (2020)
7. Eyben, F., Wöllmer, M., Schuller, B.: Opensmile: the Munich versatile and fast open-source audio feature extractor. In: Proceedings of the International Conference on Multimedia, pp. 1459–1462. ACM (2010)
8. Fufurin, I.L., Golyak, I.S., Anfimov, D.R., et al.: Machine learning applications for spectral analysis of human exhaled breath for early diagnosis of diseases. In: Optics in Health Care and Biomedical Optics X, vol. 11553, p. 115531G. International Society for Optics and Photonics (2020)
9. Gosztolya, G.: Using fisher vector and bag-of-audio-words representations to identify styrian dialects, sleepiness, baby & orca sounds (2019)
10. Gosztolya, G., et al.: DNN-based feature extraction and classifier combination for child-directed speech, cold and snoring identification (2017)
11. Han, J., Brown, C., Chauhan, J., et al.: Exploring automatic COVID-19 diagnosis via voice and symptoms from crowdsourced data. In: Proceedings of ICASSP, Toronto, Canada (2021)
12. Hessel, N.S., de Vries, N.: Diagnostic work-up of socially unacceptable snoring. Eur. Arch. Otorhinolaryngol. **259**(3), 158–161 (2002). https://doi.org/10.1007/s00405-001-0428-8
13. Kaya, H., Karpov, A.A.: Introducing weighted kernel classifiers for handling imbalanced paralinguistic corpora: snoring, addressee and cold. In: INTERSPEECH, pp. 3527–3531 (2017)
14. Markitantov, M., Dresvyanskiy, D., Mamontov, D., et al.: Ensembling end-to-end deep models for computational paralinguistics tasks: compare 2020 mask and breathing sub-challenges. In: INTERSPEECH, pp. 2072–2076 (2020)
15. Qian, K., Schuller, B.W., Yamamoto, Y.: Recent advances in computer audition for diagnosing COVID-19: an overview. In: 2021 IEEE 3rd Global Conference on Life Sciences and Technologies (LifeTech), pp. 181–182. IEEE (2021)
16. Ringeval, F., Schuller, B., Valstar, et al.: AVEC 2018 workshop and challenge: bipolar disorder and cross-cultural affect recognition. In: Proceedings of the 2018 on Audio/visual Emotion Challenge and Workshop, pp. 3–13 (2018)
17. Roche, L., Zhang, D., Bartl-Pokorny, K.D., et al.: Early vocal development in autism spectrum disorder, rett syndrome, and fragile x syndrome: insights from studies using retrospective video analysis. Adv. Neurodevelop. Disorders **2**(1), 49–61 (2018). https://doi.org/10.1007/s41252-017-0051-3
18. Schuller, B., Batliner, A., Bergler, C., et al.: The interspeech 2020 computational paralinguistics challenge: elderly emotion, breathing & masks. In: Proceedings INTERSPEECH 2020, ISCA, pp. 2042–2046 (2020)

19. Schuller, B., Steidl, S., Batliner, A., Bergelson, et al.: The interspeech 2017 computational paralinguistics challenge: addressee, cold & snoring. In: Proceedings INTERSPEECH 2017, pp. 3442–3446 (2017)
20. Schuller, B., Steidl, S., Batliner, A., et al.: The INTERSPEECH 2015 computational paralinguistics challenge: degree of nativeness, Parkinson's & eating condition. In: Proceedings of Interspeech, Dresden, Germany, pp. 478–482 (2015)
21. Schuller, B.W., Batliner, A., Bergler, C., et al.: The INTERSPEECH 2019 computational paralinguistics challenge: styrian dialects, continuous sleepiness, baby sounds & orca activity. In: Proceedings INTERSPEECH 2019, ISCA, ISCA, Graz, Austria, pp. 2378–2382 (2019)
22. Schuller, B.W., et al.: The INTERSPEECH 2018 computational paralinguistics challenge: atypical & self-assessed affect, crying & heart beats. In: Proceedings of INTERSPEECH 2018, pp. 122–126 (2018)
23. Schuller, B.W., Batliner, A., Bergler, C., et al.: The INTERSPEECH 2021 computational paralinguistics challenge: COVID-19 cough, COVID-19 speech, escalation & primates. In: Proceedings INTERSPEECH 2021, ISCA, Brno, Czechia (2021)
24. Tzirakis, P., Zafeiriou, S., Schuller, B.W.: End2You-the imperial toolkit for multimodal profiling by end-to-end learning. arXiv preprint arXiv:1802.01115 (2018)

Author Index

Printed in the United States
by Baker & Taylor Publisher Services